DANCING INTO THE UNKNOWN

By the same author

The Little King, the book of twenty nights and one night

Tamara Tchinarova in Léonide Massine's *Les Femmes de bonne humeur*, 1936

DANCING INTO THE UNKNOWN

My Life in the Ballets Russes and Beyond

by

Tamara Tchinarova Finch

DANCE BOOKS

I would like to dedicate this book to all the strong, talented dancers who never achieved worldwide fame, but who were quick learners and therefore indispensable to choreographers.

First published in 2007 by Dance Books Ltd
The Old Bakery
4 Lenten Street
Alton
Hampshire GU34 1HG

ISBN: 975 1 85273 114 1

A CIP catalogue record for this book is available from the British Library

Printed and bound in Great Britain by Latimer Trend Ltd, Plymouth

Contents

Foreword

I do not pretend to be a writer. My grammar is bad and my turn of phrase appalling, and I will never solve the mystery of English spelling. I tried to teach myself the language by pledging to read from cover to cover the longest English book I could find. That, at the time, was *Gone with the Wind*. I was still struggling with the thousand pages when my husband-to-be laughingly confiscated it and produced *Winnie the Pooh*. I did not realise that I had been reading a book written mostly in the idiom of the southern American states.

My education started with *Winnie the Pooh*. Every simple sentence was understood and read with joy. 'How cold my toes, tiddly pom' became the Ballet Company's favourite verse. I then read *The Wind in the Willows* and finally graduated to *Gulliver's Travels*. By then I was well on my way to appreciating the beauty and finesse of the English language – but, as I was already in my twenties, it was too late to achieve perfection.

These memories came flowing back when I was asked to talk about Peter Finch. Questions arose, cases and trunks long neglected were opened again. Photographs were found and articles re-read, and the whole of my life, like a large woven tapestry, was exposed to me and I was able to stand aside and reflect on it. It was like contemplating the lives of two strangers; and yet I could recall so much detail, relive so many feelings, that I decided then to write down some episodes of my life. The narrative is not always strictly chronological: it jumps about a bit sometimes. But then, that is truly the story of my life.

There is another reason for writing. In 2004, when I was eighty-five, the National Library of Australia called me to say that someone from Russia was asking for my address and telephone number. Was it all right to give it to them? 'Of course', I said, amazed. When the phone rang from Moscow, a voice said, 'I am your half-brother Alexander. I've been searching for you for sixty years, and at last have traced you through the internet.'

He then told me that my beloved father Evsevy Rekemchuk, who had left my mother and me to return to Russia when we were all living in Paris in the 1920s, had remarried and that Alexander was his son, ten years younger than me. I loved my father very much and his image was often present in my mind. He was magic to me, but left when I was six. My parents' separation was very painful to me. I knew that Mama loved him but did not want to follow him to the Soviet Union. She never remarried, and reverted to her maiden name, which I had taken too.

Alexander told me that Father settled in Harkov and became well known through the many articles he wrote. Because of his knowledge and education, he was appointed co-director of Kiev's Museum of Eastern and Western Art, and later became the editor, producer and scenarist of the Kino Studio in Odessa.

Then the Soviet Foreign Office offered him the opportunity to travel to Poland, Romania, Czechoslovakia and Hungary to propagate Soviet culture. They gave him a new passport with a new name and trusted him with secret papers to deliver to offices there. He decided, without their permission, to travel to Paris on several occasions to see Mama and me – a dangerous thing to try, and one, it seems, that was observed by agents of the KGB.

He bought me lovely clothes, and finally took me to the ballet, which made me decide to be a ballerina. He always encouraged me to read, particularly Russian and French writers, and to study, to dance, and to try to be the best at it.

In the late 1930s, Stalin ordered that all high-ranking officers of the Tzar's army were to be arrested and imprisoned. Father was arrested in May 1937. I prodded Alexander. What exactly was my father accused of?

Alexander answered that Father's dream had been to write articles demanding education for the ordinary people; but once in Russia, he found the regime and the conditions it imposed so cruel that he became a double agent, bringing reports of Soviet barbarity out to France and elsewhere in Europe. Alexander said that no one outside Russia at the time could imagine the conditions of ordinary people.

Father was interrogated: why had he gone to Paris without permission? He told them he was visiting his wife and child, but they did not believe him. He was charged with being a double agent and spying for both Russia and France. After being tortured, he was executed in October 1937. His second family were persecuted: they lost their rooms or homes, they lost their jobs, and their possessions were confiscated.

When confronted with shocking news, I turn into stone. Alexander's phone call struck me dumb. The reality was hard to absorb. Could I now finally close the door on that part of my past, now that I knew what had happened to him? But how could I? It was all too sudden. In my mind he had always remained a poetic idealist wanting to bring culture to Russia, to open up schools to the masses.

After Father had been executed, his meagre possessions were returned to his son. There were very little, mostly just parts of a diary. But there were two photographs of me aged six, one alone, the other with my faithful pointer dog

Nanka. When Alexander emailed these two photos to me, my tears started to flow, as they do now when I think of it.

I did not want to hear any more. I just wanted to sit and write, and – who knows? – I may have inherited some of his journalistic skill, as Alexander has: he is a successful author in Russia, with some ten books published. I have always wanted to write down my thoughts. I have a vivid imagination, full of hopes and dreams; but life for me has been full of realities. This is my story.

Tamara Tchinarova Finch

Chronology

1919 Tamara Tchinarova born in Bessarabia, Romania.

1925 Father Evsevy Rekemchuk moves to Paris to find work.

1926 TT and mother Anna move to Paris, to join father. TT is placed
      in a convent school.

1928 Father takes TT to see Diaghilev company performing in Paris. TT
      decides she wants to dance.
      Parents separate, father moves to Soviet Union.

1929 TT joins Preobrajenska's ballet school in Paris.

1930 TT's first appearance with students of school at charity functions.

1931 TT does a tour of North Africa as La Plus Petite Danseuse du Monde.

1932 TT returns to Bessarabia with her mother, to do a dance recital
      for her relatives. Mother and father see each other for the last time.
      When she returns to Paris, choreographer Balanchine visits
      Preobrajenska's studio and selects six girls (including TT) to perform
      in the operetta *Orphée aux enfers*. The same girls then go on to
      join the Ballets Russes de Monte-Carlo.

1933 Edward James founds Les Ballets 1933 with Balanchine as
      choreographer, TT leaves Ballets Russes and joins Ballets 1933. That
      same year, after the demise of Ballets 1933, TT returns to Ballets Russes
      and tours America with the company. Massine joins Ballets Russes,
      choreographs *Les Présages*, *Choreartium*. TT is in every movement of
      each ballet.

1936 Ballets Russes splits into two companies. Some dancers, including
      TT are sent to Australia and New Zealand on tour. TT dances many
      leading roles.

1938 TT rejoins original Ballets Russes in France and later tours Australia
      with them. Fokine is now chief choreographer.

1939 TT and mother decide to stay in Australia.

1942 TT engaged to Australian Fred Breen. He is shot down in bombing raid over Germany.

1943 TT meets and marries Peter Finch.

1944 TT joins Borovansky Ballet in Australia.

1947 Peter Finch demobilised.

1948 TT and Peter move to London.

1949 Peter has great success in Olivier production of *Daphne Laureola*, with Edith Evans. TT and Peter's daughter, Anita, is born.

1953 Vivien Leigh visits in the middle of the night to insist that Peter star with her in the film *Elephant Walk*.
Later that year TT and Anita join Peter and Vivien on location in Hollywood.

1959 TT and Peter divorce, after three years of separation.

1961 TT first works as interpreter, at the British Trade Fair in Moscow.

1977 Mother Anna's illness and death.

1997 TT retires as interpreter.

2004 TT moves to Spain.

Bessarabia

The exorcism

I remember clearly that when I was six my parents were persuaded to let me spend the whole summer with Grandfather and Grandma at the family dacha in the country. After a winter in town I was thin, had no colour in my cheeks and was in need of building up.

It was a few years after the Great War and we were living in Bessarabia, which had been Russian but was now part of Romania, as laid down in the Treaty of Versailles. The landowners, returning home from the war or from exile, had had their property restored. Romania was happy to have people managing the land and taking responsibility for running the country.

Nothing had changed much, except for the holes in the walls made by shell fragments. Life restarted exactly as it had been in Tzarist Russia. Romania had a King and a Queen and, as previously, the society consisted of intellectuals, landowners and peasants.

Grandfather was a landowner. He stayed at home during the war, being too old for service. He said that intellectuals were a nuisance: they agitated and confused the peasants. He took great pride in his vineyards and winemaking. He had two town houses, one to live in, one as an investment, and had a country dacha at the seaside. Halfway between town and the seaside were his vineyards. He owned four very old horses that knew their way everywhere, two wagons for gathering grapes, a carriage that he insisted should be polished once a week, and a small boat. He had also owned the town's biggest restaurant; but as his eldest son had been killed in the war, he had sold it.

He was an energetic Armenian, clever, shrewd and very generous, with a soft, smartly trimmed white beard parted in the middle, and a moustache. There was a permanent twinkle in his large blue eyes, and even when angry he could not disguise the laughter lines on his temples.

Grandma was round, as short as she was wide. Her hair would be plaited firmly every morning and arranged into a crown on her head. She was a placid woman, and when not making jam or baking crescent-shaped cinnamon biscuits she would go into the library and spend hours reading. She would say, 'What is the use of thinking? Turgenev, Tolstoy and Dostoevsky have thought it all out for us.' She chuckled at Chekhov's short stories, but not at his plays; she had never seen one performed. Grandma promised me I could borrow all the books when I could read, but not Dostoevsky. She wouldn't tell me why.

Their house was near the mouth of the River Dniester, in a town that, before the war, had been called Akkerman, but which the Romanians had renamed Cetatea Alba. At the entrance to the Black Sea was a big white fort that had stood there for centuries and had seen many invaders. On the other side of the wide estuary one could see houses, people and cavalry. Our street and Grandfather's house were the last spots on earth this side of the Russian border. The border was the river: over the water, the Russians; on our side, the Romanians. That frontier was more formidable than anything made of walls and barbed wire. There were soldiers on both sides, observation points, guns and round-the-clock patrols. There was no crossing, under penalty of death; no fishing, swimming, walking along the shore. Keep off, or else...

Both sides had orders to shoot at the slightest ripple in the water, and occasionally at night one heard firing. My grandfather wondered whether Russians were trying to escape from terror and famine, or anarchists from Europe were infiltrating into Russia. In winter when the river froze, whole families crossed over to Romania, and many times Grandfather would secretly give them refuge, although had he been discovered it would have meant trouble, confiscation of property and jail as a traitor.

The house was near some army barracks – good for business. The officers would go into a glass conservatory where Nanny served them with glasses of wine. Grandfather grew fig trees and oleanders, oranges and lemons. The basement cellar was for the soldiers, who were usually joined by Grandfather's younger son, Evgraf.

Grandfather, being a rich man, was always buying the latest gadgets, and one of his favourites was a cupboard looking like an upright piano. You opened the top to find the inside divided into two compartments – one for cold water, one for hot – and two taps that let water into a large basin. Nanny had to pour buckets of water until it came through the taps. Grandma said it was silly, but Grandfather was interested in progress. His library was his pride and joy; all the volumes were leather-bound and arranged in glass cases. He also had a collection of coins laid out on satin and kept under lock and key. In the middle of the room stood a grand piano that no one ever played except an aunt who visited occasionally and sang arias out of *Bohème* and *Butterfly* with a trembling voice.

All the rooms were built around a large central stove that was always kept warm. In the kitchen, which was also the dining room, a samovar was always on the boil. Nanny was mistress there – indeed, she took charge almost everywhere. She was strong and domineering; I wasn't sure that I liked her. She had been a wet nurse to two of Grandma's children, and had stayed with the family ever since as general help, cook and boss. In the summer she would stay with her fisherman son Stepan. We always had fresh fish, salted fish, smoked fish and fish soup. And Nanny in summer always smelt of fish.

She didn't so much put the fear of God into me as the fear of the Turks. According to her, they had been known to boil naughty children in big copper pots and eat them. There were also witches that danced in the woods at night, and the glow-worms were not worms at all but the eyes of witches who could make themselves invisible when it pleased them. When Grandma told me that I'd soon be off to school to learn to read, Nanny said I didn't have to learn: she could tell me stories better than any book. I suspected that she couldn't read.

I was worried about my pointer dog Nanka, given to me when I was three. At age four I would walk alone through the town from my parents' house to Grandfather's. Nanka would lead me there, let horses and carriages pass by, then take the edge of my dress in her teeth and take me across the road. She was my guardian and my friend; she understood my every word, even my glances and my thoughts. She never strayed, never ran loose and never left my side. But I feared that in the country she might go wild.

In the summers that I spent at Grandfather's house by the sea, I became his favourite grandchild. My hair was so dark that his pet name for me was Jook (Russian for 'beetle'); he preferred this to Tamara – a Georgian name of a powerful queen of the twelfth century who colours many Georgian legends. My father chose the name because of his love of Lermontov's romantic poem *The Demon*. I spent those summers bathing, picking cherries and apricots, sleeping and being loved and fed by everyone. My only battles were with Nanny; she was strict, forcing me to wash and to wear shoes – she said only peasants run barefoot. I missed the feeling of soft grass between my toes. And there were eternal battles because of my dog.

Setting out for the dacha was quite an event, involving four old horses, the strongest two pulling a wagon, with the other two assigned to the carriage. The wagon was laden with mattresses, pillows, goose-feather quilts, blankets, barrels of wine and kvass, lard, sausages, tea, sugar loaves, jams, barrels of pickled cabbage and apples, live chickens tied by their feet, and a crate with a sow and her offspring.

The seaside was twenty kilometres away and the horses knew their way. As we rode through small villages, the villagers would know that we were moving to the seaside and would start bringing cream and butter to sell to us.

The dacha was a simple, whitewashed, four-roomed house with wooden verandas on which were benches and rocking chairs. In the evenings the family sat there talking and watching the sun set into the sea. The acacia trees moved gently in the wind and cast dark sweeping shadows over the house. There was a large kitchen, built separately, with huge stoves, copper pots for jam making, black pots for fish soup, and various samovars. Not far from it was a deep well with a bucket hanging at the end of a long rope.

The dacha was set at the end of an alley of blooming acacia trees; nearer the house there were apricot and cherry trees and, my favourite, a lovely old twisted mulberry that I loved to climb. I tried to hide from Nanny but never succeeded. She always found me. On the other side of the house was an apple orchard with pumpkins, marrows and melons growing between the trees, then a field, full of sweet corn swaying softly in the breeze.

Inside the rooms the walls were white, with Moldavian rugs on the floors and walls. In the corner of my room was an icon, and under it a red glass vessel filled with oil and a floating wick that burnt with a flickering light. There were brass oil lamps everywhere and moths flying around them.

I was happy there, except that Nanka was uncontrollable. She would 'point' at anything that moved; the chickens were scattered and the piglets chased under the horses' hooves, the white doves flew for their lives, and a vole who made the mistake of peeping out of her hole was killed after a savage fight, then eaten all except for the head. I was very distressed.

Nanny would kick the dog when I wasn't looking, and Nanka would bare her teeth and growl at her. Even the placid horses were frightened. One day, Nanny announced that she was resigning if the dog was not taken back to town. She had been threatening to resign for thirty years, but it never failed to work.

Nanka was chained to the top of the wagon that was being driven to town. To my horror, she tried to jump off when the horses started and hung by her neck, howling with pain. She was then put into the crate that had brought the sow and her piglets, and was driven away. I could hear her barking and howling for a very long time. I hated Nanny and felt very lonely without my dog.

Grandfather, I think, understood my feelings and made a great fuss of me. He took me by carriage to visit neighbours and let me hold the reins. We went to one of his nearest vineyards and gathered watermelons that grew between the vines. The horses loved these and bobbed their heads, asking for their share. Grandfather smashed a large melon on the ground and I gathered up the pieces and fed the horses.

Back in the house I climbed into my mulberry tree, missing my dog again. From there I saw an old woman in a black shawl. She rang a little bell, and had a basket over her arm covered with vine leaves. Her nose touched her chin, her eyes were hollow. I sat very still in my tree. Was she a witch? Nanny went to meet her; no, she was a peasant. She had brought jugs of cream and sour cream to sell. Nanny made the sour-cream test: standing a wooden spoon upright in it. Grandfather came to look, then sent the old woman on her way with her basket full of apricots and cherries. She thanked him and smiled a toothless smile that made her look even more frightening.

That evening Grandfather made us taste wine that was ten years old, and then another vintage twenty years old, sweet and thick. Grandma protested that I was not to taste it, but she lost the argument. Grandfather wanted me to learn the difference, and I was to take a small sip of each.

After Nanny put me to bed, the full moon filled my room with beautiful moving shadows; the icon light was bright; the air was heavy with the scent of acacias. I missed my dog desperately. I could hear faint voices on the veranda. All went blurry, then, suddenly, on the opposite side of the room, I saw an enormous lion. He was sitting and growling, just as Nanka did when Nanny was near: teeth bared and chest rumbling. I would always press Nanka's lips down over her teeth, but I was scared of the lion – he looked ready to eat me. As I watched in fear, he rose on his hind legs, towering above me. I remember screaming, covering my head and sobbing in terror. Nanny rushed in and pulled me out of bed. She forced me out of the room and dragged me around the house. I remember the sharp stones under my bare feet, the moon's terrifying shadows, the cold of the night, my fear of the dark. And then suddenly, Nanny was shaking me by the shoulders; she took hold of my nightdress and in one sharp movement tore it from top to bottom. The tearing sound, like that of a screeching bird, woke me up completely. She then pushed me back into my room and made me kneel in front of the icon and pray. Grandfather and Grandma, who had come running, were furious and shouted at her that what she had done was nothing but superstition. But Nanny said I had been taken over by bad spirits, devils and witches, and that the icon would chase them away.

From then on I slept in a room with my cousins, who had joined us for the summer. There was no more wine tasting.

A week after Nanka was taken away, while Nanny was washing my long hair, I was knocked off my feet. A heavy, furry body was attacking me. My heart raced in fear, my breath caught in my throat. My dream had become a reality – it was the lion!

But no, it was Nanka. She had escaped. She was thin, almost a skeleton, dirty, her ears caked with grass seed, muddy from head to tail. Her paws were raw and blood had dried in the cracks. But she had found her way back to the dacha and me. We both cried with joy: her whining, me sobbing. She was not going to be sent back any more; she would sleep at the foot of my bed, protecting me from lions, Turks, witches and devils.

Nanny remained slightly scared of Nanka, whose chest rumbled at her sight and who bared her teeth, in spite of my pressing her lips down to keep us both out of trouble...

Karapet

Karapet was an elderly man, a beggar of indefinite age but considered by the children to be very old. They were afraid of the way he looked, and they scattered at his approach. He was bald, with a pointed chin and no teeth. His deafness meant that he only succeeded in producing weird sounds when he spoke. He was dressed in rags and had a wooden leg, which he used with strength and vigour. When fighting, he used it as expertly as the stick that he held in one hand; the children were quite convinced that he was a monster with three legs. Around his neck on strings hung his possessions: a tin jug, a saucepan with a handle, and a bell that he would ring when begging for food.

He had a faithful, dirty-white dog with pale eyes called Klop, a tough fighter himself with an ear missing. The dog had a black spot over one eye that gave him the look of wearing a patch.

Both Karapet and Klop wandered from door to door begging, doing the same rounds week after week. Monday was their day to come to our kitchen door for their provisions. The jug would be filled with wine and the saucepan with buckwheat gruel, and Klop would get the remains of the family soup.

Once Karapet had a battle with Nanny, who would not let him come to the door of her kitchen because he was so dirty and smelly. She wanted to pour kerosene on his head, which was covered in lice. She started pulling at his shirt, wanting to force him to wash, but he hit her across her bottom with his stick and across the shins with his peg leg. Klop bit her. After that encounter, no more attempts were made to clean him up. Nanny would grumble under her breath and keep her distance.

Karapet ate in privacy, huddled against the wall of the house that had given him food, and then would resume his wandering and ringing his bell, at the sound of which all the children would clear the streets and run back into their homes shaking with fear. The bravest older children threw stones at him and took long sticks to poke him with, to push him off balance. He always looked surprised at that; he loved children, stretching his arms to them, smiling his toothless smile, but the noises he made, his smell, his peg leg, frightened them away.

I was afraid of him too at first, but Nanka made friends with Klop; she greeted him and his master with pleasure. It gave me confidence, and although Karapet's hands outstretched towards me were scary to start with, I understood that he was just simple-minded and would never hurt me.

He had a particular attachment for Grandfather. They were both Armenians, and, as with all Armenians, old traditions survived. At annual festivals a lamb was sacrificed and roasted, with food shared by rich and poor after the blessing. Both men were refugees from the great Turkish butchery of 1895, when the massacres perpetrated by Sultan Abdul Hamid aroused horror all over the world. The extermination of the Armenians by the Turks was savage, and those who had escaped were fortunate. How Karapet escaped no one knew; how he found Grandfather's house no one knew either, but perhaps it was because Grandfather understood the sounds he made. Karapet would try to say 'Ararat, Ararat' when ringing his bell. (The Turks had conquered Mount Ararat from the Armenians.) It came out more like 'Awawart', but Grandfather knew what it meant.

Karapet had lost his leg through being run over by horses and a carriage while drunk, and now his only aims in life were eating and drinking. If he collected a few coins, he wanted to give them away to the children; he would grin and stretch out his hand, and the bravest of the children, when not hitting him, would snatch the coins from him.

He slept in Grandfather's stables on the straw, his dog cuddled up to him. The horses were restless until he came to settle and then the large, wooden stable doors would click shut and all would be quiet for the night. Grandfather offered him a proper bed near the stove in the vast kitchen, but Karapet did not seem to understand, and he certainly wasn't going to wash to keep up Nanny's standards. He loved the horses and would often brush them and talk his weird talk to them.

Sometimes the militia would arrest him for getting drunk. They said he was a menace in town, but he would never be taken to the police station without a fight. Karapet would be thrown into a cell to sleep it off, while Klop would spend the night whining outside the prefecture. In the morning Grandfather was informed that Karapet had been arrested and there was a fine to pay. Grandfather always paid.

The most enjoyable time of the year was mid-September, when everyone prepared to gather grapes. Young and old peasants came from faraway villages to get work and offer a helping hand. During the week before, the house, yard, stables, cellars and kitchen were full of activity. Nanny was baking bread, Grandmother was making jam in large copper pots, onions were packed into sacks, barrels of salted mullet were fetched from the cellar. It was well known that the villagers, when picking, ate grapes all day long, and the onions, the black bread and the salted fish were just the food to take the sweetness away.

Large open vats for the grapes were fitted to the wagons, with long benches for the pickers. With a lot of noise, bustle and excitement the crowd departed, to be away at least two weeks, sleeping in the open under the stars.

Karapet and his dog Klop never missed the departure to the vineyards. He claimed his place on the wagon and, like everyone else, was given an old army blanket, his parcel of salted fish, onions, a loaf of black bread and a large lump of lard that he liked particularly. Klop's rations would be supplied by everyone: fish heads, tails and gruel.

All hands available were recruited for grape picking – even small children did their share. At the end of a day's work one's limbs ached, and having eaten one's fill of sweet grapes it was so wonderful to sit around a bonfire in which potatoes were roasting and to cut the thick bread and skin the salted mullet, holding it by the tail and pulling it apart, so that one would be left with a strip of fat salty fish to swallow before biting into a sweet onion. The men produced bottles of vodka, but the women were content with hot tea.

Karapet loved to join in the singing late into the night; although his efforts were not melodious, a beaming smile would appear on his face, and as he clapped his hands he looked very happy. I longed to stay late, listening to the singing, but I was never allowed to stay the night in the vineyards; so every day Grandfather, my dog and I travelled there and back.

The working day went quickly. I was allowed to help Grandfather pick the grapes that were reserved for the table. We had special sharp, stumpy scissors and I was warned not to snip my fingers off.

One particular section of the vineyard had many varieties of grapes. Muscat grapes were grown for the family, to be stored for winter; before the Great War, another variety, Ladies' Fingers, used to be packed in tissue paper and reserved for the officials in Odessa, but now was grown and gathered for the Romanian Chief of Police, who sent armed militiamen to collect it.

When the grapes were all gathered, there were usually a couple of days of celebrations. First, Grandfather distributed the wages, reinforced by bottles of wine for everyone, and then huge tables covered with food were unveiled, the result of days of preparation: enormous meat and cabbage pies, roast chickens and grapes in great cascades. In the courtyard the large vats were waiting for their fruit to be squeezed. The children were allowed to trample the grapes, and great fun we had! Someone would produce an accordion, someone else a guitar, last year's wine was tasted, exclamations of appreciation were heard, songs were sung again and I was allowed to stay up late into the night.

One year, on the second night of festivities, Karapet was missing. He had not slept in the stable the night before, nor had he been seen all day. Karapet never missed the grape festival, so Grandfather was surprised. He went to the prefecture in case there was a fine to pay, but no one had seen him. People called at every house, and even the children who had been cruel to him looked everywhere – in the stables, the lofts, the gardens, the sheds, everywhere.

It was Nanka who found Klop. She heard him howl: long, piercing howls interrupted by loud barks. As Nanka rushed to Klop, we followed her and found Karapet, clutching his bell, lying in shallow water at the river's edge, dead. Grandfather wondered if he had been pursuing his vague dream and shouting, 'Give us back Awawart!'

The Armenian Church was not keen on giving him a Christian burial, as he had never attended any services. Grandfather was not spared the sermons and was rebuked for not having brought Karapet 'to church'. Now he wanted a Christian burial? Well, if he paid handsomely, they might consider it. So it was done; after all, the Church was always short of funds, and a sinner's soul could be saved. A solid coffin was made, and Karapet, washed and lying all clean and calm with his bell on his chest, was carried along the main street in the open coffin. He looked very peaceful, and was even kissed by old women in the church. No children followed the procession; even I, who was not afraid of him, peered from behind the window. The coffin was carried on the shoulders of the village youths and behind it marched a military brass band. They had been rehearsing a waltz for days in readiness for the Mayor's daughter's wedding party, and Grandfather had persuaded them to play that waltz at Karapet's funeral.

All the mourners returned to Grandfather's cellar and drank to the peaceful rest of Karapet's soul. Later, a stone was put up, with the inscription, 'Here lies a good, simple man who did no harm to anyone'.

Klop adopted the stables as his residence, and Nanka always shared her food with him; they were great friends. A few months later she produced a litter of strange-looking pups, not at all like her, all with pale eyes.

Tall, dark and handsome

My father, Evsevy Rekemchuk, was Georgian, tall, dark and handsome. His face was thin, his cheekbones prominent, his eyes shiny, black, slightly slanting. He was an army Captain in the Ismailovsky Regiment, nicknamed 'the battalion of death'. Its officers were chosen for their courage, drive, education and leadership. He rode perfectly, and in his well-fitting uniform, with riding boots and stick, he looked and was strong, disciplined and a war hero. He was wounded three times, in the neck, leg and shoulders. He received ten decorations, amongst them the supreme St George's Cross.

In 1916 the war against the Austrians had gone badly for the Russian troops – indeed, it was a bad time for both fighting sides. It was during the Russian retreat, near Minsk, that Mother and Father met. She was a Red Cross nurse, tending him while he recovered from a sword wound in the leg. The hospital was vastly overcrowded, operating with a tremendous shortage of medical supplies and food. Typhus and cholera took heavy tolls, and there was no way of separating the wounded from the sick. My mother was one of eight nurses looking after 4,000 patients.

When Mother was eighteen, just out of school at the outbreak of the war, she had volunteered for the Red Cross. She underwent a three-month course in first aid, was shown how to bandage a limb, to give an injection, to take a temperature and to clean a wound. She was told how and when to administer various drugs and, before she realised it, she was at the front line.

The Russians were retreating and suffering vast casualties. The wounded were lying shoulder to shoulder on the ground. The overworked doctors had to make quick decisions either to amputate limbs or to leave soldiers to die. Father was recovering, walking around, helping, talking to the wounded. He had kept his horse, as did other officers; the dozen or so horses were used for reconnaissance and to bring supplies.

My father taught his nurse how to ride, and in the process their romance developed quickly; soon promises of marriage were exchanged. They were from vastly different backgrounds. My Georgian father was brought up on the legends and stories of his nation: the Georgians were slim, muscular and long-lived and rode elegantly, their heads full of dreams of romantic chivalry, of unfulfilled desires. His ancestry dominated his character, although by 1916 he had realised that the war was not romantic. He found love and poetry in a meeting with his nurse, an 'angel of mercy'.

Mother was Armenian. Her father, like many Armenians, could have succeeded in business even on a desert island. He was practical, acquisitive, generous, envied and loved. He moved to Bessarabia, a fertile and rich region on the north-west border of the Black Sea, and acquired a plot of land cheaply, giving a written pledge to cultivate it.

He planted grapes and fruit trees, found a healthy young Ukrainian wife and settled there. Soon he was buying more land, and his grapes and wines became known all over the region. He woke at dawn; inspected his cellars; gave orders to the servants; checked the stables, the kitchen and the yard; saw that the horses were harnessed; and went to the marketplace to buy produce that he chose carefully, with love and interest. He would come back with a carriage full of friends and laden with figs, nuts, dates, Turkish sweets, Armenian spice, newly killed lamb, crayfish from the river and red mullet. His kindness and hospitality were renowned. Grandma occasionally sighed in disapproval, but had to admit that he knew how to make friends and run a business.

She had been afraid when, in 1905 after a pogrom of the Jews in our region, Grandfather took considerable risks. All Jewish people were being either deported or killed, by order of the Tzarist authorities; but Grandfather kept whole families of Jews hidden in his cellars. To feed them he would fill my mother's deep apron pockets with food and send her, aged eight, into the cellar to distribute it.

By the time the Great War started, Grandfather had three large vineyards, had built his own house, had bought two other houses (let to tenants), and had a hotel with a restaurant. Business was very good. Because so many people came to eat in the restaurant, the borscht often had to be watered, but his instructions were to make it very thick and to have some cut cabbage ready, with fresh dill to float on top and lots and lots of sour cream. He said that more profit could be made on soups than on anything else. Grandma had to agree.

They had four children. His eldest son, Pava, his pride and joy, had been killed at the front. The other son, Evgraf, went to the front too, and was shattered when he returned to find that the woman he loved had not waited for him. In desperation he married the first girl he saw. She was a good, simple, uneducated woman, who gave him healthy children but whom he never really loved. Because wine was so easily available, Evgraf drank to excess, and eventually became an alcoholic. My grandparents' other daughter, Lydia, was just a little girl at the outbreak of war.

In 1917 Mother came back home, but the shortage of nurses was great, and she again volunteered to be sent to the Turkish front. She resisted pleas from her father, who begged her not to go. His fears were because of her Armenian origin, even though the family name had been changed from the traditional ending in -*ian* into the Russian ending in -*ov*.

Then terror struck again – this time from the Russians. Villages were pillaged, and wounded officers were killed. The doctors advised the nurses to go home. Mother set out for Batum, on the Turkish border, right across the other side of the Black Sea from where she wanted to be. At night in a fishing boat, with fifteen soldiers and officers all disguised as fishermen, they crossed the Black Sea from east to west, occasionally seeing a warship, not knowing whether the captain and crew were White Russians or Red. They landed in Odessa exhausted, hungry, ill and shattered. But the fishermen looked after their boatload, some of whom were suffering from wounds. Mother returned, to be met by the Captain who was to become my father. She had come back from the war a mature woman, wanting independence and able to make her own decisions. He had left the army, tired of the butchery of the Revolution, though not disagreeing with the ideals. He had lost both his parents; their home had been razed to the ground; he had no profession. He had come to claim Anna. He loved her, and wanted to be with her.

Life came back to the town and the countryside around it. The soil was fertile and corn grew fast, giving two crops a year. The fruit trees produced their yearly crops. The Revolution was miles away. People had come home, tired of fighting; they wanted to start living again. And then in 1919 a treaty was signed in Versailles and the province of Bessarabia became Romania; and the river that flowed right outside Grandfather's house was going to be the border between Russia and Romania.

The Romanian side was recovering, and Grandfather was trying to reassemble his mini-empire. But his heart was heavy. His favourite son was dead; the other was an alcoholic. Moreover, Mother's fiancé did not appeal to him – he was a Georgian, a dreamer with no inclination for business. There was so much to be done: the vines to be attended to, the houses repaired. There was no time for dreams. My father saw only the need for reform. He was a radical, and knew that much had to be changed in Russia. He did not agree with the killing, the blood, the tears inflicted on the people, but he argued that the old system needed to be changed. Grandfather was disappointed in Mother's interest in 'the Georgian'. Why did she want to marry him, when there was a man with an adjoining property who had a perfectly good, handsome, wealthy son?

When Father and Mother married, against her family's wishes, my father did not want to be tied up in business: no houses, no flats, no vineyards, nothing. His Georgian pride stopped him accepting anything from Grandfather. He wanted to write, and to be a journalist. The young couple rented – temporarily, they believed – a room and a kitchen, converted from a cellar.

When I was born a year later, the family strife became even fiercer. Grandfather maintained that the cellar was unhealthy, and asked when my father was going to earn some proper money by doing a proper day's work, and not just sitting and writing bits and pieces that could not be sold anywhere. Not only were these articles political (and no one wanted politics, having lived through an upheaval), but they were written in Russian, and Romania was trying to suppress the Russian language. The official language had become Romanian, and children had to go to Romanian schools, where the alphabet used was Roman. The by-laws were written in Romanian, streets had been renamed, newspapers were purely in Romanian. The common language between educated Romanians and Russians was French, so Father could deal with the authorities. But the peasant population was lost and puzzled when dealing with the police or the law, or even when reading posters. Nonetheless, they accepted the change, and were happy to be at peace.

Grandfather's opinion of Father remained unaltered. How could this young man miss such an opportunity? He knew that his father-in-law was old, approaching seventy, and would be happy to hand over everything to my mother and him; how could my father not want it?

I remember our home, especially the cellar, with holes in the mud floor where the rats lodged. I remember hearing them squeak, remember being sick with tension, and Father pouring boiling water down the holes. I remember wetting my bed night after night in fear, and being ashamed of it. I also remember choking and wheezing, coughing and fighting for breath, my chest congested; and Nanny coming over, boiling milk, putting a towel over my head, making me inhale the steam and 'cupping' my chest and back, warming glasses on a flame and applying them on my body, watching the purple marks rise. It was after my recovery from that illness that my parents gave me my dog Nanka – white with brown spots and patches and a very wet, cold nose – who thereafter slept at the foot of my bed and protected me from all harm.

Lydia

My Aunt Lydia was fifteen at the end of the war. She was small and pretty and always looked a child even when she was a woman. She dreamt of a career on the stage and was considered talented; she taught herself to recite and sing, and would ask people for music scores. She had a fine collection, her favourite being *Madame Butterfly*. She knew it was about a Japanese girl in love, and had begged Grandma to make her a kimono; once she had learned to pile her black hair on top of her head, she would sing 'One Fine Day' with tremolos in her voice.

Grandfather was amused, but thought it was all childish nonsense. Yet he could not disguise a flicker of pride, and one day an upright piano strapped on a cart pulled by two horses arrived on the doorstep. This purchase had been kept a secret even from Grandma, who was always protesting against extravagance. Grandfather said he had got it from a house that was being demolished, and that he had rescued the piano from being chopped up for fuel. Lydia's reaction was immediate: she was going to be a singer, and she wanted to learn to play the piano. What was the use of having one if she could not play it?

In a small town, there was no conservatoire. Going to Bucharest was out of the question. Grandfather found an old, impoverished Jewish musician, who came to the house twice a week to teach her and always arrived in time for a meal. He was an old friend, rescued from the pogrom and then hidden in Grandfather's cellar, and was overjoyed to be able to help a blossoming talent. Lydia progressed well, and soon could accompany herself. All day long it was scales and arpeggios, chords and melodies. Grandfather sighed: where would all that lead to? Lydia grew up singing and fell in love with a wealthy man. In one way, that pleased Grandfather, but in another he had a nagging feeling: who was going to take over from him?

On Lydia's twentieth birthday, Kolia asked Grandfather for her hand in marriage. Kolia had been an officer during the war and had become a landowner. He was not an Armenian, to Grandfather's sorrow, but to his joy not a Georgian either. He was Russian, and not a dreamer: practical, efficient, and obviously destined to become wealthy. Grandfather organised the biggest, smartest wedding since the end of the war. It took three months' planning; geese were fattened and pigs kept for the occasion, to be roasted whole and served on huge platters garnished with sour apples. There were large sturgeons with parsley and lemon, and crayfish from the river – big basinfuls of them, red, with their claws open to be cracked. From a secret part of the cellar that opened only with keys that Grandfather kept on a leather strap around his waist came very special wines, the pride of the vineyard. Those wines were never sold but kept for favourite guests and special festivities. The staff was supplied with barrels of wine, and their relatives and friends were all welcome.

Everyone who could fit into the church went to the wedding ceremony. Lydia looked tiny in a white dress with a long train, wearing a crown of white flowers. I, aged four, had to carry the train. Her husband was very tall; the marriage service of the Orthodox Church requires that holy crowns be held over the couple, but it was impossible to find a best man tall enough to hold the crown above Kolia's head. So a stool was placed on the bridegroom's side to enable the best man to stand on it and hold the crown during the very long ceremony.

I could not understand why Grandma was crying. I wanted to go out, because I was worried about Nanka. My dog had been locked up but had escaped, and was outside the church barking all through the ceremony. A verger was sent out to catch her, but she bit him, ran away, and came back to resume her barking.

When the wedding party came out of the church, with me holding the long train of Lydia's dress, Nanka made an enormous leap, landed on the train and knocked me over with joy. I was shocked. It was such a happy day that no one minded – except Nanny, who continued to hate that dog and look for reasons to get rid of her.

Lydia moved into her husband's town house. He bought her a piano so that she could practise at home; and from her wedding day, Grandfather's piano was neglected.

Their summer residence was near the Black Sea, at a spot where a freshwater lagoon had formed centuries ago. This lagoon, the bottom of which was black mud, was a stone's throw from the sea. Lydia's husband had observed that local women applied the black mud to various parts of their anatomy and then swore that all their aches and pains had disappeared. They said that they felt invigorated and younger. Kolia's business sense made him build a small dacha there; then, after exploring the possibilities of these magic cures, he bought a large plot of land and built a sanatorium and rest hotel, with hot and cold mud baths, hot and cold freshwater and saltwater baths, a pool, a solarium for sunbathing in the nude, showers and a restaurant. It became a fashionable place to come for a cure for everything. Women from Bucharest swore that even their wrinkles disappeared, and they lost weight on the watermelon diet – and of course Kolia and Lydia prospered. It became a resort, where many people built their own summerhouses. Grandfather was happy about it but a little disappointed that he hadn't thought of starting the business himself.

When I went to my grandparents for summer, one week at least was spent at Lydia's. I didn't like it at first, as I was frightened by all the women looking strange, covered in mud, with nothing but white circles for eyes.

Evenings at Lydia's were very grand affairs. Everyone dressed well, large tables were covered with the best embroidered tablecloths, candles were lit. The guests picked at the food rather than ate it, and no one drank tea out of a

care had brought all the way from home, not wanting to leave a wedding present behind.

There was nowhere to go. After sitting in the park, we knocked on the door of Sonia, one of Mama's childhood friends, who was living in another small hotel. She was kind and understood our problem. She took Mama and me in to sleep on her floor. Father slept at railway stations.

Sonia

Mama and I continued living with Sonia for a while. Sonia was enterprising, and as she was friendly with her concierge and had a large, tidy room, she had made it into a workshop. She had bought a sewing machine and took any work that came her way. We fitted into the room well – even Mama's plates in their suitcase were accommodated under a large bed.

In the evenings Sonia cooked delicious stews: big chunks of meat in thick gravy with wine and herbs. She had a large primus stove with a strong flame, and the tantalising aroma filled the hotel and made me feel hungry. She loved food and served it well. Father was invited to eat with us before going to work in the evenings, and praised her culinary achievements. One evening Sonia waited for us to finish our meal, then informed us that we had been eating horse flesh. I didn't know the difference, and Mama did not mind. Indeed, she asked for the recipe, and said that during the war she had eaten horse meat at the front during the famine. But Father turned green in the face and went out to be sick.

On Sunday Sonia took us to the flea market and fair at Clignancourt. There were merry-go-rounds, shooting stands and big revolving wheels with numbers on. Bets were made on numbers and if the wheel stopped on your number, you could win sugar, dolls, wine and chocolates. Sonia had a friend operating the wheel, and would come home with kilos of sugar. She had many friends at the fair, and offered to make dolls at a reduced price for one of the stands that was giving them away as prizes. Her offer was accepted, and Sonia and Mother were in business. These dolls consisted of pink silk stretched on a head and torso. Sonia bought hundreds of these. One had to paint eyes, cheeks and lips carefully on the face, then sew silky blonde or black hair on the head, and cover it with a wide-brimmed hat. The dresses were frills, frills, frills. The dolls were used as decoration either to hang on walls or to sit on beds and chairs. Sonia bought yards and yards of bright materials, and Mother's first job at the machine was to make frills. I was allowed to gather the frills and spread the gathering evenly. I remember Sonia's room littered with dozens and dozens of dolls, the bed and floor covered with them. Business was good.

But Father grew impatient. He said I had to go to school, and he wanted to live with Mama. He found a room in another hotel, so we collected our crockery and china, and moved. And soon, of course, we were broke again.

The convent

We were very short of money. One day, Father took the bracelet that Grandfather had given Mother and went out. When he came back, he had food and money to pay the rent. He produced a small ticket and gave it to Mother, saying that some day he would sell articles to the papers and she would get her bracelet back. She cried, but seemed more upset about sending me to boarding school, now that they had money for the train fare. Father had been given the address of a convent in Versailles and this was the day that Mama was taking me there. I was very apprehensive. I could not speak French and I did not know what boarding school meant.

We walked from the little station of Versailles to the convent, Mother clutching a piece of paper with the address on it, and, after circling around a tall wall that enclosed the convent, came upon a large iron gate. Mother rang a bell. The gate swung open and a very old, toothless man limped towards us. He pointed the way across the yard to the cloisters, and there waiting for us was a woman dressed all in black with a crucifix on a chain hanging around her neck. She opened a few doors and Mother and I were in a large room facing another woman in black.

Mama was asked many questions that I did not understand, and filled papers with my name and age, and her and Father's names. She gave the woman some money and then embraced me, crying. All I understood was that she was leaving me. I wanted to know when she was coming back. She said in Russian, 'Sunday'. This was Monday. I clung to her, sobbing. I was gently led behind a heavy door, and she was taken out.

I was left with these two women in black speaking to me in a language I could not understand. One of them took me by the hand and we entered a chapel, which was full. There were nuns dressed in black and nuns dressed in white; there were many girls, most of them older than I was, and a few small ones like me. They all looked round at me with great curiosity. I was still crying but did not want anyone to see it.

After the service, we all formed ranks and went to a long room with enormous tables and benches. I was given a tin plate and waited for my turn to be served with soup. Eventually I found out that the soup was called Napoleon and consisted of thick liquid with large pieces of stale bread floating in it. After the meal, an older girl, Marie, was told to take me to Sister Marcelle for my uniform. I was given a black overall and a white coarse nightgown, both fastened by tapes at the back – and then I was led into a large dormitory with about twenty beds, covered with grey blankets. Marie was to be my guardian; she was fourteen, and talked a lot. She knew I could not understand French, so she showed me six fingers and said, '*Maman reviendra dans six jours, Dimanche.*' I understood. She was smiling and friendly and took on the task of teaching me French. I cried in bed a lot and Marie got out of her bed and sat with me holding my hand, until she was told by a young nun to get back into her own bed.

The next morning a daily routine was established. We were wakened by loud church bells at 5:30, were made to wash our faces and hands in cold water, got dressed and went to pray. The morning service was very long. It was cold in church and I felt hungry. Some of the older girls lined up at the altar and were given large white biscuits and a drink. I tried to join them, but was quickly pulled back and told '*Pas pour toi*'; later on Marie tried to explain that it was the flesh and blood of Christ, and when I was older I would be allowed to swallow it. I could not understand: how could there be so much flesh and blood of Christ?

After that, the refectory again. Then learning to read and write, praying, food, praying, peeling potatoes and stringing beans, praying, then at last bed. It was the only time when girls talked to one another, and Marie taught me a song, '*Frère Jacques*'. She taught me to call her Petite Mère, and showed me how to string beans. She used to peel potatoes in the afternoon, and the task of all the little ones including me was to string the beans. To this day, the smell of green beans reminds me of this. The scent of lilac in the spring also reminds me of the convent garden, and the smell of melting wax of the chapel. It had undertones of guilt for me: guilt for not being a Catholic, resentment against being rejected for not being one, and a vague fear of burning in hell when I died – all non-Catholics did.

Marie lived for the day when she would be eighteen so that she could take the veil. The ambition of every senior girl was to become a nun. Their prayer books were tattered with use, with almost every page containing a coloured image of a saint. They knew the lives of the saints, their sacrifices, their martyrdom. Each girl had a favourite one whose name she hoped to adopt. They dreamt about their saints and secretly kept metal rings in a drawer, wearing them at night to pretend they were brides of Christ.

Little by little their devotion and dedication affected me. I imitated their zeal. We filled our shoes with sharp little stones and spent the whole day walking and running in discomfort. In the evening, our bleeding toes were proof of our sacrificial offerings as we showed one another our martyrdom. The story of Saint Catherine who was sacrificed on a spiky wheel filled our imagination with horrors – she was '*vièrge et martyre*'. Marie nightly reread her story and cried every time. My favourite saint was Bernadette Soubirous.

I missed my mother and father. Every other week they would collect me on Saturday afternoon, take me home and bring me back on Sunday afternoon.

On alternate Sundays we were only allowed out for the day, and we always took a picnic to the garden of the Château de Versailles. Father explained to me about the kings who had built it and lived there. I loved the fountain with the horses most of all. The days in the Parc de Versailles went quickly, and all too soon I was back to *soupe Napoléon*.

Something had happened at the Convent. I never knew what it was, but when we went into the chapel a nun was lying spreadeagled on the floor, her arms opened. She was covered with a black cloth with a big white cross on it. We smaller girls were given baskets of flower petals, and while the nuns sang we had to walk up and down throwing the petals on her. This affected the senior girls that night and they all cried, and I was told that we must all pray for her salvation.

It was Saturday and Mama's day to take me home. She wanted me to go and visit friends with her, but I said no; I had been told to pray for the salvation of the nun's soul. I asked for money to buy some candles, turned a chair upside down, made an altar out of a table, put Mama's coat over my head and spent the Saturday afternoon on my knees chanting. That had a terrifying effect on my mother. She asked me about my schooldays and found that my vocation was to be a nun. Marie's example was shining in front of me and I wanted to be like Bernadette, who appeared in a grotto and had the power to cure people.

My first obstacle was that I was not a Catholic. Marie had said I could never know the joy of being a bride of Christ. I could never wear the lovely white dress that girls wore for their first Communion. Mama bought me a doll that Saturday. I did not want it; all I wanted was to pray, and now that I was seven-and-a-half I wanted to become a Catholic.

Mama was disturbed. On Sunday she asked to speak to the Mother Superior, who was very pleased that, only a year after I had entered the convent, not only could I speak French, but I also had such well-formed ideas. The Mother Superior, looking very severe, said that my mother ought to consider having me change my religion. There wasn't a truer vocation than to become a bride of Christ and pray for all the sins and sinners of the world. As the word 'sin' in French sounds like the word for fishing, I could not understand why it was so wrong to fish that one had to pray for fishermen. What would happen when all the other girls took their first Communion, and I alone would not be allowed to wear a white dress, to confess my sins and to have them absolved so that I could be pure again?

She reduced me to tears. I had looked forward to swallowing the wafer in the mornings. Other girls had told me that you felt a burning sensation and then the host dissolved in your mouth like a miracle happening, and you felt it go down into your body, giving you a sensation of joy and satisfaction. I was sobbing now. Obviously I was not like other girls; I was a freak, a monster. I could promise I would never go fishing, and I would pray for other fishermen, but why was Mother being so stubborn and not agreeing to do as she was told?

Next Sunday was dramatic. Father wasn't home. I wouldn't talk to Mother, and just prayed until it was time to go back to the convent. But my mother had taken her decision. She delivered an ultimatum to the Mother Superior in her very poor French. She said: 'Me, Orthodox, family Orthodox, Tamara Orthodox, no change, Tamara no Catholic, too much church, Tamara stay like that or Tamara go.' The Mother Superior understood. Softly, she gave us both a pitying look. She was very sorry, but it was: 'Tamara go'. At this moment Marie had come to take me to the refectory. She saw me sobbing and was told I was leaving the convent. She burst into tears and ran away, then came running back to give me a holy picture of St Bernadette. We embraced one another, both sobbing. She didn't know why I was leaving: I could not understand why I wasn't good enough to stay. I was angry with Mother – why did she have to interfere, and where was my father anyway, I loved him much more than I loved her... Why hadn't she asked him?

Institut de Barrall

I was now moved to a good school, but I knew it was an expensive one. It too was a boarding school, but because it was right in the centre of Paris I could see my parents more easily. I noticed that my father was not always there at weekends, and to my pressing questions Mother gave vague replies. He would be there next week, he was away for a few days, he was travelling, he would be home soon. One weekend he was home; it was magic. He bought us everything we wanted and many things we didn't want, took us to restaurants and the cinema, paid the rent and all the debts at the grocer's and then went away again, leaving Mother a big bundle of money. They had had rows and disagreements; he was begging her to go away with him, though I did not know where. She didn't want to. She stayed in Paris, and tried her hand at any kind of work she could do secretly. As a foreigner, one had to have a permit to obtain work, and one had to have work to obtain a permit.

She was glad that she had learned to sew. She went to small manufacturing firms and agreed to work for low wages, employed illegally. She ironed men's suits for Jewish tailors, sewed fur cuffs for a Polish overcoat factory, machined underwear cut on the cross, cut paper patterns, cut out dresses, embroidered chrysanthemums and great golden birds on Japanese kimonos made in Paris, and put frills on lampshades and cushions – she was good with frills.

But her father had always advised, 'Be your own boss. Then the profits are your own.' She decided that what Paris needed was a shop that sold salted herrings. With all that Jewish community living around her, surely they would buy salted herrings, home-made pickled cabbage and salted cucumbers? She rented a cellar a few doors away from our hotel, bought four wooden barrels and talked two Serbian colleagues into going to the dawn market at Les Halles to buy herrings, cabbage, cucumbers and coarse salt. I was on holiday from school and witnessed the pickling. It was a weekend of stench – people walking in the street covered their noses with their hands. She had large hoardings painted with the name of the shop, '*Poisson d'Or*', informing passers-by that pickled herrings were for sale. The venture was a complete disaster. We ate herrings, pickled cabbage and cucumbers for months and couldn't get rid of the smell from our clothes, our hair and our room. Mother finally had to tell our Jewish neighbours to help themselves to the fish. Then she bribed her Serbians to borrow a wheelbarrow and dispose of the barrels at night. The cellar had to be abandoned. They wheeled the barrels in darkness and dumped them with the rubbish of the flea market.

Mama made friends with many Serbs, who were also political refugees struggling to make a living. They specialised in making soft leather shoes with plated uppers. She soon learned to do the leather plating. The shoes were entirely handmade, very fashionable and soft, and sold well in expensive shoe shops.

I was again being persuaded to become a Catholic. Mother was summoned every weekend and told that it was bad for me to be different from the others. There would be no place for me in heaven; indeed, there would be punishment in hell when I died. I remember at the time learning geography and being astounded at the millions of Chinese and Indians who were not Catholics. One day, I raised my hand in class and asked how God could be so unjust as to let all these millions and millions of Chinese and Indians burn in hell for ever and ever. My question was reported to the Directrice. Mother was told that I was a bad influence on the children.

Parents' separation

Mother was going through a very difficult time. I saw Father less and less during my weekends at home, and when he was there, Mother was crying and there were rows. He was often away; Mother said that he had become a successful journalist. He had sold some articles to one of the two Russian newspapers published in Paris. These newspapers were a lifeline to the hundreds of thousands of Russian émigrés in France who had taken refuge there from the Russian Revolution. Paris was full of them. They frequented their own cheap restaurants, clubs and cafes. The shabby hotels held many of them, most living very poorly and having to take any job they could find. Trying to keep up a certain grandeur was essential if they were to retain their past status. They had to work as taxi drivers, doormen, waiters. There was a fashionable nightclub called the Sheherazade that was completely staffed by ex-members of the personal Imperial regiment and guard of the Tzar.

The refugees lived with their illusions from day to day, with hopes of change and return to 'Mother Russia'. They bought and avidly read the two newspapers that nourished their hopes. But Father's articles spoke of the reality. In his opinion, the changes and reforms not only were happening but were necessary. He explained that he himself was an educated White Russian ex-officer and that his articles were not propaganda for the Red regime – he detested and abhorred the means used by the Bolsheviks. But he wanted to establish in the mind of the White Russians that the reforms were a fact: education, houses, work, equality. There would be – the leaders said – schools and hospitals for all, and plans for agriculture, rebuilding homes, looking after children and homes for the old. Father emphasised that the leaders were strong and knew how to influence the vulnerable, simple people. The days of wealth and glory for the émigrés were over. The editor published the articles, but Father was told not to upset the readers any more. Mother called him a Bolshevik. She had seen too much butchery and misery.

Father became very mysterious. He went out at night to secret meetings. He stayed away for weeks, coming back with pockets full of money. He did not tell Mother what he was doing, nor for whom he was working. So she refused to take any money from him. Mother was terrified of anarchists; a couple of White Russian generals had been kidnapped in Paris. Of course, Father had nothing to do with that, but she rejected his ideas and his money. All he could do was to send us beautiful presents from overseas: exotic dolls, leather bags. These Mother had to accept, as there was no way of sending them back.

He returned one day, and secretly, without Mother knowing, took me to Galeries Lafayette and equipped me with a full wardrobe: new dresses, a coat, shoes that pinched my toes. I did not mind that – I loved the shoes and offered my misery to my saint, hoping that my sacrifice would keep Father with us. Then Father took me to the circus. We watched the Fratellini Brothers in their sequinned costumes playing different instruments, and then the famous clown, Grock, with his tiny violin. Father, who could always conjure up magic in my mind, told me of the tradition of minstrel clowns performing in public squares, of the *commedia delle'arte*, of the misery of disappointment that clowns portrayed. Sad faces, tears rolling down their cheeks.

Then some Georgians and their horses performed impossible feats. Their costumes were black *cherkeskas*, wide in the shoulders, narrow at the waist, and they had wide pantaloons tucked into their soft leather boots, rows of cartridges on their chest, and tall black sheepskin hats on their heads. It was a performance full of tricks. They were riding like devils, whipping their horses into a frenzy; they jumped across their backs and rode under their bellies, and as a grand finale eight horses galloped abreast, long curved silver scimitars at their sides, while the men on the horses' backs formed a human pyramid. They looked as agile as cats, as fierce as tigers.

Father's eyes were shining; he tapped the ground with his feet, he talked to me in a very animated way, saying that there were many other tricks that riders could do. He missed Russia, missed riding, Russian music and Russian friends. He must have made a decision that day, because when we came back to Mother after the circus, they spoke for a long time, and argued. She couldn't stop him doing what he wanted to do, and as I snuggled in between them in our large bed in the hotel room, I could hear my mother crying and felt my father stretch his arm under her shoulders and draw her head towards him. I just fitted in between them and found comfort, warmth, love and security being close to these two people I loved most in the world.

Father's return and a visit to the ballet

I was told that Father was going to Russia for two weeks. He was away five months. He eventually returned looking thin and tired, having suffered the fate of every White Russian returning to their homeland: detention, solitary confinement, intense questioning. Every White Russian was suspected of being a spy, and writers were under particular suspicion. He told his questioners that what had lured him was the promise of being free to return to France to report first-hand on the progress in Russia. There he saw a car factory being built under the supervision of Ford's specialists and then was taken to a writers' conference, was introduced to them and arrested for propagating anti-political thoughts. Later during his confinement he was treated with respect – it was explained to him that a check-up on his character had had to be made. He was not allowed to communicate with anyone and spent days of anxiety, misery and loneliness. One day, papers arrived authorising his release. He was put on the train and returned to Paris. We were overjoyed at his return.

Mother was working as usual and earned a small but steady income, making shoes with her Serbian friends. She advised Father to write about the arts, not about politics. On Mother's insistence, Father concentrated on writing about ballet and the arts. He found contemporary art hard to understand. Cubism puzzled him. He was not familiar with Western music. He loved everything Russian: Russian music, Russian paintings, Russian opera and ballet. Dancing had always been Father's ancestors' favourite pastime. The men danced on the points of their toes, showing their intricate steps to the girls, who glided softly, silently forming patterns of circles on the floor, hiding their faces; and when couples danced together, although in close proximity, men never touched the women, out of respect.

Father had heard glowing reports about Diaghilev and his famous Russian ballet company. He knew that he was ignorant of the art of classical ballet and therefore could not write about it to his satisfaction. Nevertheless, he wanted to put down his initial impression of this illustrious company, which was at the time the rage of Paris. So he chose a matinee performance and took me with him. We climbed endless flights of stairs, sat in the gallery of a beautiful theatre, and once again my father had conjured up a magical experience for me.

The curtain went up on a ballet called *Chopiniana*. I was transported into a dream world. The setting was a misty wood in the moonlight and the music was romantic Chopin. The sylphs glided smoothly across the stage on the very tips of their toes. Their movements were effortless, yet they jumped, and were lifted by the man. They floated, appeared and disappeared. I had never seen such a perfect combination of music, movement and beauty of the sets. I experienced that inward excitement that one feels when one discovers perfection.

I wanted to cry at the sheer beauty of what I was seeing, and had to be restrained to prevent my falling off my seat. In the interval, I could not come back to earth from my elation, and even my favourite chocolate *esquimo* was eaten impatiently.

The second ballet was *Petrushka*. Tamara Karsavina danced the doll, whom Petrushka the puppet loves although the doll prefers the black Moor. Father told me that the decor was by the Russian artist Benois, and that the sets represented a fairground in Old Russia. There were nannies, big fat coachmen, a large performing bear, street dancers and gypsies. When the snow started falling it was like a fairy tale, and when Petrushka died it was so sad I had to hold my father's hand. He was moved too, although what moved him the most was this picture of Old Russia. For me it was a unique experience. The art of Karsavina, so different in both ballets, so skilful, so artistic... I didn't want to be a nun anymore, I wanted to dance.

I asked my father first, then my mother, then I asked them both together. I begged and pestered daily. They promised to enquire. They had heard of ballet schools in Paris run by famous Imperial Ballerinas. I dreamt of my obsession every night, spoke of it every day. Little did I know that several roles of the great Tamara Karsavina would one day be mine.

But Father's efforts to write about the arts were not rewarding. Politics to him were more vital. He wrote for a magazine about his experience in Russia. The first outburst of success led to nothing. The White Russian newspapers would not forgive him for having travelled to Russia, and did not want his articles anymore. He was out of work, frustrated, once again kept by Mother's work. She did not mind as long as he did not meddle in politics. Unknown, mysterious-looking Russians approached him again. He was invited to go back to Russia with his family and was offered a job as a correspondent. He was to travel in European capitals and write reportage, but his base was to be Moscow.

The job was a six-month try-out. He begged Mother to go with him and take me. He said that the best ballet schools in the world were in Moscow. Mother would not listen. He then begged her to return to her family in Romania, but she wouldn't do that either: it would be admitting defeat. So in 1929 my beloved father went away. He assured me that it was only for six months. I never saw him again.

First steps

On the great ballerinas of the past

In the late 1920s in Paris, three ballet schools were teaching the Russian method. All were regarded as excellent, as they were run by great ballerinas of the past who had achieved fame and glory in the days of the Tzar. Paris had now become the world centre of artistic activities. In the previous decade, Diaghilev had introduced his ballet company to Paris, with its vivid decor, costumes, original music and very brilliant dancers. Not only were the dancers' technique and artistry unique, but the whole spectacle and unison of sound, movement and visual beauty captured the imagination and enthusiasm of artists, painters, musicians, critics and public alike. It was logical for Monte Carlo and Paris to become homes for those refugees and artists who had fled their homelands.

The three ballerinas who had opened dancing schools were Lubov Egorova (Princess Nikita Troubetzkoy) of the Imperial Maryinsky Theatre, a woman in her forties who was reputed to be an excellent teacher for advanced pupils; Mathilda Kschessinska (who was then the morganatic wife of the Grand Duke Andrei of Russia); and Olga Osipovna Preobrajenska.

These last two famous and respected ballerinas, by then in their fifties, had always been fierce rivals as principal dancers of the Imperial Maryinsky Theatre. This was mainly because of Kschessinska's jealousy; she had been the power behind the administration of the Maryinsky Ballet from the year 1890, when she graduated, until the days of the exodus following the Revolution.

Kschessinska had had no difficulties entering the ballet school, as her father had been a very popular character dancer. She became ballerina in 1892 and prima ballerina, a very high status in the Imperial system, in 1893. In 1895 she was given the title of Prima Ballerina Assoluta. She had been the mistress of Nicolas II before he became Tzar. She used her status effectively and, according to the Maryinsky's director, became the dictator of policy. Her whims were orders: programmes had to be changed and the repertoire altered according to her wishes. Her special status had made her extremely wealthy; she owned a mansion in St Petersburg. During the Revolution, it was from the balcony of that magnificent house that Lenin addressed the citizens of Petrograd. Kschessinska also owned an immense quantity of jewels many of which she insisted on wearing when dancing the role of Princess Aurora. She was a superb dancer, always keen to improve her technique.

The great Italian ballerinas who were engaged by the Maryinsky as guest artists were an inspiration both to her and to Preobrajenska. They were also a challenge, and made the Russians work harder. Christian Johansson, the Swedish maestro, had taught the Maryinsky dancers softness, fluidity, beauty and grace. Now the important thing was to concentrate on precision, pirouettes and brilliance in complicated jumps. Their Italian maestro, Enrico Cecchetti, was known to develop strong point work: 'points of steel', it was said. In comparison with the Italians, they were conscious of lacking an elusive quality called *brio*; but with Cecchetti's help they were able to improve their technique.

Kschessinska was first to succeed the guest ballerinas. She was brilliant and ambitious. After three years she had mastered a number of *fouettés* (turns non-stop on one foot as the other whips through the air) just as the Italians had done. She then included *fouettés* in everything she danced, even in *La Fille mal gardée*, where it was out of character. She gained a reputation as a sublime technician. Her appearances were great social occasions attended by the Tzar, his entourage and St Petersburg high society. By Imperial command, Riccardo Drigo, composer and chief conductor at the Maryinsky, had to compose special music in order to include her in his ballet *The Pearl*. The dance was introduced as a separate number, a procedure often used.

The teacher whom my parents and I chose for me to apply to, however, was Preobrajenska. She was no less well known and her popularity in Paris was even greater amongst the Russians. She was renowned for her generosity, providing pupils to dance at benefit balls, charity functions and bazaars in aid of refugees. We had chosen her because of her reputation as a warm human being, and because her studio was on a direct Métro line. We read what we could find about her; in her memoirs she said it was a miracle that she had succeeded in graduating at the Maryinsky School. She was too small, too frail and too thin. She had something not quite right with one foot and doctors thought that she had a curvature of the vertebrae. Years later, a book about the Maryinsky ballet school said of her: 'This feeble, sickly child adored dancing and with the whole of her soul tried to get into the ballet school. The school's commission choosing the candidates said her hips were deformed and that she did not have the essential qualities for ballet.' For three years her parents' efforts were of no avail. No one believed in this child with her ordinary face, unattractive body and thin legs. The qualities she had were not noticed. But finally she was accepted; her legs became pliable, her jumps light and soft, her points 'as strong as steel', and she was extremely musical. Her teachers in the early years were Ivanov, Johansson and Marius Petipa, and then Cecchetti for final perfection.

She dedicated herself fanatically to learning, as she did later to teaching. She studied complete music scores, and extracted from her teachers the best of the foundation of French and Danish dancing, amalgamated in the great

Russian classical style. She travelled to Paris for further tuition, and to Milan for private lessons.

Having started in the corps de ballet at the Maryinsky, she learned all the solo parts and was ready to replace ballerinas. When, after prolonged applause, she repeated variations, the audiences admired her skilful improvisations. She shone in *Coppélia*, *Raymonda* and *Paquita*, but the role of Lisa in *La Fille mal gardée* was monopolised by Kschessinska. After a decade, it was given to Preobrajenska, but her rival stopped at nothing to spoil her performances. Mysteriously, the door of the cage holding live chickens was unlocked, and during Preobrajenska's solo variation they came out onto the stage and created a panic amongst the people in the wings. Preobrajenska did not bat an eyelid. She smiled charmingly, pretended the chickens were part of her solo and, dancing carefully amongst them, received one of the biggest ovations of her career. Valerian Svetlov, the great ballet critic, was rapturous:

> She is bubbling with a sense of humour, she is gay, joyful, has a gift of comedy, she was graceful, her dancing was above praise. Virtuosity, technique, hand in hand with pure classicism and inborn musicality. Her dancing is as natural as breathing. She was Lisa personified, not a prima ballerina who took off her sables and diamonds. She wore the bonnet and apron of Lisa as if it were her own...

In 1902, Pavel Gerdt choreographed Saint-Saëns's *Javotte* for her. Saint-Saëns said she was the embodiment of his music. Andre Levinson, a very famous and important critic in Russia, said, 'She is the spirit of classical dancing'. In *Chopiniana*, Fokine created the prelude for her. The ballet is now called *Les Sylphides*. Fokine recalls:

> In this dance, I explained her unique capacity for balance. She froze for a moment on the toes of one foot and, in a dance almost devoid of jumps, succeeded in giving the impression of being borne aloft. In the following runs on the stage, in her flights interspersed with moments of immobility, there were no sudden spasms of movement. She floated, as down, from one flower to another, attaching itself for a moment in passage to a stem or to a leaf. The first breath of breeze projecting it on again further...

She danced in Italy, France, England, Germany and South America, and was often a guest artist in Monte Carlo. Then she devoted herself to teaching as wholly as she had done to dancing, always being generous; and when the young Egorova was given her favourite role to dance, *Raymonda*, she taught her the part. She organised ballet performances at the front line during the Great War as late as 1917, when Russia was in complete chaos, then moved to Paris and opened a studio there. A most successful school, its reputation was worldwide. The Italians described her as 'the little Russian woman full of grace and brilliance, a tiny woman but a great artist'.

That was the teacher for me, if only she would accept me.

Into ballet school

We went to meet the great Preobrajenska in her studio. We were ushered in by a plump secretary, shown to some chairs and told to watch the class. Preobrajenska came in. She was a tiny woman, the same height as was I, then aged nine. About twenty girls of all ages and a few boys were waiting for her. All stood along the walls next to a barre built along the length of the studio, their feet turned out heel to heel, one hand extended, the other resting on the barre. Olga Osipovna watered the whole of the floor with a small watering can, to make it less slippery. She then took a long, heavy stick and gave the floor three knocks. It was a theatrical signal for the curtain to go up.

She said, 'Into the first position, *pliés*.' The pupils bent their knees and went deep down, scooping the air with the free arm. Olga Osipovna was counting aloud, rhythmically knocking her long stick on the floor. The chubby secretary was also the pianist, and was playing a tune on the piano without looking at any written music. Occasionally Olga Osipovna would gently tap a bottom with her long stick and say, 'Tuck it in! I don't want to see it sticking out', or she would get hold of a pupil's shoulders from the back and wrench them straight, or a tense wrist and say, 'Soften that hand up'. She was incessantly walking around instructing, correcting, very rarely praising. I could tell that she had her favourites amongst her pupils, and that there were others, not the very good ones, of whom she was not taking much notice.

After her pupils had worked at the barre, changing sides to exercise both legs, she called them all to the centre of the room. Each girl and boy had a particular place. The best dancers were in the front row; for the others, the weaker their technique, the further back they would stand. Olga Osipovna showed a series of steps that she called *enchaînements*: a *port de bras* for an arm exercise, an adagio for balance and beauty of movement, an allegro for speed and precision, and then the turns.

She split her class into two and gave the girls from the back rows easier steps, one at a time. There was a *glissade*, sliding along the floor, and an *assemblé*, a jump with a 'swish'; Olga Osipovna became very angry when they did this without keeping their heels on the floor. I thought that she was naming these steps in French because we were in Paris, but later found out that the ballet terms all over the world were in French as a universal ballet language. There were *pas de chat*, and *pas de bourrée*, *sissonnes*, *jetés* and *emboîtés*, and finally spectacular *fouettés*: one girl would come into the centre of the studio, move into a preparation, find her balance and proceed to turn on the toes of one foot, keeping the other foot in the air. The first girl did thirty-two of these, the second girl sixteen and then the others all tried at the same time. That movement was a technical achievement that not many could do.

I was fascinated, and with trepidation waited till the end of the class. The fat secretary then put my mother and me at the end of a line of girls who had danced in the class and now were thanking the teacher, some kissing her, some shaking hands with her, but all curtseying. When it was my turn, I curtsied too. The chubby pianist-secretary told Olga Osipovna that I was a young candidate. She looked into my eyes, then lifted my skirt and looked at my knees and said, 'You will have to straighten these', turned me round, looked at my back and said 'Your back is straight, that is fine', then asked me, 'Why do you want to learn?' I said, 'Because I want to dance more than anything.' She smiled and all her face was transformed and lost its severity. She spoke to me in Russian; I, having been for three years in French schools, replied in French.

'Is your daughter French?' she asked Mother.

'No,' said Mother, embarrassed.

'Why does the child answer in French? Do you not keep up her Russian? It is such a beautiful language – she is not to neglect it.'

'I will try,' answered Mama.

'It is essential to learn music too. Does she play a musical instrument?'

'Yes,' Mother said, lying.

'Good, which one?'

'The violin,' one lie leading to another.

'Violin is hard to play, unless she is extremely talented. I would recommend the piano.'

'I will change her teacher immediately.'

I was amazed at Mama's sangfroid.

I was told to come to class on the following Saturday, as it was my half-day from school, and so my ballet days started: a world that was to be full of elation and depression, high hopes often dashed to the ground, disappointment and fulfilment, days of frustration, years of hard work, slaving, crying, and aching limbs and bleeding toes. But it was a new world, with new friends, new horizons, new ideas, new striving for achievements. For my mother, new worries too. If I were talented, I would have to study ballet full-time – daily classes, never-ending exercises. I had to be taught music. If I were to be taken out of my good school, I would have to have private tutors; that meant teachers coming to my home. Where was home? A small garret in a tiny, shabby hotel? Where would we put the piano, if indeed we could buy one? Where would the money come from to pay for all these lessons, tutors, clothes, food, rent, ballet shoes? I knew the difficulties, and did not want to show my eagerness too much. But Mother, with her impulsive, enthusiastic nature, did not hesitate. She was like that; she plunged into the unknown, she was generous, energetic, and never thought that she could make a mistake. She said she was just going to work harder. Everything would be all right; we would worry when the time came. We had made a decision and there was no turning back.

The first few months

My first few lessons were very disappointing and even frightening. Olga Osipovna took no notice of me. Nothing had been explained to me, including the positions we were supposed to keep our feet in. My limbs were aching at night. My teacher's system in the beginners' class was one of repetition, the same exercises every time. Eventually I learned the names of most of them. I realised that every step that we did in the middle of the classroom had to be done with the feet and legs going through the positions learned at the barre. But I was disheartened; I had a feeling that I was clumsy, stiff in my limbs with enormous knees and unpointed toes.

I attended two classes a week, one on Saturday afternoons at her studio at La Madeleine, another an evening class in a studio at Rue de la Pompe. She lost her patience often, shouted at pupils, grabbed chairs by their backs and slammed them on the floor with force, and once even broke a mirror in a temper. I was petrified at these rages and was happy that they were not directed at me. Mother found out that my teacher, loved by all, full of charm, grace, generosity and goodwill, was going through a difficult time in her private life. Her companion, a Russian man, was giving her trouble.

A few months went by and both Mother and I were discouraged at her lack of attention towards me, when she suddenly said, 'If the child wants to be a dancer, she will have to attend daily classes.' She took me by the hand, moved me from the back row into the third row and said, 'This is where you will be in future.'

Her attitude towards me changed. There wasn't a day when she didn't remind me to stretch my knees, point my toes, work on my turn-out, put my heels on the floor in *glissades*, swish my foot in an *assemblé*, leave my head behind when trying to turn and bring it back quickly before my body finished turning, relax my hands, pick up my elbows, soften my movement, steady my balance in a *développé* and hold my back in an arabesque. It was torture. I did not know what to concentrate on; all parts of my body seemed awkward and not to her liking, everything I was doing was wrong. For months it was work, work, work, corrections, corrections, corrections. Mother made up her mind to let me attend daily classes.

We made new friends. A family called Sidorenko, whose two daughters were learning to dance, had a very large apartment. Mother rented a room in their flat and life became different. They were wealthy and had a piano, and we could share the teachers who called at their lovely flat. We had a piano teacher, as well as a teacher of French, mathematics and history who came once a week and left us homework. There were three of us now to go to our ballet classes; we would travel unaccompanied in spite of the constant dangers of being molested, and of men known to expose themselves to little girls in the Métro. My namesake, Tamara (later known as Tamaria Grigorieva), was the elder sister, beautiful, selfish and mean; the younger, Galina (Galina Razoumova), was warm, affectionate and sensitive – my best friend, who remained so all my life.

Mother had now perfected her skill in plaiting shoes, and was working all day and late into the night to pay for my lessons. There was never enough money, as the daily classes were a big drain on our finances. Mama was always in debt. She had to go to Olga Osipovna and ask her for credit, or to put me back on two lessons a week. Olga Osipovna, with a smile and great sympathy, firmly said 'no' to cutting any lessons and asked Mother what kind of work she did. On hearing about the shoes, she said, 'Forget about the money. Make me a pair of shoes.' Mama took the imprint of her foot on a piece of paper, drew the shape of her foot and asked her Serbian friends to make a wooden last especially for Olga Osipovna. It was a tiny one, size thirty-three, like a child's foot. The shoes were made and fitted perfectly. They were soft, pliable and comfortable, and as soon as she put them on she stood on her toes, making a series of *échappés* where the feet on points are spread slightly apart and then the heels come back on the floor in a perfect crossed-over fifth position. I was hypnotised. My teacher then went to the far end of the classroom, took a preparatory position and proceeded to make a perfect series of turns in a diagonal line, called *piqués*, finishing up with fast turns called *chaînés*, all on the tips of her toes. She was very pleased; apparently the sole of the shoe was soft but supported her foot as a real ballerina's toe-shoes did, and she had been carried away showing us her skill in a way that none of her young pupils had seen before. She was then in her late fifties but that did not stop her. From then on she wore only Mama's shoes for classes, folding them into a box carefully after use, and Mama made her many pairs in different colours. Many of the mothers gave Mama orders too. But life was costly and we were always short of money.

First appearances

We pupils of Preobrajenska became involved in charity work for White Russian refugees. She could never refuse a plea for us to perform for a worthy cause. I had been privileged to be included in her arrangement of a special version of *La valse des fleurs*. I had been learning ballet for only a few months, so was thrilled to be selected, even though I was dancing in the back row.

These annual winter balls were grand charity affairs. The publicity spread far and wide so that the event would attract, as well as Russian émigrés, wealthy society people who could contribute generously. The Russian aristocracy who attended wore their uniforms, medals, insignias, orders and decorations.

We girls were impressed at hearing a live major-domo announce, in a thunderous voice, '*Le Comte et La Comtesse* so and so', '*Le Prince et La Princesse* so and so', 'His Imperial Highness *Le Grand Duc*'. There always was a Grand Duc.

We were hidden behind a velvet curtain, peeping at the ladies and gentlemen. It seemed to me that I recognised in one of the Comtesses a cashier from one of the cheap Russian restaurants near the Place Clichy. This could well be so, but tonight she was La Comtesse, reliving the splendour of her past. These evenings, when the cream of Russia met, were a pretence that nothing had changed. The men clicked their heels on being introduced, or on asking a lady to dance. The women wore long white gloves and held their heads erect. The string orchestra played polkas, mazurkas and waltzes. The ball opened with a polonaise.

All of Preobrajenska's best pupils were there as soloists. I was at the back, being very raw still. We wore ethereal, pale green tunics, the skirts scooped as petals so that our legs would show, but there was a great discrepancy in headdresses, which represented different flowers. Irina Baronova was a marguerite, Tamara Toumanova a rose, Ienakieva a cornflower, Nina Youshkevich a lily of the valley. I represented the grass. My hat had no flowers, and consisted of greeny-yellow artificial grass, looking more like hay. One mother said about me, 'Poor, miserable dried-out grass. Poor child.' That upset me even more. But Olga Osipovna took me aside and said, 'You must work. When you are as good as the others, everything will fall into place.'

She gave me the will to improve myself, to try to be as good as Toumanova and Baronova, who were in the advanced class. They were already strong, confident dancers and my admiration for them knew no bounds. I couldn't make up my mind which one I preferred. Toumanova was lovely to look at, dark with wonderful sad eyes, her movements full of intensity. Baronova, in pigtails and with a retroussé nose, already had a clean technique and a pure style that made her steps look effortless.

These first appearances were disasters for me. A German grand-opera company from Berlin was scheduled to perform *Der Ring des Nibelungen*. We were recruited for the first opera, *Das Rheingold*, to appear as the Nibelungen, the little dwarfs in the earth caverns, mining gold for the Gods. The complicated scenery presented acute difficulties. Some boxes in the dress circle were removed to produce the effect of the depths of the Rhine; green gauze was stretched over the wide stage, and moving shadows projected on it to portray the movement of the water. In the depths of the water, maidens swam guarding the gold. It took hours to work that scene successfully. The caverns of the mining Nibelungen were dark, gloomy, as black as the bowels of the earth.

During the dress rehearsals, we sat around for hours half-listening to the orders shouted in German, a language we could not understand. The singers, Wotan and his wife Fricka, sang what seemed interminable arias. Other people dashed about: giants with swords, helmets and shields. The lower boxes in the audience were requisitioned too, to accommodate an overflowing orchestra. The French stagehands swore at everyone, calling them '*sales Boches*'.

The waiting was endless. I had a personal difficulty: I had two long black plaits that I couldn't hide under my gnome's peaked cap.

We had strict instructions to listen for our cues. We listened to all that German singing, not being sure what precisely we were listening for. All we knew was that we would be called for a *tableau vivant*, before the music started with the clicking sound that was our signal for mining. I was busy hiding my hair because it didn't match the red beards we had stuck on our faces, and must have missed my marching orders. When I looked around, my bearded companions had disappeared. I made a dash for my rock. The curtain went up and one red-bearded dwarf with black plaits was left standing in the wings.

The rocket I received from the stage manager was in German. I couldn't tell exactly how nasty it was, although the tone spoke for itself. My beard had been so saturated with glue that it could not be completely removed afterwards and I had to suffer the added humiliation of walking about with the shadow of a beard from ear to ear.

Another disastrous appearance was at the Russian Opera season in Paris, the opera being Mussorgsky's *Boris Godunov*, with the great Russian bass Feodor Chaliapin singing the role of Boris. Chaliapin adored Russian music and popularised it all over the world. He was a brilliant actor as well as singer, and Boris was his favourite part.

Being an artist and a sculptor, he drew and sketched his face in various roles, mastering his make-up to such an extent that he became the character that he was portraying. Not only did he look fierce with his vibrant eyes, his thick eyebrows, his cropped black beard giving his face a haggard look, but he was strong and majestic. He acted the part in a grandiose way. His sheer size was dominating.

There is a superb portrait of him, looking regal, perturbed and imposing, his golden robe embroidered with pearls, sapphires and rubies, the huge Holy Cross of the Tzar on a heavy chain on his mighty chest.

Chaliapin sang this opera many times. It was not considered that a costume rehearsal was needed. As pageboy, I was to hold the train of his robe during the biggest scene in the opera, the coronation of Boris. The beauty of the singing was overwhelming – the chorus and the extras were all Russian refugees. I was entranced. The orchestra and even the stagehands were aware of this great moment: the Mighty Chaliapin's important entrance.

I had been instructed to hold his train with one hand, and in the other to carry an incense burner, swinging it to create a religious atmosphere. I was to march behind Boris in the procession, followed by a crowd of extras carrying icons.

The wardrobe mistress saw my long black plaits hanging down my back, and with a piercing yell of 'Where the hell is your wig?' disappeared into the wardrobe department, and came running back panting, clutching a tiny, blond, pudding-basin wig, suitable for a small boy, but too small for my long black hair. 'Put it on.' I tried. If I put it onto my forehead, my plaits were hanging down the back; if I tried to arrange it to the back of my neck, my forehead was showing, with black hair tidily parted in the middle. I needed at least three hands, one for Chaliapin's train, one for the incense burner and one for the minute, slippery wig.

The mighty Chaliapin swept out of his dressing room a few moments before his eagerly awaited entrance. He wasn't known for his delicate language when angry. He looked at me from head to foot and to my head again, and with his fierce, resonant basso profundo voice, shouted to the stage manager, 'God almighty, by the bloody Virgin, what kind of a scarecrow have you given me here?' I stood paralysed for a few seconds before bursting into tears, decided in a flash of panic to put my wig forward, grabbed his robe and my incense burner, and, hoping that in the dazzle of Chaliapin's entrance no one would notice me, walked behind him sideways like a crab, sobbing.

La plus petite danseuse du monde

It had been firmly established in the ballet world that the more experience a dancer had on stage during the initial learning period, the better it would be for dealing with technical difficulties later on. Difficulties arose often, such as stages with no side wings so that various entrances were impossible, stages with steep slopes affecting one's balance, strong projector lights blinding dancers, sticky or slippery floors, and erratic musical accompaniment. Preobrajenska's own childhood and adolescence in the Maryinsky Theatre dictated to her that she should give her pupils every opportunity to perform and better themselves.

For this purpose, Olga Osipovna allowed into the studio where she held daily classes a stream of onlookers: ballet directors, impresarios, choreographers and many other people. They were allowed to watch the classes and select dancers for a project or a venture, and often even propose contracts to them.

One of the visitors was a Russian named Orlitsky. He was recruiting new dancers for performances in Algiers and Morocco. Using the best theatres,

dressing room to say that it wasn't the kind of show he wanted. Couldn't we change the programme, wear more revealing dresses, bare our bellies and wander around the tables before and after dancing and talk to the men? It would be better for business; men liked dancing girls, and if the girls were prepared to sit at the tables with the men the proprietor would pay more money to the company.

Orlitsky drew himself up. 'My girls – never', '*Jamais*', '*Nous sommes des danseurs classiques.*' A violent argument followed.

Mama joined in the row, took the hysterical girl to her large bosom, pacified Orlitsky and told him to stop shouting, and it was decided that we would wait until the morrow and seek advice from our impresario, who by then, we hoped, would be back from Marrakesh.

Le beau légionnaire

Our contretemps had been overheard by two men in uniform, who had followed the proprietor and were standing outside our dressing room. One of them clicked his heels and introduced himself: 'Captain Morosov, Foreign Legion, and my batman Alexei. Can I do anything to help you?' He knew the country. He thought we needed protection. No young girls should be allowed into such an establishment. Did we have proper accommodation? He clicked his heels again to Mama and I saw immediately that he was overwhelmed by her plump loveliness.

That evening, under his supervision, we changed hotels. We had apparently picked the wrong hotel – one for short-term clientele who hired rooms by the hour.

Our Captain was on a month's leave. His regiment was stationed in the desert, defending forts and fighting attacking tribes. He was of Russian origin, had fought in the war and had escaped during the Revolution with his faithful batman. He was so happy to have found us and to be able to speak his native tongue. We told him that we had to continue our season if we were to get paid. He became the mediator, our impresario not having turned up. It was arranged that we should dance the more lively national numbers of our repertoire: a fast Russian dance, an Italian one with tambourines, a Spanish one with castanets.

The proprietor never spoke again of sitting at the tables to entertain the customers. We never knew what the dashing Captain had said to him. The reputation of the Foreign Legion men was that they were brave and ruthless; they were always armed and stood no nonsense. From then on, every night the cafe was filled by men from the Foreign Legion, in clean sandy-coloured uniforms, caps decorated with red and gold and flaps fluttering at the back of their necks. Morosov, we knew, gave orders to his friends to protect us. No

Moroccan dared touch a girl. We were escorted to the cafe and to our hotel after each performance.

In the daytime, cases of oranges were sent round to the company, delivered by Alexei. Our days were filled with invitations to visit various places around Casablanca. I guessed that the Captain had fallen in love with my mother; but, being a gentleman and very conventional, he expressed his love by organising outings for all the girls Mama was saddled with.

He planned our meals and hired three horse-drawn carriages for us. Mother, he and I would be at the head, and in the other two carriages the ten girls and Alexei – shy Alexei, never daring to look into a girl's eyes. We went to the edge of the desert and to the foot of the Atlas Mountains; we saw caravans of camels driven by black-dressed Arabs, faces hidden, eyes flashing. We saw donkeys being maltreated, some having large sores on the side of their bellies and heavily laden with goods, with a man riding on top as well, pushing a metal rod into the wound. Their women walked behind carrying heavy earthenware jugs on their heads, faces hidden, bodies draped in white cloth, like walking tents.

We filled ourselves with dates, figs and watermelons. We saw what was to us the horrible sight of a live kitten being torn to pieces and eaten by dogs.

When we stopped anywhere, a crowd of little boys clung to our carriages asking for coins. The way Morosov treated them made me think him cruel. He had a little stick and beat them on their fingers with quick, sharp blows.

We were frequently amazed by the sight of men relieving themselves in full view in the busy thoroughfares of the city: not by stepping out of the way, but squatting on their haunches with their robes pulled up.

During this season another misfortune happened. My mother's handbag was stolen, with her passport and personal papers. That seemed a dreadful disaster. There was no Romanian consulate in Casablanca and one could not travel anywhere without a passport. As a minor, I was included on her passport.

I suspected that its disappearance was a plot, engineered by the Captain. The day before, Alexei, bringing a gift of fruit, shyly asked me a strange question: how would I feel if my mother married again? I said firmly that she couldn't, she was already married. Alexei continued that his master was a very kind man, who had saved the lives of many during the Russian Revolution. He said how happy the Captain had been looking after us. He had found in my mother a real Russian woman, warm and lovely. He had even taken up his balalaika again, neglected since his days in Russia, and sang old romantic melodies softly to himself at night.

That was the longest speech that Alexei had made during our acquaintance. It had embarrassed him; he mumbled, looking around to see that no one else was listening. He put into my hands a heavy basket of fruit and disappeared. Why had he said all that?

In our dilemma about the loss of the passport, *le beau légionnaire* attended to everything. First, he formally proposed marriage to Mama, saying that the simplest, quickest remedy was to marry him there and then. Mama wouldn't hear of it. I was not surprised – I knew that she still loved my father. Then Morosov took Mama to the police to make a declaration. She was presented with a form. She had the presence of mind to enter her maiden name and to answer the question, 'Single, married, widowed or divorced?', by putting a cross against 'divorced'. Mother had never been divorced from my father, but thinking quickly now, and perhaps prompted by Morosov, she altered her status. She did it without hesitation, and told me later that it was much easier that way than to get a legal divorce in France.

No questions were asked; she emerged from the prefecture a divorced woman. I had become more and more certain that her handsome legionnaire was responsible for these machinations. He was clever, positive and imposing, inspiring respect and even fear amongst the officials. Did he bribe a Moroccan to steal Mama's papers because her excuse for not marrying him was that she was not free? But we knew that without that man we would be lost. His gallantry to us was in sharp contrast with the shiftiness of the others around us. The police, the passport officials and the proprietor could all be either bought for cash or ruled by fear. It was worse than Romania because it was unsafe as well – in Romania there was no fear of being abducted.

We were able to finish our season and be paid in full, and to have an official-looking paper stating who we were, all in order, in lieu of a passport. We were able to leave Casablanca, wiser for the experience.

Next stop was Marrakesh. The Captain must have suspected that we wouldn't do any better in Marrakesh. We had the address of a so-called theatre. Once again it was a dirty cafe, right in the main square, which was a wide-open place, bubbling with life, an open market with hundreds of people buying and selling goods, bargaining and arguing. There were snake charmers with cobras in hessian bags, spoon players clicking noisily to the accompaniment of goatskin drums, grain sellers, fruit sellers. The market place was stacked with sacks of beans, corn and flour, and men's shoulders were laden with carpets and rugs.

We again relied on Morosov to inspect our unsuitable terpsichorean palace. He said we could not dance there. There wasn't even a platform to dance on, and there was no hope of finding a pianist. Morosov found a hotel for us and made us swear that we would wait for his return and not budge without him.

Orlitsky, unaccustomed to battling against the tide of life, left the management of the company to Morosov – a matter of working out a safe return to Paris, because our impresario had escaped to France, never to be seen again.

We had to make our way to one of the ports, Algiers or Oran, from where ships sailed to France. We had to transport our luggage and costumes; and, worst of all, we were very short of cash. The cheapest way to travel across Morocco was to take local buses. Morosov could not leave Morocco, but he insisted on coming with us as far as Oujda on the Algerian frontier. From Marrakesh we struggled on to Meknes, then Fes.

The further we went into the interior of Morocco, the worse the conditions of the people were. There were many blind people with flies stuck around their eyes, men with amputated legs with the bone protruding out of their limb, people covered in sores, beggars, mothers carrying babies, and children with enormous stomachs, swollen by hunger.

As we were waiting to change buses in Fes, two well-dressed men in European clothes approached my mother and offered to buy her girls. She could be included in the deal and put in charge of a harem. They would pay not only in paper money but in gold and goods and would even give our man (Mr Orlitsky) a camel, so that he could get himself into port. During the course of this proposition our Captain returned, and what he said in Arabic made the two fellows disappear.

The heat was appalling, the water scarce. Occasionally one could buy some from leather bags suspended at the side of a camel's saddle, but the water was dangerous to drink. The Moroccans ate a kind of flat cake as hard as a stone, but we existed on watermelons and dates. The last part of the journey was the hardest of all; there was no possibility of washing, and no toilet. When the bus stopped, one had to take refuge behind a tree, if there was a tree to go behind, while the eyes of the bus passengers followed our efforts to hide. The drivers were like lunatics; the more dangerous the road, the faster they drove.

Our two large wicker baskets of costumes were secured on the roof of the bus, which annoyed the other passengers, who wanted to put their bundles there. Morosov argued, swore, manipulated and saw to our food and our comfort, while Orlitsky sat brooding in a corner of the bus. Nothing like this had ever happened to his classical troupe before.

In Oujda we had the whole day to wait for a direct bus to Oran. Captain Morosov bought all our tickets. Mama, accompanied by the girls and me, went to visit the town. Mama's curiosity had always been aroused by tales of life in the harem, and she wanted to visit one. We were taken into a courtyard in the centre of a cool house. On every side of the courtyard were rooms with barred windows. We were not allowed to go into the rooms; but women, like monkeys in cages, came to their windows and spoke to us, covering their faces. Mama went to one face and uncovered it. It belonged to a lovely young woman, with dark almond-shaped eyes encircled with black. She blushed, while the others laughed a lot, stretched their hands and touched our breasts.

Once again Mama was propositioned to sell some of the girls, this time by the fat old woman in charge. She spoke a few words of French and said, '*Moi, acheter les grosses filles*'. She was only interested in the fat ones. Mama laughed, gathering her brood to herself. We were given beads and jingling bracelets. I was worried that some heavy door would click somewhere behind us, so that we would miss our bus and be locked up for ever.

It wasn't at all like the *Thousand and One Nights* oriental tale I had read. It was dirty, sordid, and smelled of sweat. The cats and dogs in the courtyard looked starved, the women's hands were filthy, and most of the women had no teeth and looked very fat.

Our bus to Oran was waiting. Captain Morosov kissed my mother's hands many times. He did not speak much, just cleared his throat a lot. And begged her to write.

We did get to Oran, and a ship took us back to Marseilles. Orlitsky explained to the authorities our difficulty and lack of money. Many papers were signed and the shipping-line officials agreed to repatriate us.

Mama was very quiet. I saw her eyes looking into the distance, appearing to be very misty.

Return to Romania

Back, then, to the Studio Wacker, but not with our pockets full. Mother had formed the idea of becoming reconciled to her parents and paying them a visit. They had never stopped writing, and the relationship, in spite of Grandfather's disapproval of her departure, had remained affectionate. Mother had to hold on to her pride and convince them that it was essential for us to go on living in Paris because of my 'chosen vocation'.

She set to work very hard once again to save for a fare back to Romania. She had an idea that I could give a few dance recitals over there, so that the grandparents would be convinced of my talent. For that purpose, Preobrajenska worked out a full dancing programme for me. She always enthusiastically approved of any project. She dug into the repertoire of the ancient ballets and produced a series of dances, to be fashioned into a programme with an interval. The first half would include my Russian dance and finish with a romantic Strauss waltz in which I was dreamily pleading for my hero to come back to me. The second half would have my doll's dance, and after a few other pieces the finale would be a new number, a foxtrot being hummed by the whole of France: 'Happy days are here again'.

I had been very good at doing the Charleston; one day Olga Osipovna caught me before class showing off, and I think it inspired her. For my foxtrot I wore a saucy feather hat and a boa round my neck and moved my hips like a flapper. I loved that and really threw my classical inhibitions away.

Mama, wanting to prove that she too had had productive years, made shoes for all the family from scraps of leather handbags – very fashionable in Paris. Olga Osipovna, too, was paid by a new stack of shoes.

We had been away five years, and my grandparents were looking older. We were met with tears and hugs, then climbed into the horse-drawn carriage, Grandfather holding the reins, me next to him. The hood was down and we took many detours to come to our destination. Grandfather obviously wanted to show the town that his daughter and granddaughter were back from Paris, France.

The guest bedroom had been redecorated for us, and a feast of bulging tables prepared for our first meal. Relations, friends and business associates had gathered to welcome us. Grandfather used the occasion to display the wines from his exclusive cellar. I hadn't eaten so much for a long time, and I was eager not to offend the cooks.

At the end of the four-hour meal, Grandfather pulled some documents out of his pocket and announced that, as his daughter had come back, he was celebrating the event by handing over to her the deeds of a block of flats transferred into her name. He was now dispersing his assets, having given to Lydia a house that she chose herself in Galatz; in spite of her husband's wealth, this was her family inheritance. Evgraf, the only surviving son, was going to inherit the vineyards and the town house. Evgraf's family lived with my grandparents now, in a large separate wing. The grandparents adored their two grandsons, my cousins, now aged ten and twelve.

Grandfather was happy at the family being together again. His only niggling feeling of unease was that Evgraf was missing. He'd called the reception 'bullshit', then had gone into the cellar to hold his own celebration...

The next day Uncle Evgraf, sober, embarrassed, hugged me to his heart and asked if I would like to ride with him to the vineyard – I could hold the reins. Yes, I would. Mama asked Grandfather whether I was safe with him or if there was a risk of his getting very drunk and frightening me. No, no risk. He had his bouts of despair and frustration, drank to excess and had taken now to hitting his wife when drunk, though she accepted that situation without complaint. But nothing would happen to me: he never drank while attending to the vines, which were now entirely looked after by him.

Evgraf showed them to me with pride. He lectured about grafting and told me the history of vines: how their cultivation started in the Caucasus, had been flourishing in Egypt, was taken up by the Romans, and then spread to the rest of Europe. He told me how the monks kept the grapes going during the Dark Ages. Later it was discovered that wine matured better in bottles, but we still sold a lot directly from barrels. Our simple people loved it that way; bottles were for the refined customers.

He loved looking after vines, watching the tender shoots in April turn into leaves in May. He had to be alert during the flowering period when hail or heavy rain could destroy the whole crop. In September he battled with the birds: children made festoons of coloured paper attached to branches, men dressed scarecrows in hats, but birds were hard to fool.

That afternoon Uncle Evgraf and I became firm friends. I do not suppose that anyone else listened to his lectures on the history of grape growing. He asked me a lot about Paris and the thousands of Russian refugees there. I said that most of them were waiting for a political change so that they could return to their homeland, but his comment was that they were fooling themselves and it would never happen.

On the night that we returned from our vineyard expedition, my uncle got drunk again. We could hear the noise of smashed crockery, abusive words, shouting, crying. We ran into their part of the house. Uncle's sons were trying to cope and lift his heavy body from the floor. The white tablecloth on the table had red wine spilled all over it, the plate of soup was upset, the chair had fallen, and he was lying on the floor, having knocked his head on the edge of the table. His wife was nursing a bruised face. I was stunned. I could not believe that the same person, the gentle, talkative man patiently explaining to me about the cultivation of the grapes, had turned into this gross beast, who had hit his kind wife and beaten his children, made this mess on the tablecloth and now was smelling vile, and looking bloated, dirty and revolting.

Recital

Mama set out to plan three recitals. One was to be at Grandfather's dacha in the village of Serguevka, by the sea; another in Aunt Lydia and Uncle Kolia's bathing establishment on Boudaky, ten miles further along the coast; and the main one in our town of Akkerman.

We had to find two good musicians: an accompanist to play the piano for my numbers, and another, a brilliant soloist we hoped, with a classical repertoire to play during my changes of costume.

The town's only piano teacher was proud to have been asked and showed her skill admirably, but no other talented musician could be found. Then, as though by magic, a family of gypsies walked into our courtyard. They were in rags, barefoot, hungry and tired. The woman offered to predict our future by reading our palms. The children begged for bread, and the man took a violin out of an old case that he put on the ground in preparation for a coin collection.

I stretched out my palms, curious to hear about my destiny. She looked at them, seemed very surprised at what she saw, and told me that I would spend my life away. I was to cross seas and oceans, learn other languages, live in other countries and communicate with people through the arts. In faraway continents, unknown to me, people of various nationalities would applaud my work. My destiny was different from those of other people whose palms she read in our town. She had never seen such an amount of travelling. I would marry in my early twenties and have a child, a girl. She could not tell me anything beyond the age of thirty-five, though she saw a great change, a withdrawal, a loss and separation from the world. I was to work hard, always, but be rewarded by success. I was elated by her predictions. Hard work and success were exciting. That must mean ballet. The age of thirty-five did not worry me – it was so far in the future.

As I went into the house to get money and food for the family, the man started to play his violin. The most artistic and passionate melodies came out of his fiddle. He played what I guessed was a Turkish lament, the sound of his violin imitating the sound of shepherds' pipes in the mountains. Then he played a Romanian dance melody, a *doina*, starting with a slow tempo, evolving into a frenzy that merged Eastern and Western music, Arab quarter tones and European tunes. He then played a jig in which his bow, moving in fast semicircles, called for the participation of all the strings in quick succession as his foot was beating the ground.

Everyone came out into the courtyard and stood listening in amazement. At the end Mama declared, 'That's the man for us. He will play at Tamara's recital.' The proposition was accepted immediately.

There was no trouble about the gypsies moving to the seaside; they knew the district well and slept under the stars anyway. What must they do? Work out a programme, with the names of the composers. Impossible! Don't know the names of the tunes, or the composers; can't write, don't read music. No matter, just play five different tunes, don't repeat them, start with a slow one, then a faster one, then a sad one, and keep your most lively one for the end. Come back at the end of the week. You will be well paid.

Every condition was accepted, except that they should come back at the end of the week. They wanted to stay. They could sleep in the courtyard; the stables would be even better, as they loved horses. They were not asking for anything but to be fed and given old clothes and blankets.

Nanny, supported by Grandmother, argued to keep them out. It was dangerous to have gypsies sleeping on our premises; everything was liable to disappear – clothes hanging on the lines, chickens, piglets. There was a way, Nanny knew, that by throwing a rag over a piglet's head and smothering his squealing by squeezing the jaws together, they could stick a knife into its head. Those gypsies could even fool a guard dog.

But these arguments were overruled. There was no mistaking whose daughter my mother was: she was every inch like her father – energetic, taking quick and positive decisions, never admitting that they could be mistakes, just charging forward with good humour and determination. The problem of the virtuoso musician settled, she threw herself frantically into preparations about the 'cultural' event. A photograph of me balancing on points was to be printed in the middle. The text would be 'A dancer straight from Paris, supported by the brilliant Magyar Gypsy Koka playing Romany violin melodies whose origins stretch from Hungary to Turkey'. Mama also placed a large notice of the forthcoming attraction in the local paper.

When the posters were ready, she sent our groom to plaster the town's walls with them. She went at night from street to street with a brush and a bucket of paste, checking that it all had been done properly.

The Sunday before the mid-week recital, children were given stacks of prospectuses and posted at strategic points to distribute them. The children had been rewarded with coins and tickets to the show and there was no shortage of volunteers.

The only cinema in town had been hired for the evening. Mama was at the box office and had to open it early, as queues began to form an hour in advance. The gypsies brought some friends along, claiming they were relatives, so they had to be let in. We were apprehensive about pockets being picked or homes ransacked during the show while the houses were empty, but we received no complaints later.

The enthusiasm for the performance was stupendous. Mama had charged twice the price of normal cinema admission. It had all been organised for a good cause – in aid of the local orphanage – so the mayor and his wife were in the front row, looking magnificent in their regalia, war medals and jewels.

I was in a daze, I was dreaming. It may have been my twelve-year-old's enthusiasm, but the tiny figure of the middle-aged, long-nosed, fierce-moustached Koka – bending over his violin as if embracing it, head swaying, eyes closed, his bow brilliantly conjuring up sounds of caressing and weeping on the strings – produced a deep impression on me. I was inspired by his playing and danced as well as I could.

Later on in life when I listened to Russian gypsies performing in Paris night clubs, I was never as impressed as I had been by him. Romania is rich in folk music, with the Turk–Arab influence evident, and the *doina* expresses both love and mourning. Because of the large, wandering gypsy population, there is a medley of races, and the Magyars have added an intense vitality.

The performance itself went very well. After Koka and the accompanist had been paid, the proceeds were handed over to the mayor, who made a moving speech praising the artists, the organisers, the audience and the town. My accompanist, in a generous gesture, gave her share to the mayor too, and with tears in her eyes and a lump in her throat said it had been the happiest day of her life. After the mayor ceremoniously departed, having shaken hands all round, I could feel my grandparents' pride. Surely they would now see the sense of us living in Paris: Mama had proved her point.

Next she planned a show at Grandfather's dacha. A wooden rostrum had to be built, strategically placed at the end of an alley framed by acacia trees in Grandfather's garden. The young men of the village enthusiastically joined in and, having built it, left their shirts behind on the grass to claim their places for the evening performance.

As my uncle had worked out an elaborate arrangement of lights while he was sober, the local generating station was checked in case there might be an overload. As a precaution, paraffin lamps were placed on the stage. People brought their lamps, blankets and even chairs for the show.

In the afternoon, suddenly, as though driven by a sixth sense, another gypsy family joined our original one. There were three men now, one carrying a *nai*, a sort of pan pipe that he played like a mouth organ. Another had a *zymbalom*, a kind of dulcimer consisting of stretched wire over a base; the man played it by lightly striking it with small soft hammers. They offered their services for the evening performance. Koka did not mind, and I saw him wink at them. Mama agreed to have them play the last number, a medley of tunes, but insisted that Koka was to remain the soloist.

The gypsies wore short red embroidered jackets, sashes round their waist, a large earring in one ear and brightly coloured kerchiefs. We repeated our phenomenal success, but this performance was not so formal. As the gypsies played their last number, a little girl aged three came onto the stage. She was barefoot and wore a bright blue skirt, and on each hand, secured to her forefinger and thumb, was a miniature pair of cymbals that she banged together, always in time with the band's fast rhythm.

The park was full of non-paying customers, and even the church vicar came. We gave the gypsies' families half the proceeds, while the other half went to the vicar. He was delighted, although Mama had not been able to control the audience and make them all pay. With the lamps blazing, I was devoured by mosquitoes.

The third recital was in the bathing establishment belonging to Lydia and Kolia. We expected a more sophisticated audience, since the clientele for the mud cure came from Bucharest and every other big city. They would be used to recitals, concerts, and classical and gypsy music. The prospect made me nervous. The rostrum was very well placed, surrounded by trees, and my uncle again did wonders with the illuminations. Ropes were stretched between trees to keep the public in order and all tickets were sold in advance.

Gypsies arrived en masse. We never knew how they communicated with one another; they just appeared on the day. We now could form an orchestra of ten. They took it for granted that they were wanted.

My final dance, the foxtrot, could no longer, alas, be the last number of the programme. The colourful gypsies would kill it dead. They stood around the rostrum waiting impatiently for their turn to go on. They outshone me. I capitulated; it was a gypsy invasion, a Magyar concert, and I was their supporting artist. For the evening to be a success, they, and not I, had to do the last number.

A quick rehearsal was organised. One of the gypsy women told me that she could show me how to do the gypsy's 'shake'. It is as if shoulders and breasts are seized by a tremor, but the rest of the body must not be affected below the shoulder blades. It took some practice. While I rehearsed to join the gypsies' finale, everyone who was watching joined in, the peasant women in shawls laughing so much that tears rolled down their cheeks.

But I finally mastered the movement; and on two occasions years later, great choreographers asked me how I learnt to do that. One was Michel Fokine, who was rehearsing me as the gypsy in *Petrushka* and bent down and whispered something into his wife's ear – she always sat next to him at rehearsals. They were curious about my skill. The other choreographer was Bronislava Nijinska, sister of the famous Vaslav Nijinsky. She brought me right into the front line of her ballet called *Danses Slaves et Tziganes* and put the same question to me. I gave the same reply to both: I was taught by the wandering gypsies of Bessarabia.

Summer drama

That summer, a dramatic event happened of which I learned only thirty years later when my Aunt Lydia told me about it in London. I remember vaguely that, late one evening, Uncle Evgraf arrived unexpectedly at the seaside dacha, riding a horse. He was extremely agitated, and the horse, steaming and panting, looked exhausted. Evgraf leaped off the saddle, ran to Mama, and, after a whispered conversation, they both harnessed Grandfather's two horses to the light carriage. It took a few minutes, and they were gone...

In 1962 Lydia told me what had happened that night. She had decided to spend an evening in Grandfather's house visiting Evgraf and his family. While they were having dinner, they heard a sudden scratching sound on glass that froze their conversation. On looking at the window, they saw a hand outside, palm flat, pressed against the pane. It remained there for a while, motionless, and then the fingers scratched again lightly on the glass. They all sat transfixed, unable to move, seized by an unreasonable fear.

The hand persisted, and a second hand appeared, gesticulating, signalling, knocking at the window with despair. Evgraf, sober, decided to investigate, taking a paraffin lamp with him. Outside in the street, under the dining-room window, he saw the shape of a man crouching low against the wall. Evgraf watched him stretch out again, just able to reach the high window. Evgraf approached nearer, touched him, and found that the individual was soaking wet. He lifted his lamp to the man's face and almost dropped the lamp with shock. He couldn't believe his eyes. The man was my father.

Evgraf took him into the house. He looked thin and haggard and his hair was beginning to recede. He was dried, given food and drink, and asked innumerable questions. He said he had bribed Russian fishermen to take him across the patrolled river, but had jumped out of the boat before it approached the shallow waters. He had swum into the thick bamboo and waded through the reeds and tall swampy grass.

He had come because he wanted to see Mother and me. If we were not there, he had brought letters to be sent to us, as it was forbidden to mail letters overseas from Russia. He took a bundle of soaked letters out of his shirt pocket. His aim was to beg us to join him there – not to risk our lives and cross the patrolled river as he had, but to ask for a visa, a legitimate entry from Paris into the Soviet Union, claimed because he was living there.

He was an established writer now, living in the Ukraine. He had to return the next night to be picked up by the fishermen at the same place amongst the bamboo and reeds. He had only some twenty hours to spend here hidden. He couldn't let the fishermen down, as they were risking their lives coming so near to Romania. Evgraf had then galloped the twenty-odd miles to the dacha to bring Mama into town.

Lydia told me that while they were waiting she asked Father whether he wanted to come back to the West. He said, no, not now, he was too involved in life in Russia. It was a very hard time. It was now 1932, and for the last five years Stalin had been in power. He was suspicious of the thinking people, and restricting the freedom to write; but artists and writers were struggling to do so.

Russia was non-literate. This gave great hope to writers and teachers, because the persecution could not last. Stalin approved of literacy, stating that 'writers were the engineers of the human soul'. Writers could help to inform people of the progress in the country and keep up their morale. Some writers had become desperate about the restrictions over writing about industrial achievement, and Mayakovsky had committed suicide; but the struggle was going on.

Father told Lydia that times were harsher than ever. People still lived in overcrowded hovels, had hardly anything to wear, had to wrap their legs with rags against the cold. But now the Second Five-Year Plan was to start. It was to cover industry, machines, tractors, electric power stations, the building of great dams, and a metro line that was to encircle the whole of Moscow. These were enormous projects. To put them into operation, strength and moral support were needed. It was a mistake for Russia to cut herself off from the world. The world would help if they knew of the suffering.

But the West only saw harm in Communism; and Russia, for her part, mistrusted the West. Many mistakes had been made, but Father stood by his idealism: writers were needed. He could not go back now and sit idly in the West while Russia was just finding her strength after such a holocaust as the war, revolution and the famine.

When Evgraf brought Mother to him, she and Father embraced, crying, hardly able to believe their unexpected happiness – neither of them had dreamt of this reunion. The family left them alone for a few hours. My father asked Evgraf to call him in good time so that he would not miss the boat that was to take him back, as the fishermen would be waiting for him. As the hours went by, the family joined in debate about the couple's future; but the agitated conversation could not move my mother's adamant refusal to live in Russia. The West was safe, people were free: free to work, to earn a living without being directed. Mama had me to think about, and my ballet; no amount of Father's persuasion about better ballet schools in Russia would convince her. Besides, it meant never seeing her own family again, not even communicating, being shut off from the rest of the world.

Lydia remembers how lonely, sad and desperate my father looked. His hopes had collapsed. He argued that we all belonged there: we were Russians, couldn't we see that, didn't we feel any pity for the people's plea? No amount of begging could made her reconsider. It was the end, really the end of their union. Father, after a last tearful embrace, gave Mama a letter that he had written for me. I was given it much later in Paris. In it, he said I should read the articles that he had left in a case in Paris, read Gorky, and try to understand his motivation. He was not one of the Communists that one read about in the Western press, cruel, ruthless and violent. He was a romantic, an idealist, a patriot, and above all, he loved Russia and its people.

He told me to read, read, read. French literature was so rich – Anatole France, Victor Hugo – and so romantic: the poets, de Musset, Lamartine – the great Lamartine being the nearest he had found to equal Pushkin, who could not be translated adequately. He told me to read Turgenev and Tolstoy – Tolstoy above all understood Russia.

By the time Mama considered it right to hand me his farewell letter, I had discovered many of these great writers myself, having always been an avid reader. I even kept notebooks with copied verses, phrases and sayings that had particularly moved me. The beauty and magic of the poets made me a romantic person. I never realised how like my father I had become. Much later, on reading the wonderful epic of Pasternak's *Doctor Zhivago*, I often thought that his motivations were very akin to my father's.

That night, an hour after darkness, Evgraf escorted my father to the edge of the river. The two men embraced with great emotion. Little did Father know then what fate had in store for him. The last thing that he said, tears streaming down his face, was, 'At least I know that I have tried'.

Further steps

The Studio Wacker

Olga Osipovna was at the peak of her teaching career. The Studio Wacker in the Rue de Douai, near Place Clichy, became the centre of the dancing world. On the ground floor was an exhibition of pianos for sale, on the first floor a cafe-restaurant. It had a notice board with information about events, recruitment and work offered to ballet dancers. It was a meeting place for dancers, choreographers and teachers from all over the world. It dominated the dancers' lives. It was the core of their very existence for pupils, teachers, experienced dancers, choreographers, impresarios, and – most lively and active of all – the young pupils' mamas, who participated fully in every facet of the development and technique of their children. They whispered to one another about progress or failure in dancing achievements, and created an atmosphere of competition amongst the children unequalled by any exam grade, medal, diploma or graduation certificate.

We had no exams. Olga Osipovna worked out her own system. When she considered a pupil strong enough to be moved into a more advanced class, she did so. On such a day we felt that the heavens had smiled on us; we walked about with our heads lifted high.

For over a year now we had been waiting to be promoted, changing into our practice clothes early, so that we could watch the last half-hour of the advanced class. Their work included more practice on points to achieve speed, control and precision. It was part of Olga Osipovna's policy to allow us to watch the progress of this class. The door of the studio was always left open and each junior girl had a place for her head and shoulders within the frame of that door, as long as the threshold was not over-stepped, and silence was kept. We had our positions worked out, two girls lying flat on their stomachs at the bottom, two kneeling, two standing, and the rest using stools. Twenty heads peeped out of the door. It was a pyramid of sighing, criticising admirers, inwardly envying, dreaming of achieving the same standards.

Inside on a row of chairs sat all the dancing girls' mamas, eagerly watching every movement, suffering with every unkind remark of Olga Osipovna's, swelling with pride at every word of praise, eyeing one another, twisting their lips slightly at another child's mistakes, but keeping their criticism for after, as it was strictly forbidden to talk or whisper while watching the class. Olga Osipovna was severe, but she always wanted this spirit of competition to prevail. An audience watching, praising, criticising was keeping up the performing spirit.

One was always on show, striving for perfection, never relaxing the discipline. Every hair had to be in place, tightly arranged around the face, with no loose coiffure wobbling on the neck to prevent the head from turning. Every shoe had to have its ribbons perfectly sewn, with the ends tucked away on the inside of the foot. The great moment when our admiration had no bounds was at the end of the class, when Olga Osipovna announced, '*Fouettés*'. It was the cue for all the girls to show their skill one by one.

There was no doubt that Tamara Toumanova was the budding genius. She was the star par excellence, and her mama the uncrowned queen of the mamas. Tamara had a fascinating aura of mysticism surrounding her. She was born in a train while her parents, both Georgian, her father a prince, were fleeing the Bolsheviks. As a child dancer aged eight, she created a sensation on her debut at the Paris Opéra. *Le tout Paris* was raving about her. Her mama, after that, adopted the regal 'we' when speaking of her. She spoke in the Russian way, with foam on her lips. 'We danced', 'we wore', 'we said', 'we made 64 *fouettés* today.' Mama was undisputedly the most informed, the wisest, the most experienced of the whole studio.

The other mothers could only listen. This was the way to mend your toe shoes, this was the way to reinforce them with shellac, this was the way to pad your toes with cotton wool. Never cut your toenails close to the corner, never push back the cuticles on your toenails – this weakens the nail. If a nail comes off (as it very often did), wait for it to be outgrown by the nail forming underneath, and never tear your old nail away. Do not drink water after class; suck an orange. Eat all you can, but not before class; horse meat is cheap and good. Beware of macaroons and buns – they are all right for skinny girls, but not for short stocky ones.

Mama Toumanova carried Tamara's toe shoes under her arm. She explained why: when Tamara had danced at the Paris Opéra, her shoes had been left in her dressing room. When she tried to put them on before she went on stage, nails had been hammered into them so that Tamara would lacerate her toes. The dancers of the Opéra, motivated by jealousy, had done that.

There were stories of trapdoors on stage mysteriously opening, projector light bulbs suddenly exploding, glass and nails being spread on the stage, and – the worst story – of a ghost engineered to appear with malicious omens. But all was conquered; 'we' danced, blessed by the sign of the Cross, and 'we' stunned Paris. Our admiration was unlimited. We and our mamas had to agree that this was the voice of experience.

One day, Mama Toumanova came to the studio with the new idea that, as we were all entering our teens and our breasts were developing, we should take measures to prevent over-developing. We were advised to wear towels tightly around our breasts at all times, as a sort of straitjacket. Damp towels were even better – never mind the torture of it, it was all part of discipline.

Like fools, we went through this process until Olga Osipovna put a stop to it. She said that breasts had to be supported, but by firm brassieres. Our organs inside had to withstand the shaking from our dancing steps. Our wombs, ovaries and bladders had to be tightly held. She told us the shape of the underwear that we should wear from the waist down while dancing: briefs, a triangle of satin with the sides made of very firm rubber like an athlete's jockstrap.

My mama immediately began to knit the bras – circles of mercerised cotton – and to make the briefs. The whole studio went to her for fittings. Other mothers took to baking buns for the thin girls, selling oranges and sweets for a bit of profit.

The studios occupied several floors and were rented by the hour, every room reverberating with echoes of piano, violin, gramophone and voice, but the largest one was Olga Osipovna's. Downstairs the Café Wacker was a hubbub of activities: people crowding around the notice boards, writing down times and places of auditions, inquiring about opera companies recruiting for provincial theatres, about small unknown ballet groups luring dancers for one or two performances with no guarantee of pay or railway fare. Older dancers who did not consider that they should attend classes any more occupied tables at the cafe, sitting for hours with one cup of black coffee, the cheapest on the price list, in case a notice should go up that the millionairess Ida Rubinstein was recruiting for one of her extravagant appearances.

Rubinstein was often forming companies, reviving *Cléopâtre*, putting on *Sémiramis*, employing the famous choreographers Massine and Fokine, commissioning music, paying the dancers fabulous amounts that enabled them to live for months. If she wasn't forming a company, there were rumours that she soon would. When she did, all the habitués of Studio Wacker ate cakes, bought clothes and ballet shoes and took additional lessons to brush up their dancing. Otherwise there was little hope for work.

The Folies Bergère and the Casino de Paris were recruiting occasionally: one featuring Josephine Baker, a black bombshell appearing half-naked covered in feathers, a singing and dancing sensation; the other featuring Mistinguette, a mature, cracked-voice music-hall artiste, performing encircled in an aura of masculine admiration. These two fashionable music halls were looking for beautiful girls, who had to be statuesque but not necessarily good dancers. All they were required to do was to stand on stage as still as mannequins, wearing ostrich feathers or crinolines opened up in front, revealing a sequinned G-string. Their breasts were bare. The girls had to stand with their arms up, often holding a lit candelabra, and on no account move.

At the time, nudity was considered very daring, and only the most unambitious girls who were in show business for the money or desperate for it agreed to do that kind of work. Often the older girls, lured by an audition that promised dancing, were talked into appearing and only baring one breast. The money was less for one, but the management worked on the theory that when a girl reveals one breast, the other will soon follow.

Vera, a beautiful girl of eighteen, was the highest-paid performer. Her act was called 'Vera and Vania'. She was employed by a nightclub in Pigalle. Vania was a boa constrictor. She had trained him to slide along her naked body, hiding the parts that she didn't want to reveal to the audience. She used sculptured artistic poses set to exotic music, with subdued lights shining on her body. The act finished with the boa entwining her body, being held by his neck and with her bending his head on to hers and being kissed by him.

She never had to give an audition. She had stunning photographs of herself naked with the boa. Her prepared speech at the interview suggested that one day the boa might not hide some parts of her body, might even be angry and squeeze her to death. It was an added excitement: the suspense of perhaps seeing more of her and the possibility of her being strangled.

She went from nightclub to nightclub, working by night, sleeping by day and only waking up in time to attend one ballet class, because her ambition was to dance in classical ballet. She was generous and friendly, bringing sweets to us all, for ever answering questions about her pet boa, inviting us into her hotel room to look at him. Her small room was like a miniature jungle. She had secured a dead tree trunk with branches on a wooden stand, which served the boa as a resting-place. He could be seen entwined and coiled, partly hanging from it. She said that in the middle of the night he often slipped onto her bed and coiled himself at her feet. He was affectionate, and often she had to push him down so that he would keep to his part of the bed.

She fed him on rabbits once a week; she had to buy a live rabbit and let it loose in the room. She had watched once, but after that couldn't do so again. The rabbit hid at first, but then in fear was cornered, sat motionless and let himself be swallowed without a squeak of protest. The jaws of the boa extended to a formidable size and the rabbit disappeared in little jerks. Vera shuddered at the memory. On those nights a grateful Vania would slide into Vera's warm bed, but she, pushing him away, would spend the rest of the night not sleeping, her big eyes wide open, staring at the wall of her room, counting the flashes of light reflecting the neon signs of Gay Paris.

Balanchine

Georgi Melitonovich Balanchivadze, at the age of twenty-seven, was already a noted choreographer. He, like Olga Osipovna, had studied at the Imperial Ballet Academy of St Petersburg. When he auditioned for entry to that illustrious school, Olga Osipovna, by then an established older ballerina, was amongst the judges. She was particularly interested in him. He showed a grace and concentration that arrested her attention, and even as a child his sensitivity to music was visible. He listened. He had been taught the piano by his mother, who herself played very well. This appealed to Preobrajenska, who all her life had studied the theory and understanding of music in depth.

One of his first appearance on the stage in his school years was as Cupid in *The Sleeping Beauty*. Tamara Karsavina was Princess Aurora. The stage production of the magic fairy tale fired his imagination and inspired him to perfect himself.

As a young student, he appeared in various ballets: *The Pharaoh's Daughter* (in which Kschessinska showed her complete dominance as prima ballerina assoluta), *Paquita* and *Esmeralda*. The ballets with their lavish decors, transformation scenes and brilliant costumes, the sound of the orchestra, the audience enthusiasm, all reinforced his determination to do well. But suddenly the school was shut down; the upheaval of the Revolution had affected the Tzarist establishment. Pupils dispersed, and in his early teens Georgi, like many others, lived through a time of privation and starvation, taking what jobs he could, often in exchange for scraps of food. Money in those days was meaningless.

Later, when the school was re-opened after the Bolsheviks had decided that not only the aristocracy but the people of the proletariat too could enjoy the arts, Georgi was back, eager to continue. The Maryinsky Theatre was used for Communist Party meetings, at the end of which a few ballet numbers were performed.

Georgi was very active; not only did he play the piano for older dancers, but he also tried his hand at choreography, and as such made his mark in school performances. He graduated in 1921, joined the Maryinsky Ballet Company and found time to study at the Petrograd Conservatorium. At a charity performance when Preobrajenska was a guest artist, aged over fifty, loved and respected, she chose Georgi as her partner in a tarantella. The audience was rapturous.

Then Balanchine gathered together a group of dancers, young, eager and dedicated, under the name of Evenings of Young Ballet. They made their own costumes, and he arranged the choreography. It was a time for him to experiment with his talent. The key to his creativity was his understanding of music. He rejected the approach of having ballets with a story, but kept the fundamental technique of ballet itself. This, and his ability to invent movements, made his new work unique; it was a new form of classicism.

In 1924 a small group known as the Soviet State Dancers succeeded in getting a summer engagement abroad, in Berlin. Balanchine and three other dancers, amongst them Alexandra Danilova, chose to stay in Europe afterwards. They continued touring and came to London, dancing in a music hall. Diaghilev was at the peak of his popularity and, being always on the lookout for talent, sent the small group money to come to Paris and audition for his company. What he saw pleased him and he engaged them on the spot. As the Diaghilev Company had an annual obligation to dance in the ballets of the opera season at Monte Carlo, Georgi was asked to choreograph these short ballet interludes. It was Diaghilev who changed his Georgian name of Balanchivadze to Balanchine, having found that his real name was regarded as unpronounceable in France.

When Diaghilev's resident choreographer Bronislava Nijinska left the Company, Georgi was appointed in her place. At twenty, he was ballet master to the famous Diaghilev Company. Bernard Taper, his biographer, says that it was during his four-and-a-half years with Diaghilev that Balanchine's aesthetic outlook was shaped, his canons of judgement were established, and his taste was refined. He became an artist as well as a technician. He choreographed *Le Chant du rossignol* in which Alicia Markova, a girl of fourteen, made her debut. She was the very first of the 'baby ballerinas', the nickname for young dancers that became so popular a decade later.

Balanchine created *Apollo*, in which Serge Lifar shone in all his youthful beauty. His broad shoulders, narrow hips and perfectly shaped legs emphasised the purity of his dancing. Diaghilev, after the first performance, went on his knee and kissed the leg of Serge Lifar, something that he had done only once previously, when Nijinsky danced *Le Spectre de la rose*. The ballet was a masterpiece and earned Balanchine tremendous respect from the composer Stravinsky. This developed into a friendship that was to endure for the rest of their lives. Balanchine's analyses, understanding and interpretation of music were such that Stravinsky enjoyed collaborating with him.

After Diaghilev's death, Balanchine, already suffering from an operation on his knee that considerably weakened his dancing, contracted pneumonia. After a while it turned into acute pleurisy and then developed into tuberculosis. A spell in a sanatorium was prescribed. When he left there, after months in the snows of cold mountains and with his silhouette slightly altered because of the food he had had to consume, he found himself in Paris looking unsuccessfully for work. Looking elsewhere, he moved to London, where he arranged small, spectacular ballet scenes for the Cochran revues. These were lavish, with no money being spared to produce intelligent, contemporary, witty shows. They amused and appealed to the sophisticated audiences that were devoted to them. Cochran also employed highly skilled set-designers, and Balanchine produced artistic little ballets for him.

Our Studio Wacker was alive with rumours about Balanchine visiting ballet schools, selecting girls for Offenbach's *Orphée aux enfers*, an operetta to be produced at the Théâtre Mogador in Paris.

The day before he was to arrive, Olga Osipovna prepared those she considered her best young dancers to be auditioned by him. I was amongst

expenses were minimal and no choreographer came on that tour; but there was no guarantee that the dancers would get paid.

The repertoire consisted of the ballets from the previous Monte Carlo season. The transportation of the whole company was to be in two buses, supplied courtesy of an uncle of one of the principal dancers, David Lichine. The girls who had been with Balanchine at the Mogador had no difficulty in being accepted into the company. I was taken on without an audition.

As the average age of the youngsters was thirteen or fourteen, the mothers refused to let the girls go unless they went too. No mama, no girls; no girls, no ballet; de Basil capitulated. Additional seats were fitted into the aisles in the buses for eight mothers: Mmes Toumanova, Riabouchinska, Baronova, Sidorenko, Kobseva, Semenova, Volkova and Tchinarova. Mine made herself useful straight away, volunteering for the upkeep of the wardrobe, and she soon became indispensable to Grigoriev. She was the only one who knew how to pack costumes fast, and which basket to open first on arrival at the other end. She held that post for ever after.

I was given the tricky task of dancing turns in *Concurrence*. It was a difficult assignment: three of us, in line, had to do sixteen *fouettés*, the fourth, eighth, twelfth and sixteenth being double ones. Toumanova was in the middle, with Tatiana (Tassia) Semenova and me on each side. Mme Toumanova's eagle eye watched us every night, always instructing us beforehand not to crowd Tamara in our display, to remain firmly on our spot. This unnerved Tassia, who started to lose her balance.

In a damp Dutch town, on a small stage with a slope, with the spotlights unusually placed, she lost her focusing point and swirled towards the centre and Tamara. Mme Toumanova was furious; the next night, dreading that moment, and having received a further warning, the girl was even worse. Mme Toumanova had a violent row with Mme Semenova. On the third night Tassia crashed into Tamara. The two mothers behaved hysterically, shouting at one another. Grigoriev, master of discipline, calmed them down, offering to resolve the problem by placing Tassia on the other side of Tamara, swapping places with me. As she had been drawn to the left while turning, if she did so again she would disappear into the wings. But it didn't happen that way: as if drawn by a magnet, Tassia crashed into Tamara again. There were screams of resignation and shouts of a career being ruined, and the arbiter Grigoriev decided that Riabouchinska would have to do the turns instead of Tassia.

The grand tour was memorable for many things, apart from the experience of dancing in cold theatres to half-filled houses. Holland seemed to have more water than land. The landscape was flat, the sky grey in autumn, and it was cold, damp and monotonous. There were rivers, canals and large expanses of water beside the muddy roads. Exhausted and sleepy, we still had to attend morning classes: Grigoriev accepted no excuses. Discipline never eased, hard work never ceased. A few times when we were travelling during the morning and had asked for the bus to stop so that we could answer the call of nature, Grigoriev gathered us young ones together, told us to use farm gates as practice barres and, clapping hands, made us exercise our limbs so as to loosen up and not forget that we were dancers. All this to the stunned surprise of the cows in the fields and the constant amazement of passing motorists, sometimes just managing not to crash into one another.

Often, at night, when we had been scheduled to motor to the next town, we were hurled out of our buses, warm and sleepy, by our driver, who had come upon a floating bridge a mile long, and, having considered that a fully loaded bus would be too heavy for it, made us walk behind the bus. In the drizzle, shivering, we must have looked like a group of refugees. Mme Riabouchinska alone, a frail, elderly lady, was allowed to stay in the bus.

Some theatres were decrepit, but we danced in them because they were cheaper to rent. The worst of these was the Theatre Carré in Amsterdam; it had at some point been used as a circus, and there was straw on the dressing room floors. It was approached by a series of little bridges over dirty canals, tucked away in a shabby district. Refuse and dead rats floated in the canals, and live ones established themselves in our ballet shoes left in the theatre overnight, the shellac-reinforced toes of which were chewed away. Greasepaint was nibbled.

The public stayed away. Amsterdam, Rotterdam, Zwolle... In Eindhoven, a town that proved difficult to find, we drove around, asking for directions, and located the theatre by 8 p.m. Mama opened the basket of costumes fast, and within ten minutes sixteen girls dressed as sylphides were taking their starting positions.

For the sake of economising, the accommodation for our stay in a town had mostly to be found after the performance, in private houses that were pointed out to us from the stage door. There were always people eager to let rooms near the theatre: clean rooms, icy rooms, rooms on top floors reached by amazingly steep steps. When the front door of a house opened, one was confronted by a straight staircase, each step of which was equivalent in height to two in other countries. One of my memories is of a dancer, Jan Hoyer, having gone up the stairs holding a precious radio that he had nursed throughout the tour – no one knew why, as it only crackled – but then deciding that he preferred another house he had seen. He lost his balance and toppled onto his back, holding his heavy radio on an extended arm above his head and landing at my feet.

The financial situation was drastic. Grigoriev could be approached for a small 'advance'. The main cash was held by de Basil, but we could never catch him, as he was travelling ahead of us in his own car. The 'advance' was really money that already had been earned; but while Grigoriev kept the accounts diligently, the problem was that he nonetheless ran out of advance money.

It was fortunate that we all loved the Dutch pickled herrings; they were cheap and could be bought from barrows on the streets. This kept us nourished. For years afterwards, I could not face pickled herrings.

However, the experience of the tour was worthwhile. We learned to overcome difficulties, to dance under any conditions, and learned full ballets with just the minimum of rehearsals. Having covered twenty or so towns, we motored back through the industrial part of Belgium. After two flat tyres, the door of the bus flew off and had to be secured by string.

We returned sadly to Paris. In spite of the rows and jealousies, we had become accustomed to living as one large family. We had developed loves and hates, made close friends, made enemies. The days and nights had been spent in intimate contact; we shared hopes, fears, common problems. We were linked together, and now we were parting. We were asked where in Paris we wanted to be dropped. Most people chose Place Clichy near the Studio Wacker. Hardly anyone had a home, so most of us had to look for accommodation.

Pigalle, the district around Clichy, was full of cheap little hotels. We all had our favourites. In ours, the proprietor did not approve of cooking in the rooms, and did not allow a primus, the precious possession of every Russian living in a hotel. Bearing that in mind, Mama had bought a collapsible folding spirit stove and a supply of dried blocks of spirit; the whole could be hidden at a few seconds' warning. On the way to Paris she had bought some Belgian sausages, and they were soon sizzling in our room. I went to open the window to get rid of the smoke; seeing in the street some people dressed up in evening clothes, I remembered that it was Christmas Eve 1932.

Les Ballets *1933*

Studio Wacker, our lifeline, was seething with rumours that the Monte Carlo ballet would be calling us back because of their contract for the opera and ballet season there, and that Balanchine was forming his own company. He was asking Toumanova, Jasinsky (a Polish classical dancer) and six of us girls to join him. Within a day, de Basil was calling as well for a Monte Carlo season.

Our instinct and heart were for Balanchine, but common sense said de Basil: he had a definite contract. We went to Olga Osipovna. Her opinion was that each of us would gain much more working with Balanchine in a small company, where he would be creating new ballets for us under his own supervision. We seized the chance – this was what we wanted anyway. My mama went back to working in Paris, making ballet dresses for charity performances.

Because Preobrajenska was preparing excerpts from the ballet *Paquita* for her pupils, I travelled daily to Balanchine's studio and worked there. It proved to be the most interesting, fulfilling and developing period of my dancing life. Each morning we started with an extended class; the exercises Balanchine gave us varied each day and were new to us but derived from our pure classical training.

Our shoulders, hips, heads, bodies and arms were directed into postures unknown to us; we were becoming more adaptable, softer, with our *demi-pliés*, so important for a dancer's elevation, developed to such an extent that each of us covered the length of the studio in a few jumps. Balanchine improved our turning technique immensely, at first by forbidding us to do more than one turn to the left, one to the right, then only two to the left, two to the right, for months, until he unleashed our turning possibilities. He demonstrated a lot himself: his power in effortless jumps was amazing. He had to protect his injured knee, but he dazzled us with his leaps, his balance, his supple body. His attitude to us always remained patient; he never lost his temper, never raised his voice, but also never praised.

When our master started the choreography of *Mozartiana*, he arranged for each of us girls to have a phrase of the Tchaikovsky music to interpret; each was shown to her best advantage, performing new steps suiting the music perfectly. He would pick a girl and spend hours working with her, trying various combinations of steps. The others danced them too, but the one who had been chosen for the day remained his source of inspiration. As a partner in these rehearsals he was superb, able to think of what seemed impossible lifts and poses, complicated linked arms unfolding into simple classical poses, entwined arms and legs forming sculptured groups. It was a new dimension, and his inventiveness in shape and form was unique. He gave us enormous confidence.

Toumanova was the leading dancer, but he worked with each of us. Mme Toumanova assured us that he was in love with Tamara, but we had our doubts. He seemed to be totally absorbed in choreography. He was concerned about our health, reminded us to wear warm scarves to cover our mouths and throats after rehearsals, and once gathered all the mothers together to tell them that they were to see that outdoors in winter all the girls wore tight, knee-length woollen knickers. It seemed impossible to draw him close as a person. He never became familiar, which was perhaps his greatest and most mysterious charm.

A cherished memory of that time is of the midnight Easter Service in the Russian Cathedral in Rue Daru: the congregation crowding outside, our little group with Georgi Balanchine keeping together, the deep voices of the choir singing, the power of the service, the praying of the priests, the gleam of icons, the smell of incense, the illumination of the candles held by each worshipper, lit from one candle, passing the flame along until thousands of little lights flickered in the darkness, the clergy circling in procession around the Cathedral, the proclamation that Christ had risen, the joyous feeling of greeting: 'Christ has risen' and answering, 'Verily, he has risen', exchanging three symbolic kisses, and Georgi Balanchine there, smiling, kissing, friendly, visibly moved by the service. The adolescent, overwhelming joy we felt, that now, after being kissed three times by him, we didn't want to wash our faces anymore...

Every day during rehearsals, spectators were present: Boris Kochno, slim, elegant, cultured; André Derain, massive, enthusiastic; Darius Milhaud; Georges Auric. Derain, a staunch friend, suggested we perform in public squares or at village fairs. He would procure a little wagon for us, decorate it gypsy-style so that we could travel as *danseurs ambulants* as mimes and troubadours did in centuries past.

Months went by. There were financial difficulties. The studio filled with even more guests: Coco Chanel; writers and artists, including Tchelitchev; critics; and Edward James, a shy young Englishman of wealth, taste and culture. He was married to a Viennese dancer, Tilly Losch. Edward James was to finance our ballet company: his wealth was reputed to be unlimited.

Tilly Losch joined our classes. Although beautiful and having a powerful fascination for men, she could in no way be considered a classical dancer. She walked with feet firmly planted on the floor, threw her body about in jerky, violent movements and used her hands fussily. New ballets were to be created for her.

With finances reinforced, our ballet was widening its sphere, and dancers from Marie Rambert's London Studio joined us, amongst them Diana Gould, tall and beautiful; Pearl Argyle, a fragile-looking, ethereal dancer; and Prudence Hyman, a strong dancer. Balanchine incorporated them into the ballets. We Russians felt jealous: these girls were old, all of eighteen, nineteen. They were sophisticated and worldly, and Balanchine arranged steps and variations for them.

The master's ability to be oblivious to anything showed when he had to choreograph ballets for a scheduled season. *Errante*, to Schubert's *Wanderer Fantasy*, was his creation for Tilly Losch, with costumes by Tchelitchev, who explained with outstretched arms the effects he planned – the lighting, the wind machines, the movements of the dancers in huge, floating robes, carrying big banners flowing in the wind. Tilly was cast as an enigmatic woman struggling against the world, and carried a long train that she manipulated expertly, supported by Jasinsky in passionate encounters. We were the faceless crowd around her. The choreography suited Tilly superbly, as she wrung her hands and threw her body around, desperately searching, fighting. Balanchine's ability came to the fore again.

Les sept péchés capitaux was another creation for Tilly Losch, with text by Brecht, music by Weill and decor by Caspar Neher, and with Lotte Lenya singing. The story was told by two characters, a singing Anna and a dancing Anna, travelling to seven cities and encountering a sin in each of them. Again it was all for Tilly. There was no technique, but there was charm, sex appeal and beauty, plus the talents of librettists, musicians, set designers and above all choreographer. We, dancers of the traditional school, preferred *Mozartiana*, *Songes* and *Fastes* (in which I had a solo); and in spite of the lavishness of the newly acquired wealth, we wished we were back in the old poor days just working, undisturbed by all the glamour supplied by Edward James's contribution.

We opened in the Théâtre des Champs-Elysées on 7 June 1933. It was a brilliant first night, a social event of importance, but to our dismay the season was not a success. The important critics found *Errante* scandalous, *Mozartiana* dull, and *Les sept péchés capitaux* unpleasant. Besides, in competition with us at another theatre, the Châtelet, de Basil's Ballets Russes de Monte-Carlo were having a successful season. Léonide Massine was their ballet master, and, as the critics praised their work, the public flocked to see them.

We, with Balanchine, went to London and opened at the Savoy Theatre. Our troupe was reinforced by the brilliant dancing of Lifar and Doubrovska in a *pas de deux*. The same lack of enthusiasm for the new ballets prevailed, and de Basil's company was again competing with us: they were at the Alhambra Theatre, where they stayed for twelve weeks playing to packed houses.

Sadly, we had to fold our season, the last performance being particularly dramatic. Nerves were tense and dancers were disillusioned, dancing with despair. Lifar for some reason had slapped Edward James's face, calling him 'nothing but an amateur', and indeed challenged him to a duel in the Bois de Boulogne. Georgi had danced the leading part in *Errante* with Tilly Losch himself, having had to replace Jasinsky, who had suffered an injury. He was magnificent. This, the last night of our long and dedicated venture, was the only time we had seen him perform on stage. Balanchine could not offer us anything for the future, although there was vague talk of going to join him in America, where he was starting new work. But money for fares, visas, permissions – all that was impossible. It was a parting of the ways.

Edward James, upset at the failure of the season, in a moment of wild generosity asked the whole company to spend a fortnight at his family's stately home, West Dean Park, near Chichester. Our mamas were included in the invitation. It proved to be the most luxurious two weeks in our lives. We were in palatial surroundings on a vast estate, the park of which stretched for many miles.

We were free to roam, ride and use the marvellous library and music room, and each of us was allocated a room with a four-poster bed and gilt antique furniture. My mother and I slept in a bed that had been occupied by King

Edward VII (there was a rumour that James was his illegitimate grandson). The only time we were required to make a formal appearance was for the evening meal. Mr James dressed in evening attire, while other guests, his friends, also changed into more formal wear.

Diana Gould and Prudence Hyman told us that in England changing for dinner was de rigueur. The two dresses I had bought in the 'ten shillings, one pound store' made their evening appearances in turn. Mama had two blouses and switched them nightly.

The butlers serving us wore spectacular livery, worthy of an eighteenth-century play, and impeccable white gloves. The placing of the guests was another ceremony. Each night a different guest was selected to sit on the host's right – a position we dreaded, as the lady on his right was the first to be presented with the silver platter by the butler. The problem was knowing how to serve oneself, what amount of food to place on the plate, and how to deal with it all tidily, not appearing to be over-hungry. Diana and Prudence were invaluable to us: we watched them for cues. The only accident occurred when Natasha Krassovska, on being presented with a large platter of turbot covered with sauce, decided that the fish had been sliced, and pushed the servers under it, displacing the whole lot onto her own plate. It overbalanced, of course, landing on her lap. She burst into tears and the butler was mortified; but Edward James behaved as if nothing had happened. He assured her that it was of no consequence and made a sign to proceed with the roast.

After dinner the form was to play hide and seek in the shut-off wing, the legend being that a ghost was in residence there. Edward James, the ideal host, took part in these noisy games. The unoccupied wing became alive: doors creaked open, revealing figures covered in sheets and screeching with maniacal laughter; piercing screams were heard; people in the dark were pushed into mouldy cupboards where heavy keys with padlocks locked them in. It was frightening, exciting, producing hysterical laughter, fear, screams and sighs of relief at reaching safety.

We all knew that Edward James was not happy because his beloved wife Tilly was not at West Dean Park, and our hearts were full of sympathy for him. The fact that he was such a generous host, not requiring anything in return, moved us deeply. Subsequently, we learned that he had spent a tremendous amount of money financing the ballet and paying off musicians, librettists and artists. A few members of the French *beau monde* who had at first promised to share the expenses withdrew, leaving him with the whole burden of the debt. When he had paid for everything, he found that many of his commissioned drawings had disappeared. Edward James was one of the theatrical 'angels' with a big heart, but he was not tough enough.

After two weeks there, sleeping, eating, being lazy, our mamas decided we should approach de Basil, whose company was still dancing at the Alhambra.

All six of us, Toumanova at the head, were taken back on the spot. Toumanova was back in her leading roles, but de Basil decided to make the others feel guilty for having left him. We were treated as defectors, hearing 'I told you so' all too often. We had let him down, we should have stayed with him, by now we would have been leading dancers, now all places were taken, he was short of money and could only offer us £5 a week. The others in the corps de ballet were getting £8. Even mama had now to give way to Mme Larose and take second place in the wardrobe.

Money never troubled dancers. We were ready to dance for any amount, and jumped at the opportunity. Mama and I would make £10 a week between us. We signed a contract for the rest of the Alhambra season.

Toumanova and her mother shared a room in Arthur Street, near New Oxford Street. Mama and I had the room above. Their rent was £1 a week, ours fifteen shillings. The building was lit by gas, each floor having a meter shared by two rooms on the landing. When I came home, it was always dark and there was no gas in the gas ring. As soon as I put a penny in the slot, the man occupying the other room on the landing would frantically begin to use the gas up. His light went on, his kettle filled, his fire went on, and in no time my pennyworth was used up. I complained to Mme Toumanova, who came up, thumped on the man's door, giving him a piece of her mind in Russian, then switching to French, shouting, '*Vous brûlez* gas, *vous* put penny *tout de suite, vous cochon!*' To me she said, 'Tamarotchka, you must learn to defend yourself in life.'

We had a drunken landlady who spent her days in a filthy kimono and carpet slippers. She was on the ground floor and owned a very talkative parrot. She gave each tenant only one set of keys. As my hours were different from my mother's, when either of us was home the other had to shout for the key to be thrown out of the window. A year later, for the Covent Garden season, we could afford slightly more luxurious premises in Coptic Street, with electric light. On the way to rehearsal, taking a short cut through Arthur Street, we heard a squeaky voice calling in Russian, 'Tamara, drop the key' – the parrot hadn't forgotten us!

Irina Baronova and Tamara Toumanova shared many leading roles in common: *Sylphides, Petrushka, Concurrence, Cotillon*. The ballet critic Arnold Haskell wrote, 'Tamara is grave, tragic, intense: Irina is fair, gay'. Irina was, in my own opinion, extremely moving.

The most fully accomplished ballerina was Alexandra Danilova, trained at the Imperial School, and also a member of the Diaghilev Company. In her early thirties with de Basil's company, she was in her prime. She possessed chic, a masterly presentation, a charm and a brilliant personality, which, added to her beautiful line and lovely long legs, made her work a joy to watch and an inspiration to the younger members.

Because of my turning ability, I was told to learn the role of the Top in *Jeux d'enfants*, and then informed that I was dancing it at a matinee – Baronova had suffered a slight injury. The one and only rehearsal was on the morning of the matinee. 'What about the *pas de trois* with the Sportsman and the Child?' I asked. 'I cannot tell Woizikovsky to attend, he has too much on the programme today,' said Grigoriev. 'But what about the lifts?' 'You've seen them done, you must copy.'

Tania Riabouchinska, the Child, came to the rehearsal, and explained to me what in theory I must do. We walked about the empty stage for half an hour with her saying, 'Here you pose', 'Here you turn', 'Here you jump', 'Here you are lifted'. All this without music.

Before I knew it, the matinee was on and I felt paralysed with fear. The wings were crowded with the whole company, curious to watch my ordeal. I was seized with panic: my stomach felt as if I had swallowed a stone, my back was arched and tense, but my legs were like jelly. I also had to overcome the fact that for the two previous weeks we had had no classes; we had only been relaxing and fattening up in the luxury of West Dean Park. I knew my performance was of great significance for me: it was my debut as a soloist, an occasion that could influence my career. The role demands great assurance, perfect balance, intense concentration, keeping legs, arms and body in line and never stopping whirling on one's toes.

I went on stage with knees knocking, chin trembling, throat contracted and tears on eyelashes and made a complete mess of the part. Not only did I not turn on the same spot, but I lost confidence in myself about three-quarters of the way through and decided I could not continue to make all these double turns: I had better whirl round on my two feet lest I crash into something – no matter as long as I keep in time with the music. This brought out the fury of our *régisseur* Grigoriev, who barked at me, 'What do you think you are doing, changing Massine's choreography?'

I still had my *pas de trois* to dance, but things did not improve. To my horror, de Basil, from the audience, came through the little door onto the stage and told me I had danced like a cabbage. I burst into tears. I could not possibly survive that; it was the end of everything. Even my friends in the dressing room kept a stony silence. The only gesture of sympathy came from Massine, patting my shoulder as I was jerky with sobs, he said: 'Disasters happen to all of us sometimes in our lives. Don't cry, get on with it.'

So, it was back to the darkest corps de ballet. I never saw the role of the Top again. But soon after, Baronova took it upon herself to teach me her role in *Le Beau Danube*. I showed what I could do with proper rehearsals, and was given it for ever after. Eventually Grigoriev relented and I was given Estrella in *Carnaval*.

But the main task now was corps de ballet work, responsible, gruelling and precise. Three of us, Anna Volkova, Galina Razoumova and I, were in everything. Massine saw to it that we were in every bit of choreography he produced. We learned all the roles and could go on with one rehearsal or none. My fiasco served me well; I wasn't going to be caught out again should another chance occur.

Our memory storage seemed phenomenal, the music that we heard being instantly translated into movement. At Covent Garden Opera House, *Choreartium* to Brahms's Fourth Symphony was hurriedly prepared and a midnight performance for special guests given for charity, attended by the Prince of Wales. We danced in black tunics and pink tights, with a Grecian column for decor. It drew cries of ecstasy from the audience, and our next summer season at Covent Garden was sealed.

In the meantime, after Golders Green came Streatham Hill, Bournemouth and Plymouth. Bournemouth was memorable because Rostova, applying wax to her eyelashes, dropped the lighted candle on her *Swan Lake* dress. Screaming and in flames, she ran on to the stage, where sixteen girls were dancing. Nina Tarakanova's dress caught fire too. Had it not been for the presence of mind of Grigoriev and Hoyer, who smothered the flames by covering the girls with their jackets, there wouldn't have been a de Basil Ballet any more.

Plymouth was remembered for the terrible digs we had, where the bathroom in the back yard had not been used for ages. Narcisse Matouchevsky, a lovable, round Pole with a stutter, lit a match there and was bodily thrown out of the glass door by the force of the explosion. He became deaf for a long time and it did not do his stutter any good either.

America

In 1934 the American impresario Sol Hurok engaged de Basil's company for a short season in the United States, starting in New York at the St James's Theatre. We sailed on the French Line ship *Lafayette*. The approach to New York by water was a sight not easily forgotten. Once we had disembarked, there were the unbelievable skyscrapers, the overpowering fear of staying on the twenty-seventh floor of a hotel and being too nervous to look out of the window, the illuminations of Broadway and Times Square, the theatres, the cinemas, the burlesque shows, the lights flickering, the noise of the traffic, the crowd, the discovery of hot dogs for five cents. There were automats dispensing delicious apple pies and ice creams, milk shakes, the animation of the people in contrast to England – all the impressions of pulsating, exciting life.

The four weeks' season was received rapturously. Sol Hurok backed the performances with a full orchestra conducted by Efrem Kurtz. Illustrious visitors came backstage, including Rachmaninov and Stravinsky. New York was in ecstasy; plans were made to extend the season and go to other towns, and eventually Hurok engaged the ballet to come back for future seasons. De Basil accepted anything offered, but his problem now was that the Monte Carlo season's engagement had to be fulfilled. He had to manipulate the situation and think quickly.

In Paris, Bronislava Nijinska had a small company of dancers performing her choreography. She was to take her ballet to Monte Carlo for the spring season, but she was short of good dancers. De Basil decided that his 'fast-learning girls' would go to Monte Carlo, while the rest could continue dancing in the States.

Eight were chosen, I amongst them, headed by Danilova as principal. It was Monte Carlo for us. No amount of protest helped.

De Basil's charm and ability to talk anyone into anything worked. He talked about Nijinska: what an honour it was to work for her, what a charming woman she was, how she would not tolerate weaker dancers. He could handle people and make them do what he wanted them to do. Mama was again to be in charge of the wardrobe.

With our hearts heavy at leaving our friends and glossy America, we embarked for the unknown, reinforced by the assurance that we were to work with a choreographer of genius and a charming woman as well: Nijinska.

Reputations and reality

Nijinska

We moved from ship to train and straight to rehearsal, our legs still unsteady after the stormy crossing of the Atlantic, our hearts beating with expectation, imagining a special welcome upon meeting the charming great lady. The first sentence uttered by Mme Nijinska was, 'If you think you have come here to rescue the great Nijinska, you are mistaken! You are here to fill up the back rows of the corps de ballet.'

Nijinska was held in great respect all over the world. Having been a fine dancer turned choreographer, she produced some stunning ballets, of which *Les Noces* of Stravinsky and *Les Biches* of Poulenc were masterpieces. Her troupe had several new ballets as well as the old classics.

Her girls formed a clique into which one could not penetrate. They disliked us straight away and we returned the compliment. Madame, being very hard of hearing, spoke to us in a voice that was hardly louder than a whisper, but managed to save for us the most insulting, humiliating remarks. She was given to such nasty sentences as, 'Who do you think you are? Nobody'; 'You are looking pathetic'; 'If I were you, I would give up'. All this in a very calm, very low voice, so that to hear oneself being insulted one had to come close to her. It was doubly humiliating.

She kept us on our toes out of sheer fear. We could not deny that the precision of her work, the brilliant way she instructed us in class, could only improve our standard, but during many rehearsals tears would be swallowed, lips would be bitten hard. Her severity was fierce, but we had no alternative but to get on with the season and try to forget the insults.

The ballets were Ravel's *Bolero*, in which she worked us into a frenzy of Spanish dancing, twisting our bodies, swishing our long skirts, becoming alive with expression and temperament; *Les Biches*, a revival of the twenties, a charming, fey piece; and *Les Variations* to Beethoven, a pastoral ballet for which she took me by the hand and placed me in the middle of a circle of girls. I did not know if it was an honour or a punishment; perhaps she wanted to single me out and show the others how not to dance.

Because of this hostility, the rehearsals were torture. Our toes were bleeding because we were rehearsing on points, an effort not usually demanded from professional dancers until the dress rehearsal. The atmosphere was charged with unhappiness. One lived in fear of the next crippling sotto voce remark. The unfairness of it was that, apart from the soloists, her own company was full of dancers who were weaker than we were. A couple of them were not even able to balance well on points.

But we could find happy relief in the sunshine and mimosas of Monte Carlo, in being able to run out and sit on the bench under the orange and palm trees, and in Pasquier's patisserie, where we ate cakes until we were bursting. The hope that kept us alive was that this season would soon be over and we would be back with even-tempered Massine, who never insulted a dancer out of sheer sadism.

The season over, there was a big party at the studio. Mme Nijinska behaved in a human way: she talked to us individually, even smiled and thanked us for having worked so hard. We should have thanked her that we had learned how to carry on in spite of bleeding toes, wounded pride, diminished egos and the hate in our hearts.

Massine

We travelled to Barcelona to rejoin the main company, now returned from their American tour, in the lovely Liceo Theatre, tiered in gold and red. Our friends heard all our stories of humiliation and martyrdom. De Basil was very kind, thanked us and gave each of us presents of Spanish gold bracelets. Our little solos were handed back to us.

The season at Covent Garden was being prepared. Massine used each of us in every movement of his second symphonic ballet, *Choreartium*. He was a brilliant choreographer and dancer, with a dynamic personality. He had started a new epoch in ballet when for Diaghilev he had created *Parade*, for which Picasso designed the costumes.

In the course of the next three years he was to revive *Les Femmes de bonne humeur* (décor by Bakst, music by Scarlatti), *La Boutique fantasque* (Derain– Rossini) and *Le Tricorne* (Picasso–de Falla), as well as creating original productions especially for our ballet.

Choreartium was pure interpretation of the music of Brahms's Fourth Symphony. In the second movement, one of great beauty of composition, twenty-four girls, arms linked, entered the stage in a slowly moving procession, dressed in dark red nun-like robes, and formed incessantly changing groups (copied from religious frescoes), shaping their hands into the sign of a Holy Trinity blessing. An unbelievably beautiful effect was created, followed by contrast in the third movement, with dancers romping at a pagan village festival, full of lusty laughter.

Changes of costumes from one movement to the other were achieved with lightning speed. Each girl had made her arrangements with an assistant, be it mother, boyfriend, stage manager or unoccupied dancer, who stood prepared in the wings with the required costume opened at the back.

I was selected to be one of the original four in Massine's revival of *Les Femmes de bonne humeur*. He spent hours initiating us into the movements required, until each of us, in the lovely Bakst costumes and white wigs, looked like Sèvres porcelain statuettes.

Massine's contribution was immense: as a dancer his achievement was colossal. In *Le Tricorne* his Farruca brought the house down, with prolonged applause interrupting the performance every night. As the hussar in *Danube* he had no equal; he could hold the audience in ecstasy just by being still or by moving an eyebrow with perfect timing. His choreographic output during these years was phenomenal.

Every season in New York, our contract stipulated that we had to have five new ballets. There were two of these seasons a year, so five ballets were being prepared in Europe for the opening four weeks at the Metropolitan in New York, and five other ballets would be rehearsed during our gruelling tour of the USA so that we could show them at the Metropolitan at the close of the tour. Often we had to rehearse after performances. All the dancers, after coffee and sandwiches at the end of a show, changed into practice clothes and made themselves available for Massine to continue building his human pyramids. It was fortunate that in the USA a few theatres were part of a complex that included a hotel where the whole of the company could stay.

It was at Covent Garden in the summer months, with a full orchestra conducted by Efrem Kurtz or Antal Dorati, that the ballet achieved its most glorious days. The thrill experienced when the orchestra tunes up on opening night is a feeling that no one who has been on stage will ever forget. Among my memories are the gala performances, with the audience always in full evening dress; the Royal Family in their box, the two little princesses in pink dresses attending a matinee; the weekends when double-decker buses were hired to transport the whole company to eat, drink and be merry at a stately home – often we did not know who the hosts were, and were thankful to escape small talk with the excuse that no one spoke English.

The exhausting tours were the ones in America – one year we visited over eighty towns and cities, another year over a hundred. One night here, two nights there, a week in Los Angeles, one in San Francisco, one in Chicago, seeing nothing but train, hotel and theatre with a cafeteria in between, where T-bone steaks and banana splits were a luxury; limbering, rehearsing, dancing, sleeping, mending shoes, washing tights. A special train would take us to our next destination, often on the opposite side of the vast American continent. Our home was that train. In the daytime, seats in the open carriages could be turned into bunks, while at night a dark-skinned attendant converted our wagon into sleeping compartments, the beds separated by curtains.

On one of these tours, Massine choreographed *Union Pacific*, a ballet of American life. It depicted the construction of the railway by Chinese and Irish labourers through uncivilised territory in America, culminating in a scene where the locomotives from each end meet at centre stage. For this ballet, Massine had studied the cakewalk in New Orleans, and the strut and the shuffle in New York. The result was a colourful, fun ballet in which many of us danced the roles of tarts entertaining the builders. Baronova danced a very spicy Lady Gay. But at the start of the ballet the girls had to wear grey sacks encasing their bodies from head to foot, remain completely rigid and be carried on stage to represent the planks and rails of the railway line.

In Los Angeles this ballet was a phenomenal success. It became fashionable for film stars to attend performances: Joan Crawford, Franchot Tone, Paulette Goddard and Charlie Chaplin, all came backstage and met the dancers, but our greatest fan was Marlene Dietrich. By special permission, she secured a seat in the wings and followed the ballet to other cities in California. It was rumoured that she had lost her heart to David Lichine. Marlene wanted to appear as one of the planks in *Union Pacific*, and a great fuss was made of this event. The press was informed and came in force; photographers filled the stage. Grigoriev was unhappy: bad discipline, trivial publicity. Finally she did not appear.

But the publicity increased the ballet's popularity even more. We visited film studios, seeing the incredibly handsome Robert Taylor, who had just made a film of *Camille* with Greta Garbo. Jeanette MacDonald, all big blue eyes and curls, was practising scales. We met Cary Grant at a party given by his friend Elissa Landi, and what pleased me, aged fifteen, so much was the gallantry of Francis Lederer, who clicked his heels, kissed my hand and said I had danced superbly.

Massine continued with his productions. In *Jardin Public* he danced with Toumanova; in a fine episode depicting beggars, they looked both handsome and pathetic. We girls stuffed our bosoms with towels to appear as milk-bearing nannies with infants. This ballet did not have a long life. The choreographer who was testing his wings was David Lichine. Before he produced his best work, he made a few ballets that lived for but a few performances; in these first years of American tours he was experimenting. Later *Francesca da Rimini*, *Protée* and *Graduation Ball* became successful, but at this earlier time he was tiring, inconsistent, overbearing, demanding, constantly changing his mind. We felt sorry for him. It was Massine who was supreme maestro.

During the following Covent Garden season, Nijinska became guest choreographer, producing Stravinsky's *Les Noces* and d'Erlanger's *Les Cent Baisers*. We had warned our friends what a terrible experience working with her would be. To our surprise, she singled out the girls who had been to Monte Carlo, and rewarded us by giving us priority in small solos. Her smiles and kind words were reserved for us. This favouritism was not popular with the established soloists.

Minor and major disasters

An exhausting period of intensive work preceded the presentation of Berlioz's *Symphonie Fantastique*. The ballet depicted in five movements the agony of a sensitive young man obsessed by a love that drives him to attempted suicide. Massine danced the leading role and seemed to live the part to such an extent that he became withdrawn, brooding and morbid.

The leitmotif represents the young man's dream of his beloved, danced dramatically by Toumanova. The work on *Fantastique* started in America during one of our busy tours; on arriving in London, the company, and particularly dancers like myself who had had no breathing space at all, were extremely tired. It affected our self-control, and a period started when – despite the strict discipline, the dedication, the seriousness of the work, the inspiration of the music, the importance of Covent Garden – all was forgotten, and sixteen sylphides stood in little circles on stage giggling helplessly. Shoulders shook, faces dissolved into strained grimaces, and black mascara tears rolled down pale, trembling cheeks.

Tassia Semenova started it all with an innocent remark whispered into her neighbour's ear: 'This ethereal creature is so hungry, she could eat a horse.' Each night we expected her to give us different details of the menus she fancied, and it turned into an epidemic of laughter that we could not control. One that was fatal in breaking us up was, 'I *can* eat horse meat – it's not bad with lots of onions; but tonight, just for once, I'd love champagne and caviar spread with a dash of lemon juice.'

Grigoriev fumed, remonstrated – nothing helped. The stronger the threats, the more the sylphs shook with mirth. Fines were imposed – five shillings a performance, increased to ten shillings, going up to a pound, a large sum out of our limited salaries – with no effect at all. Finally, a notice was pinned on the board, warning that anyone laughing on stage would be dismissed on the spot.

That night, the ballet *L'Après-midi d'un faune* was performed. The six nymphs, of which I was one, had been trained for months to adapt to an intricate style of stone-like maidens in imitation of Greek sculpture. Stillness was essential to produce the effect of a frieze. The girls considered this to be a skilled performance requiring a lot of concentration. But the unexpected happened. One of the nymphs, an older dancer named Tania Chamié, was in the habit of folding her arms and having a quiet little sleep. During rehearsals it did not matter, but now, waiting for her entrance as a nymph, the same occurred: serene Tania had fallen asleep. The pastoral Debussy music had acted as a soporific. Anxious to wake her, we called, 'Tania, Tania, quick!' She woke up and, in a desperate dash onto the stage, tangled her bare feet in the electric cables in the wings. To the astonishment of Lichine, the sensuous Faun, she made her entrance on her back, exposing to the audience her posterior and ten bare toes. The entrance of us other nymphs followed immediately, and this time, even if we had been threatened with execution, we could not have retained our composure. Three young nymphs were helpless with laughter. The curtain was hardly down when a notice was pinned on the board: 'Due to lack of discipline and misbehaviour on stage, the dancers Abricossova, Razoumova and Tchinarova are expelled from the ballet company as from tonight. Signed – S. Grigoriev.' Some of the other dancers rallied round, asking for a reprieve. Tania admitted that she had dozed off. Nothing could make Grigoriev reconsider his decision.

Mama went to work next morning, helping to cope with 200 costumes in preparation for the premiere of *Fantastique*. She asked me what was I going to do; I replied, 'Sleep'. We, the three expelled girls, were in all five movements of the Berlioz.

That morning was the dress rehearsal of the symphony. The full orchestra was ready for ten o'clock. At half-past ten I was woken by loud thumping on the door. 'Tamara, quick, hurry up to rehearsal, everyone is waiting!' Galina and Kira had already been woken up and were hurrying too. Massine, seeing his dancers missing, shouted to Grigoriev, 'Where are my dancers? You should know better than to chuck them out of the company on the eve of an important premiere.' The matter was never mentioned again, and, like a miracle, the laughter stopped too.

On the opening night of *Fantastique* the girls were in a wild panic because of the change of costumes required between the first and second movements. Christian Bérard had designed stunningly beautiful white crinoline dresses trimmed with black tulle for the ballroom scene. The girls had exactly sixteen bars of music to undress, get into these bulky dresses, secure tall, wired headdresses and pull on black lace elbow-length mittens.

All the girls were identically dressed, even Toumanova, the ballerina dancing Massine's beloved. The music is a breathtaking waltz. My own partner, Valentin Zeglovsky, was relatively new in the company and was confused with the many new ballets he had to learn. He knew that he had to carry 'Tamara' – me – off the stage. As the leitmotif was played, members of the corps de ballet disappeared, so that Toumanova and Massine were to be left on in a vision of ideal love. I jumped up to be carried away, found no partner to lift me, and landed on my feet facing Massine, who glanced at me with a look of horror on his face. My partner had carried off the wrong Tamara. He had carried off the star. Above the leitmotif, louder than the orchestra, screams were heard in the wings. Mme Toumanova was beating my partner's chest, shouting, 'Let my Tamara go, you beast!' while I, putting on my best soulful smile, stretched my arms yearningly to Massine and carried on, being for a few bars of music Berlioz's and the poet's inspiration.

Friendships

Alexandra Danilova (Choura), the ballerina assoluta of the company, was effervescent, emotional, warm, gay and friendly. While in St Paul on one of our American tours, it was noticed that her passport and mine were not quite in order for crossing the Canadian border. She needed an extension that could only be handled in New York: I was still a minor travelling on Mother's passport, and Mother was in New York making costumes. It was decided that Choura and I would be left in St Paul for ten days to await the ballet's return from Canada.

Tania Riabouchinska's mother was suffering from an advanced stage of stomach cancer, and had to be hospitalised. The decision to do so was put off until Tania could be near her, and she was left in our charge. She was weak, looking like a skeleton and often unable to keep her food down. Choura booked us into three adjoining rooms, with Mama Riabouchinska in the middle one; and we began a vigil that proved to be a sad ordeal. Choura looked after Mama Riabouchinska with the dedication of a professional nurse, and after me with care and concern. We exercised together, shopped in turn, worried in unison. It cemented our friendship.

Mama Riabouchinska died three weeks after the company returned. Choura once again became busy as supreme ballerina, but always after that time had a few friendly words for me.

Girls alone in an American city, whether in a hotel or walking down the street, were open to pursuit. During the first tour, four of us stuck together and for a while battled our way clear of soldiers, sailors and drunken fools beating at our cheap hotel doors. It all became rather frightening and our sleep was disturbed. When we were staying in a city for just a few hours, we would spend them in an all-night cinema. It was economical too: for twenty-five cents we could see six films, mostly westerns – although the dialogue, consisting mostly of 'Hi, buddy', and 'Yup', considerably limited the growth of our own English vocabulary. Sitting up the whole night was tiring. When Grigoriev heard of it, he put an end to it.

We devised another stratagem for saving money. Six girls got together and booked a room with a double bed. They were given two keys. One girl would come down, then take up an additional girl with her. This was repeated until all six were in the room, and then we slept lined up across the bed. This was only possible in large hotels where the whole company and the orchestra were staying for the night. Our hairstyles and turned-out feet made us all look alike.

But soon girls had to have protectors: our own young men. The groups split into fours, two girls, two men, who made their plans together: taxis, cafeterias, hotels, help with heavy luggage, accompanying one another to stations and to rehearsals. This intimacy encouraged romance, and the familiarity promoted affairs, marriages, jealousies and heartbreak. Two girls

Grandfather Tchinarov   Grandmother Tchinarova

My mother, Anna Tchinarova, aged 18

My father, Evsevy Rekemchuk, in his army uniform

Mother in Paris, 1927-28

Father in the 1930s

Mother on the beach at Nice, c. 1930

Myself aged six

With my beloved Nanka. These are the two photographs of me that my father kept until his death

Olga Osipovna Preobrajenska, my teacher in Paris in
the 1920s

A Preobrajenska charity performance, Tamara third from right

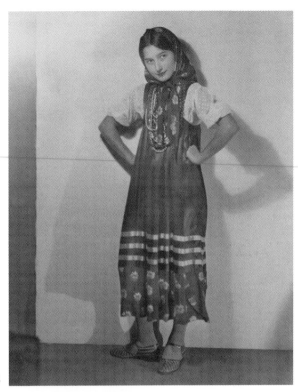

Recital in Akkerman, aged 13

Aged 15, Ballets Russes de
Monte Carlo

Midinette in *Le beau Danube*, Ballets Russes de Monte Carlo, 1935

The young Irina Baronova

Tamara Toumanova

Tatiana Riabouchinska

Estrella in *Carnaval*, Ballets Russes de Monte Carlo

Dinner at the Savoy Hotel, left to right Borovansky, Volkova, Michel Fokine, Tamara, 1936

were rushed to hospital with their wrists cut. Once our night train was delayed in Arizona because one of our number, Lulu, was missing; she was found an hour later, walking between the railway lines. She had read *Anna Karenina*, and was hoping that the train carrying her faithless beloved would run over her.

Romances blossomed: my own did too. Yurek Lazowski was waiting for me to be a little older, so that we could seriously think about marriage. I liked his warm, loveable personality; he was thoughtful, kind and very gallant. If I wasn't nursing a gardenia in a cellophane box, I would be nursing an orchid. It was accepted that we were a couple; so we did not expect the development of Alexis Koslov's hopeless attraction to me. Koslov was a brilliant dancer. Because of his technique and his unusually small size, he specialised in character parts. He was moody, temperamental and unpredictable, and drank a lot. When drunk, he became dangerously aggressive before collapsing in tears of remorse.

He had acquired a gun, carried it in his luggage, and was often seen polishing it. He declared his love for me during the ballet *Le Beau Danube*, in which he played an artist painting me. I told him it was hopeless, but had to continue smiling and flirting with him as the role required. He said that he could not bear it any longer and would do something desperate – he meant it.

He picked a fight with Lazowski in the corridor of the sleeping car and charged at him, then produced his gun and waved it in my unfortunate boyfriend's face. He was disarmed by others and collapsed on the floor in a heap. He smelt strongly of drink and the gun turned out not to be loaded. Lazowski's legs gave way under him too, and he had to be revived.

The most dramatic event was our real attempted murder. Paul Petroff, a leading dancer, was romancing with a lady, and during a most passionate moment was knifed three times by his discarded paramour. Petroff had bled profusely, and the Chicago hotel room was covered in blood. He was kept in hospital for a week.

The attempted murder could not be kept secret, and the press covered it extensively. Reporters followed us from town to town trying to get information. The FBI were interested too, and agents mingled with the company, disguised as stagehands. But although the culprit was known to all, everyone pretended not to understand English. Both the FBI and the reporters gave up in despair. Petroff recovered completely and never divulged the name of his would-be assassin.

The greatest balletomane of them all – Arnold Haskell

Everyone, sooner or later in their lifetime, has an opportunity for advancement or promotion. Sometimes difficult decisions must be made. I did not have to decide. With a dozen other dancers, I was pushed into being the nucleus of a new company, formed in a hurry, for a year's engagement in Australia.

De Basil did not want to refuse the attractive prospects there. He split his own troupe, joined forces with the Woizikovsky ballet and called the new grouping the 'Ballets Russes du Colonel de Basil'. To their repertoire of six works he added sixteen of his own. It meant that twenty-two ballets had to be cast, taught and rehearsed during the last four weeks of the Covent Garden summer season.

We resented this but we agreed, partly because each of us was to be promoted to bigger and better roles. Because many dancers were as yet unproven, all leading parts were to be shared, and dancers would alternate in each – my wonderful assignments were to be Action in Massine's symphonic ballet *Les Présages*; the Princess in Nijinska's *Les Cent Baisers*; the Queen in *Thamar*, a ballet that Fokine produced for Diaghilev with Karsavina as the Queen; and the lead in Balanchine's *Cotillon*. I was also given various solos in *Aurora's Wedding*, *Swan Lake*, *Carnaval* and other ballets.

We rehearsed with indefatigable vigour, exhilarated by the challenge. I learned the principal roles directly from Baronova. *Les Cent Baisers* had been especially created for her. *Cotillon* was hers then, too.

Rehearsals were frantic, because at the same time we had to prepare *Symphonie Fantastique* for the Covent Garden presentation and Massine was very demanding. As soon as these rehearsals were over, the *régisseur* of the new company, Jan Hoyer, would stake his claim on our time. At every opportunity, Baronova, even before her entrance for the *pas de deux* in *Aurora's Wedding*, would show me an additional movement from *Les Cent Baisers*. Paul Petroff, her partner, would support me in a particularly tricky pirouette. It must have looked like a madhouse, as odd corners were used for transmitting roles to one another at any time of day or evening. Nina Verchinina, in her dressing room, showed me athletic swings of the body that I could not manage.

Before we sailed, de Basil made us undertake a special rehearsal at Covent Garden to show a selected audience what we had achieved in under four weeks. Arnold Haskell had been invited to the rehearsal. I suspect that no one could have kept him away. In the *Daily Telegraph* of 2 September 1936 he wrote an article headed 'New Ballet Company – young dancer of rare promise':

The official rehearsal given at Covent Garden last night by Colonel de Basil's new company, which is leaving for Australia, was of exceptional interest. Ballets as well known as *Cotillon*, *Les Présages* and *Le Beau Danube* took on a new meaning when acted by fresh interpreters, although this show was designed to reveal the company rather than the works. In *Cotillon* especially, one felt that Woizikovsky's remarkable memory has restored much lost detail, and in his own work he is unique.

Once again Colonel de Basil has made a real discovery in Tamara Tchinarova, whom, although just 17, he has been carefully nursing in the other company for three years. Here is a potential star, with a strong technique, great individuality, intelligence, humour and sparkle. She has versatility too, as she showed by dancing roles created by three different artists. Australia is fortunate to witness the debuts of a dancer who represents to an unusual degree the line and style of the Russian school.

How encouraging Arnold Haskell was, and what a treasure he proved to be as counsellor, critic and champion of the newly formed company. His knowledge of ballet was tremendous. We respected him a lot and feared him a little. In his young days he knew Diaghilev's and Pavlova's ballets well. He followed and encouraged Markova's and Dolin's careers, wrote a lot about the baby ballerinas and promoted their success. He was dedicated to the cause of ballet, not only writing about it aesthetically, but having a full understanding of the technicalities both of interpretation and of production. He attended classes, rehearsals and performances, often standing in the wings. He followed the development of young dancers, watching their personalities blossom when he had predicted it. He was emotional and rational at the same time, always helpful and enthusiastic. He decided to travel with us to Australia, and by so doing, by giving interviews, writing and broadcasting, he transmitted his enthusiasm to the public.

He popularised ballet in Australia, demolishing the belief that it was an effete art performed by hefty-calved women and effeminate men. He was able, because of his reputation, to make the Australian public aware of this traditional art. The foundation he laid then for the appreciation and understanding of ballet has grown from generation to generation, making Australia now one of the most rewarding countries both from a performing point of view and from a box office sales perspective. But we did not yet know that.

Fateful steps

Australia I

We sailed on board the *SS Moldavia*. Immediately, our concern for the repertoire became acute. Space on the main deck, negotiated with the Captain, was roped off for rehearsals from 9 a.m. till 6 p.m., with a short interval for lunch. At first other passengers resented it; but within a week, in the swell of the Straits of Gibraltar, through the Suez Canal and the heat of the Red Sea, passengers were reserving their deckchairs and were at their posts before the morning class started. On landing in their homeland, they remained our faithful public.

On board ship, life was fun. We were enjoying our favourite pastime, dancing, and in the evenings were able to relax, sing Russian songs and dance again. There were magic skies, unusual panoramas, new horizons and many new love interests. The exotic ports of call were fascinating: Port Said, the canal stretching slowly, Port Sudan, Aden, Bombay, Colombo. In Bombay Arnold Haskell gave me a handsome beaten-silver necklace that I treasured till the day it was stolen from me along with the rest of my jewellery.

Once we had arrived in Australia and begun touring, the amalgamation of the two companies created strife. There was the de Basil management and the Woizikovsky one; there were two bosses and two administrative directors. Arnold Haskell did his best to remain impartial, but he was drawn into the intrigues. No sooner did he write a flattering assessment of someone's performance than he was accused of preferential treatment, of falling in love, of promoting one dancer at the expense of another. Dancers would turn their backs on him for the slightest criticism in print, and some even refused to speak to him. Every member of this company, as in all the Russian groups, was a strong individual, and this was partly the reason for the phenomenal success the company achieved. Haskell played a major role in promoting it.

The success of this tour has never been repeated. One factor was the enthusiasm of a fresh group suddenly experiencing triumph; another was its reinforcement through even more effort and confidence; and another, not least, was Haskell's indoctrination. He says in his book *Dancing Round the World* that the first performance in Adelaide was a triumphant success. He praised many, and of me personally he wrote:

> T.T., who started her career in the parent company, more than justified her promotion. As Action in *Les Présages* she gave a performance that could be compared to Verchinina, though it was entirely fresh in conception and her personality was well suited to Balanchine's *Cotillon*.

And later he said:

Les Présages was given a splendid performance. Since I have seen it over 200 times and with different casts, I speak with conviction. Tchinarova's Action is brilliant, and more than confirms what I have predicted for her. With her jet-black hair, olive skin, and the suggestion of immense nervous energy held well in reserve, one can only compare her to some pure-bred Arab horse. Her interpretation is both musical and strictly personal – an outstanding performance.

Coming from this famous author and critic, this made me dance even better, and with each performance my confidence grew.

Our principal dancers grew in stature too. Helene Kirsova took up most leading roles with confidence. Valentina Blinova was charming, a soubrette with lovely legs. Igor Youshkevich, a strong partner and wonderful dancer, had a fine classical line. Roland Guerard was a purely classical dancer. Woizikovsky himself, who has not been equalled as a character dancer, gave strong, wild interpretations in *Prince Igor*, great ones in *Petrushka* and a subtle one in *Cotillon*. He had worked with the great choreographers in Diaghilev's company, and was able to instruct us and get results.

I now felt able to attack the dramatic role of Thamar. This is the title role of a ballet based on a poem by Lermontov, depicting the legend of the Georgian Queen Tamara, who lived in a castle perched on top of the Caucasus Mountains and enticed travellers into her castle. She offered each of them food, drink and her body, and after a wild night of revelry, stabbed him and had her servants cast the body into the river. The music by Balakirev was mysterious and wild, with rhythms of *Lezginka*, the Georgian national dance, at times sounding smooth and subdued, at others frenzied. The decor, by that designer genius Bakst, was a mass of pink and purple shades. I wore a body-hugging dress in a soft lilac shade and a jewelled Georgian hat, my eyebrows painted in a straight line à la Karsavina; nerves on edge, my face was drawn and pale. I was frightened of the responsibility of that part, but I loved it. I wished I had been more mature – thirty, say. I knew I was too young for it.

In his book *Ballet in Australia*, Hugh P. Hall wrote:

Tchinarova as the Queen, having accepted the Prince's love, treacherously stabs him and is seen recoiling with blood-stained hands as he tries to struggle to his feet. This ballet is mainly drama. Bakst's clever decor and the strong acting of Tchinarova as the ultra-sadistic Queen made the gruesome story exceedingly effective. She looked positively bloodthirsty in this part, an extraordinary contrast to her gaiety in *Danube*.

The ballet critic of the *Melbourne Herald*, Basil Burdett, was most enthusiastic too.

The tour progressed: Adelaide, Melbourne, Sydney, Brisbane, New Zealand's towns and cities, return seasons, and finally back to Europe. A year had gone by. With our heads whirling with the success, with scrapbooks full of flattering notices, decisions had to be taken about whether to return to the main company or not.

Europe

Many dancers did return, but Woizikovsky with his group preferred to tour Europe. He offered me the chance to stay with him, and to Mama the opportunity to run the wardrobe; we took both. He negotiated a tour of Europe, including Berlin, Stockholm, Helsinki, Riga, Milan and Cannes. The distinguished Diaghilev ballerina Vera Nemchinova and her partner Anatole Oboukhoff and husband Nicholas Zvereff joined us.

Many roles were available again. I was tempted with the Slave Girl in *Prince Igor*, principal nymph in *L'Après-midi d'un faune*, the Princess in *Firebird*. Nemchinova and I, between us, danced all the roles – she purely classical, strong, brilliant, perfect; me, *demi-caractère*, enjoying my promotion. At the Scala in Berlin, a variety theatre, we shared the evening show with conjurers, fire eaters and performing seals, the second part of the programme being a wild *Prince Igor*. Every night I counted the curtain calls: nineteen, twenty. Our euphoria was spoiled by nagging thoughts of the growing war-fever. The city was plastered with swastikas and Italian fascist banners: Mussolini was visiting Hitler. The excitement of the population rose to hysterical heights. The radio propaganda sounded menacing, and twice, in the middle of the night, loud knocking woke us and we were told to go to shelters in the cellar. Soldiers pushed us bodily out of our rooms. We were issued with gas masks and forced to sit wearing them until a Nazi commandant came in to tell us that the all-clear had sounded.

In contrast, Riga, next on our schedule, was a charming, old-fashioned city that reminded me of Russian paintings – all onion-dome churches, snow, horse sleighs with bells, and bulkily dressed coachmen. The success of *Les Présages* there was phenomenal. From there to Helsinki, so cold that our ship, on the way back, had to get icebreakers to release it. Then to Stockholm, a fairyland of blue skies and pine trees, branches heavy with snow; and finally south again to the sun.

It was easier to dance with warm limbs, but disaster struck. Our booking was in Milan. To our dismay we found that the Quirino Theatre was an old, abandoned building awaiting demolition – dusty, dirty and damp, at the end of an arcade that may once have been fashionable, but was derelict now. The publicity for our appearance was non-existent. In a hurry, everyone from the management to the dancers took posters and pamphlets to stick on walls or distribute. The message was: 'Tonight at 8.30, a show'. Hardly anyone came. *Les Sylphides* was seen through a cloud of dust. In *Le Spectre de la rose*, the Rose leapt on to the stage and disappeared. The floorboards gave under him. He was found, by a frantic stage manager, looking for a way out of the basement, worried that he could still hear his music above, but unable to get back on again. The whole season was misery: no money at the box office, no press notices, although we tried to wine and dine a journalist, who ordered expensive dishes but wrote a nasty review.

The company relied on ticket sales for wages and transport. Now we had to get to Cannes, where a season was booked. A general meeting was called, and all pockets were emptied and the contents pooled. The only people who still had something left were my mama and Woizikovsky. It was decided that Mama, at the head of forty hungry people, would travel across the French–Italian border to Menton, select a cheap restaurant near the frontier, order spaghetti for everyone and sit there, waiting for developments. No one knew for how long we would wait. Woizikovsky remained in Italy to negotiate the transport of our scenery. But to Mama, a gambler at heart, he confided that there was only one way to rescue the honour of the company and to appear in Cannes: pay the lorry drivers. He gambled in the San Remo casino with the little cash he had left.

In Menton, we ate our spaghetti very slowly, eagerly watching the road stretching across the frontier, praying for a miracle. Suddenly we saw two lorries with the markings of the Monte Carlo Russian Ballet, wicker baskets tied on top. Woizikovsky had staked the money but turned his back to the roulette table, unable to watch the little ball stumble. The chosen number came up. He grabbed the chips and ran. He was now sitting in the cabin with the driver, grinning and waving. To the surprise of the population of Menton, forty people ran screaming to greet the two dusty lorries with hysterical enthusiasm.

But the steam was going out of the venture. We could only wish that we again had Arnold Haskell's encouragement, moral support and enthusiasm. But with him away, and given de Basil's indifference, we felt abandoned and very depressed.

Ballarat ballerina (or ups and downs): 1939–40

After reaping the rewards of the Australian season, de Basil stopped caring about supporting a second group that was hardly paying its way. Now he wanted to take his number one company to Australia and dazzle that continent still more.

Our dancers absconded in hoards. There was no alternative for Mama and me but to claim our places in the main company. We were received with open arms. But as a last recruit into the old fold, and with my capacity for quick learning, I was pushed into any gap of the corps de ballet. After two years of hard work, having been elevated to principal dancer and with scrapbooks bulging, I was back where I had started – not even in the front row, but right back, almost supporting the scenery. That hurt. I was constantly in tears! Protestations were in vain. De Basil, who hadn't seen me anyway, was unavailable for discussions.

Grigoriev took charge of the casting. He saw me as a threat to his daughter-in-law, Tamara Grigorieva, who was tall, beautiful and stately – a poor dancer, but coached by Lubov Tchernicheva, Grigoriev's wife and an influence on de Basil, who was preoccupied with financial machinations.

Plots and intrigues abounded – the ones backstage, I felt, manufactured against me alone. I weakly demanded my little solos back, but they were taken by others. Eventually, de Basil ordered Grigoriev to reward me with a good solo to be forever mine, Toumanova's vivacious Mexican girl in *Union Pacific*; but the ballet was seldom performed, having been overexposed in previous seasons when Massine was king.

Now Michel Fokine was our supreme resident choreographer. His repertoire prevailed. He was impatient, dictatorial, sharp, rude and a complete crusher of egos. He asked me to fill any existing gap. In *Cinderella* I was in the back row, frantically doing some double *batteries*, scratching the sets. In *Le Coq d'Or* I found myself on stage following sixteen other maids, never having seen the ballet: 'Do as the others do', a split second behind. Fokine said, 'She can go on without a rehearsal; she learns quickly, she won't let me down.' In *Carnaval*, from the ensemble of which I had been promoted years ago, before my 'fame' even, I was right back into *Valse noble*. Fokine pointed at me and said, 'Look at Tchinarova, everybody, she has the style I want.' I dug my heels in for the next ballet, *Scheherazade*, refusing adamantly to be a 'green wife', the least important in the harem. I had danced the small role of an odalisque for ages. My face streaming with tears, I protested publicly, sobbed about broken promises. Taken aback, Grigoriev, with steely eyes, exposed his teeth in a wolf's smile and handed me back my part.

Fokine was the next inquisitor. I had delayed the rehearsal. I was undisciplined. Now he would make me suffer. He was going to show me what a bit of spirit meant. He twisted my back, wrenched my neck, slammed my shoulder blades together. He was a monster, and called me a cry-baby, but... he was not ungrateful. He thanked me for finding my way in *Le Coq d'or*. His wife Vera, present at every rehearsal, smiled at me. I realised that working with Fokine was a rare privilege and an enriching experience.

He restored all his ballets. We had now a different conception of *Les Sylphides*: inspired, ethereal, creatures not of this world, talking to and hearing beings unseen. *Carnaval* became subtle, coquettish, gay and romantic, Sèvres statuettes come to life. *Prince Igor* men became fierce, menacing, wild, frantic; the girls became subdued slaves, soft and languorous; the Tartar girls, frenzied. Fokine's *Scheherazade* became exotic and sexy, and brought out the marked difference between the abandon of the orgy scenes and the petrified fear of slaughter in the end. His *Firebird* became a magic, mysterious fairy tale; in *Petrushka*, really Russian, the mystic of the magician was emphasised. Never had the ballets been so well presented.

Fokine's style and understanding became imprinted on us forever. I knew that, but it did not console me. When he took up the restoration of *Thamar*, I was practically a decoration on the walls of the castle. Mama was suffering for me. She happened to be in a lift carrying the costume of Queen Thamar, still with my name sewn in it, when Fokine stopped the lift. She showed him the label and said, 'My daughter danced that in Australia and received wonderful notices.' He replied: 'How interesting; yes, she is a very capable girl.' That was the end of the conversation. Poor Mama had to remove my name from the dress.

The Covent Garden season was in full swing again, with depressing days of rehearsals and miserable lodgings. I never stopped being pushed about. Someone was ill, someone wanted to get out of the back row, another was a favourite of someone with power. Tamara Grigorieva, the thorn in my flesh, sat firmly on her roles. She was now dancing Action in *Les Présages*. She was curious about my interpretation, and asked me to show her my style. 'Nothing doing,' I said, 'you go and find one of your own, or let us alternate.' But she wouldn't budge.

Australia II

We sailed to Australia again. Surely I would get my chance there: they knew me. But nothing was changed and no one cared, except Baronova. Australian friends came round full of questions: Why wasn't I dancing more? In Sydney a newspaper article appeared asking why so little of my work was being seen.

The faithful gallery audience's representative wrote a letter to the directors, signed by very many, demanding to see me as Action. The letter was passed on to our management and it was decided to grant the request. I would be allocated a matinee, put in as an extra performance. No publicity, no announcement: the spectators, mostly children, rustling sweet wrappers and talking aloud. Not my faithful crowd. I danced. I didn't shake the world, and after that I went to pieces. Tamara, my rival, had had her eyes glued to my performance. Subsequently she blatantly copied my hairstyle, my angular dancing style and my strong interpretation. I never saw the role again.

My decision to leave the company crystallised as the end of the season approached. After my return to the main company, I had experienced not only a feeling of frustration, but a smothering campaign that was soul-destroying. I was upset and depressed and felt as though I was being buried alive. Even Mama was persecuted. She had been told that she was wanted in the wardrobe but that her fares could not be paid any more. We were sure it was all Grigoriev's machinations. We hated him.

We were not the only ones. About ten people succumbed to the warmth of sunny Australia, to the friendliness of the people, to the openness of their hospitality. Some dancers left to open ballet schools or to marry. I and five others, Raissa Kouznitzova, Kyra Abricosova, Valery Shaievsky, Sobik Sobichevsky and Valentin Zeglovsky ('Giggy'), formed a group to give recitals. J.C. Williamson's Australian management company was very encouraging in employing our group; the ballet had been a gold mine for them, and they offered us extensive tours of the provincial cities and towns of Australia and New Zealand, covering territory that was as yet balletically virgin. We were to perform excerpts from famous ballets.

Sunny Australia looked promising. We found a small, cosy flat in Sydney. Mama set out to make costumes for the recitals that had been planned. We were going to do the lot: variations out of *Les Sylphides*, *Le Spectre de la Rose* in full, Columbine and Harlequin from *Carnaval*, a grand *pas de deux* from *Aurora*, another spectacular one from *Don Quixote*. We were going to show them we could do it. Rehearsals were going well, and Mama frantically sewed night and day. A new life had begun...

Mama had bought all the materials out of her frugal savings. She was a little worried when Raissa said that she and the *two* Polish dancers, with both of whom she lived, could not pay for their costumes. There was no alternative for us but to continue making them. I spent my nights drawing cherries on Columbine's crinoline.

At the same time, a man named Levitoff, who had been Pavlova's impresario, was living in chic poverty in a small back room of the Hotel Australia. His shirts were frayed, so Mama made him new cuffs by cutting the back of one shirt. He was always hungry; Mama provided large bowls of borscht.

He persuaded us to give three preliminary matinees for schools in Newcastle, a neighbouring town. He made an agreement with us that he would pay us each ten pounds a performance and keep the rest of the box-office profit himself. It was a roaring success; the theatre was chock-a-block with wide-eyed youngsters. At the end of the three days, Levitoff, now a few hundred pounds richer, was easily able to pay off his pressing bills.

He wanted to continue presenting us; with his experience in Pavlova's day, he knew just how to deal with advance publicity. However, the extent of his profit was calculated by Raissa, whose Machiavellian mind dominated the wills of both her lovers Sobik and Valery (whom she later married). The three of them decided that they were being exploited, and planned to set off by themselves, wanting to reap a higher benefit. One night, they vanished, absconding to New Zealand and taking all of Mama's costumes that had been made for them. Eventually, we learned that their tour was a fiasco, and that they had had to be rescued, cold and hungry, from a mountain on South Island. They begged us to re-form our original group, but we refused. We were happy at their total failure, and hated them for what they had done.

In the meantime, Giggy, Kyra and I worked out a full evening programme, dancing twenty numbers between the three of us. J.C. Williamson was no longer interested in our depleted group. We found a theatrical agency, pretending to ourselves that it wasn't a sleazy one. Its poster proclaimed, 'We send shows on the road, everywhere and anywhere.' The agency recommended a Mr Knight. We were asked to pay cash for advance publicity, money that was to be reimbursed from the profits. We emptied our pockets and waited.

A few days later, a phone call summoned us to Ballarat, where a theatre had been booked. Immediately we arrived, we knew that yet another disaster had struck. The theatre was a wooden shack, with a poster stuck on its front door announcing the appearance of the Covent Garden Ballet with full orchestra in a programme of famous ballets. One lonely reporter was waiting curiously, wondering how eighty people could fit onto the stage and non-existent pit. When he found out that there were three of us and a pianist, he said he would denounce the fraudulent announcements in the local paper. We looked desperately for Mr Knight and found him at the local pub, drinking the proceeds of the sixteen tickets sold.

We summoned up our courage and, fortified by the tradition that the show must go on, got in touch with a local school. Knowing schoolgirls' enthusiasm for ballet, we invited them to attend free of charge. The headmistress, overwhelmed, gave permission.

And so we danced. It was freezing, and the hollow wooden-platform stage had loose planks in it. Whenever we jumped, a wooden board shot up on the other side. We changed costumes behind a screen held by a fireman, in full view of the audience. The hall was lit by four bare bulbs. Switching the stalls lights out meant having a blacked-out stage. We could see the audience; in the front row, women were wrapped in blankets, their feet resting on hot-water bottles. They could hardly see us, though, as our hot breath created clouds of vapour and our feet lifted clouds of dust. Our noses were dripping, sending long sprays during our pirouettes; our toes were numb, frozen solid. We danced the evening away, and then found Mr Knight, staggering drunkenly around, repeating tearfully, 'It was a beautiful show, the best I've ever represented, but there's no money at the box office...'

We were broke again. It was 1940. Kyra had to return to Melbourne to start a new life. Her husband made ballet shoes from a secret Italian pattern. Giggy returned to Sydney. Mama and I were once again searching for work. But where to start? One theatre was showing Gilbert and Sullivan non-stop: the other theatre, the Tivoli, variety non-stop. On seeing their programmes I decided they could do with my services. Their shows consisted of mini-spectaculars copied out of pantomimes, operettas or ballet. The dancing was very poor: inexperienced girls climbing painfully on their toes, staggering around with frozen smiles, representing bees or butterflies, babes in the woods, or willow pattern scenes, girls in kimonos opening fans on miniature bridges. I could do much better.

I conjured up a scene where moths and butterflies formed gigantic fluttering patterns around me, the principal dancer, appearing as a bat. It would show me executing highly technical steps, turns, jumps and whirls. The music was planned to be *agitato*, hurry-hurry music, and the costumes were to be masterpieces. I designed a black costume head to toe, with tights, mask and hood included and large wings attached to my wrists, so that with every movement the wings would flap menacingly. The outline of the body, the mask and the wings were to be luminous, as were the outlines of the corps de ballet around me. At a particular moment the lights had to go out and the ballet performed, with our silhouettes picked up by special projectors. Mama had some phosphorescent paint, so my tights were decorated artistically with me inside them, standing for hours in front of the mirror waiting for the paint to dry out.

I asked for an audition, and stepped early one morning onto a stage lit by a single centre bulb. My costume looked mangy; it could only be effective when sparkling in the dark aided by that special light reflecting from the sulphur. I asked in my non-existent English that, if they had such a spotlight, the main bulb be switched off in the middle of my number. I was to have entered the stage with a huge leap, planning to be lifted from the wings by partners. I jumped as high as I could, and, unaware how slippery the stage was, landed flat on my bottom. I tried to get up, fell on my knees again. The electrician obediently switched the light off and I was left in total darkness. I had to crawl into the wings on my hands and knees for refuge. On my way out I crashed into the scenery, having completely lost my sense of direction. Needless to say, the Tivoli did not give me a contract.

Mama took a sewing job in an underwear factory. I, not trained to do anything but dance and unable to speak the language, found employment in a wireless-maintenance shop. I had to drill holes in metal nuts for the repair of old sets. I broke many a drill there. My boss, smelling of sweat, hovered over me much of the time, showing me how to drill the damn holes without breaking the needles. He had a way of leaning over my bent shoulders, embracing me from the back, his fat frame engulfing me, his head on my neck, breathing hard, pushing my left arm holding the nut, pressing my right one with the drill. After a while I noticed he enjoyed my clumsiness, and as the pile of broken needles mounted up, an invitation for an intimate dinner was whispered into my ear. My excuse was that, because I was working all day, I had to practise dancing in the evenings. After a few weeks of playing for time, I was told that the drills I was breaking cost a lot of money, and there was no profit employing me. It was hinted that I would never make an engineer.

I was rescued from the workbench by my own personal Prince Charming – a clever artist called William Constable. He was the scenic designer at the Minerva Theatre, where the producer was Alec Coppel. Bill persuaded Alec that what the Minerva needed was a spectacular revue, for which he would design costumes and sets. Bill, carrying a huge bunch of scented lilies, arrived to announce that Alec was willing to put me under contract pending the production of a revue, in the dancing numbers of which I would star.

William Constable was to remain in Australia, become a successful and influential set designer, and make a great contribution to Australian ballet.

Alas, the Minerva project never came off, but another one was on its way. Helene Kirsova had opened a ballet school and was forming a ballet company. She invited me to be one of her leading ballerinas and asked Mama to make all the costumes.

Working with Helene was a very professional affair. 'Pioneering ballet in Australia' was her motto. She was instrumental in developing strong Australian dancers, and gave opportunities to local artists and composers to create original works for her. Especially for me, she choreographed *Faust*, based on a poem of Heine where the Devil is a woman – me. Henry Krips wrote the music, and Loudon Sainthill designed the sets and costumes. I loved this intensely dramatic ballet depicting passion and death.

I had leading roles in many of her ballets, and the preparation for these involved weeks of gruelling rehearsals. She never allowed anyone to mark time. In the role of a Good Fairy in another ballet, my variation consisted of hops on points and continuous turns. These I performed every day on my toes. I was in top form and the work was stimulating.

Financially, though, she was a miser; although she spent money on giving parties, she gave us just a hundred pounds for a ten-week season. The thirty weeks' rehearsals were included in the deal. We spread our earnings and somehow managed to live on two pounds ten shillings a week.

Raissa and her two men were in the company too. I wasn't on speaking terms with her, but had to share a dressing room. She complained of being suffocated by the lilies I was getting each evening from my friend Bill.

Faust's Sydney success became known in Melbourne, where all tickets were sold in advance. Raissa and her men, displeased that they were not the bosses and envious of the benefit, decided to strike just before curtain-up. A full house was kept waiting while three principals demanded quadruple wages and top billing; Kirsova capitulated, then sacked them all.

She tried to re-cast her ballets, but quarrelled with the Williamsons' management and found herself with no theatre, so the ballet company died a natural death.

I took up the tinting of photographs; as colour film was not available and the Second World War was by then in full swing, there was a great demand for souvenir photos of loved ones, children in pretty dresses, young brides and so forth. I was getting a shilling a photo, but could do as many as I wanted.

About this time, in 1941, I fell in love with a charming, lively, intelligent press photographer named Fred. He joined the forces, and proudly came to show me his smart Air Force uniform. During his training, every Saturday a group of us went dancing at Romano's, the smartest place in town.

There were champagne celebrations when the young men became fully fledged officers. Our friendship grew closer. Promises were exchanged for after the war. Fred was posted to Canada to train as a bomber's observer. Our parting was painful: knowing anyone headed for active combat was a heartbreaking anxiety. One listened to the news, searched in newspaper lists for names of friends. Thousand-bomber raids were taking place over Germany. Fred was reported missing in July 1942. Another telegram followed: missing, belived killed. His family did not want to believe the worst. I did not have any hope, although I could not believe that he was dead. What a waste of a good young life, what a heartbreak for us. I loved him dearly. I cried for weeks.

In Sydney, the situation for us, officially, became worse. We were Romanians, and therefore enemy aliens. We were told that we were lucky not to be moved into an enforced labour camp, as many others were. We had to report each week to our local police station and put a cross against our name in a large book. Soon, the kind superintendent developed a crush on Mama. He first called to see if we were still there, and a pattern was established: we were always there, and he himself would mark our cross in his book. After a while, from the fibre suitcase that he always carried, he produced every week a bunch of squashed flowers. He was a great beefy male, and would not have been seen dead carrying a bouquet, but obviously his heart was soft. This was generally so with Australians: a rough exterior, swearing and complaining, but a warm, friendly nature. We found more sympathy and hospitality during these gloomy days. Friends made then remained friends forever.

The world turned upside-down

Six pairs of underpants

During the very hot Sydney summer, one of the pleasures of life was Redleaf Pool, a small beach in a bay that was made safe from sharks by a thick net extending from the bottom to the surface, enclosing the pool completely. It was one of the few places where I dared swim.

The pool was always full, so it was hard to find a space on the sand to stretch out and read my book. Noticing a very dirty, crumpled towel on the edge of the water, I decided that its owner must be a child, who would be spending its time in the water. I could read undisturbed... until I became aware of a presence. An extremely thin young man with large hazel-green eyes was staring at me. His face was vaguely familiar.

He took a long time drying himself, and after shaking his towel said he hoped he had not covered me with sand. He stretched out his rag next to me and plunged into a paperback of the life of Michelangelo. When he asked me if I had read it, I said I was having trouble enough finishing *Gone with the Wind* (I was determined to do so, although I hardly understood what I was reading). He was intrigued at my poor English and why I should have picked such a thick book written mostly in a Southern dialect.

Friends of the young man appeared; he obviously was popular. I recognised a couple of actors from the Minerva Theatre, and then we were introduced. His name was Peter Finch: he was a soldier, a lance corporal in the anti-aircraft division of the infantry. He asked me how often I came to that beach. I said frequently, although I was teaching ballet all the hours I could.

The actors had seen me dance, and enthused about my talent. '*Hélas!*' I said, 'in the moment I dance not.' He said, 'Alas, not *Hélas*: at the moment, I do not dance', laughed, looked at my book and said that tomorrow he would bring me another. He could speak French and knew I was translating as I spoke.

I saw him again a week later, with the same towel and a book for me that he had been carrying all that time. He said it was A.A. Milne's *Winnie the Pooh*. He told me he was on leave from Darwin, where his regiment had been sent from the Middle East. They had travelled back on an ammunition ship where his nerves had been torn to shreds. The only way to keep from going insane from fear had been to be on watch, when the mind was occupied in scouring the horizon for enemy submarines. Below decks, the anxiety was overwhelming, and to fill oneself with spirits was the only way of getting any sleep.

His regiment had been transferred to Darwin because of the shortage of men left in Australia to defend its shores from the Japanese. The bombing there was constant. He could not believe his luck at being alive. They had spent ten months in trenches, aiming their ack-ack guns at the Japanese Zero fighter planes. They were bombed regularly twice a day. The fear and frustration was total. The guns could not be manipulated fast enough to match the speed of the planes, nor could they shoot high enough.

Peter was on leave in Sydney to take part in a film made by the Department of Information. Shortly afterwards I saw the film – propaganda for the sale of War Bonds. He was playing a young soldier who had lost his sight and had to have a letter from his wife read to him. I told him I was very moved by it and cried, and that it was a pity his eyes were bandaged, as I thought they would look good on film. He laughed, said he was very flattered, and asked me to the cinema to see a French film.

I found he knew and admired many French actors – Jouvet, Gabin, Raimu, the actresses Françoise Rosay and Arletty. I was amused by his speaking French. He made a tremendous effort; his accent and intonation were perfect, but he was short of words, and expressed himself by many '*alors*', '*c'est ça*', '*oh la la*', '*mon dieu*', '*comment dire*', and the tone he used in simply saying a guttural '*ohhhh*' sounded just like a Parisian. In exasperation he could drop a perfect '*merde alors*'.

He had spent some time in France as a child, though he had now forgotten a lot of the French he once knew, but his memory had been revived recently in Lebanon when his regiment was sent there to support the Free French. They were fed on bully beef and 'goldfish', an army name for tinned pilchards. They had seen so many starving people and, unable to feed them all, the soldiers had decided each to adopt a child, whom they would supply daily with food out of their own rations.

Peter had selected a girl of eight called Marie, whose photograph he showed me. She went straight to him each morning for her food and ran away clutching and hiding it, bringing it to her mother with whom she shared it. Once she brought for Peter a holy picture of the Virgin Mary, to protect him, she said, and he had received a letter since, scrawled in her childish writing, saying that she was praying for his safety. I spoke French to him, told him of my Marie in the convent who had also given me a holy picture.

The enjoyment of seeing French films brought us together even more. *La Kermesse Héroïque* was a favourite, seen several times: *La Femme du Boulanger* another. Peter became very emotional when Raimu was distressed at his wife's unfaithfulness; it brought tears to his eyes, and he felt he was seeing a moment of sublime acting. I understood Peter's reaction. I felt I had found a man with a heart and soul, who was not ashamed to show his emotions.

Peter seemed to have a lot of free time. The Department of Information used him for war-effort propaganda. As a veteran who had been to the Middle East and had pointed guns at the Japanese, who were now advancing in the Pacific, he was detailed to speak at the Regent Cinema four times a day, in between film showings, to persuade people to buy War Bonds.

Our friendship had matured into daily meetings and shared interests; most involving of all, I realised that Peter had adopted Mother and me as his family. Our little flat was his anchor; it seemed he had nowhere else to go. When I asked him where he slept, he said there was always the army camp, but because of his activities in town, they were not strict about him sleeping there.

We spent most of our time together. I was amazed at his lack of possessions. He always carried a book with him, bulging out of a pocket, but obviously had no change of clothes. His shirt and shorts were the only ones he possessed. The shirt had a large bloodstain on the chest where his nose had bled, and the shorts were crumpled and dirty. When he crossed his thin legs it was clear that he wore nothing underneath: his private parts were loose in a very abandoned way.

When he said he was to appear at the cinema, I asked tactfully whether he would wear another shirt, or at least wash that one. Yes, sure, was the vague reply. But on the morning of his first appearance, when he rang our bell for his accustomed meal, he wore the same stained shirt and filthy shorts on which he had obviously wiped his hands many times.

There were two hours before his performance. I told him to remove his shirt, and proceeded to wash it. The shorts received the same treatment. He did not protest. I was aware that my maternal instinct had been awoken, but excused myself in my own mind by the argument that to me the stage was sacred: one should appear clean, tidy and looking one's best.

While Mama prepared a meal, he sat with a towel around his waist. Mama asked where his underpants were. He smiled vaguely saying they had been lost somewhere; he had used them when his nose had bled and then had thrown them away... The next hour was spent frantically drying and ironing the clothes, and I persuaded him to polish his boots. His socks were like mittens on his feet – all the toes were bare. I couldn't do anything about that and they wouldn't be seen anyway. Now he looked more presentable for a stage appearance. He refused to have the band on his slouch hat washed, although it was saturated in sweat marks; he said it was the proof of his desert campaign.

I went to listen to his speech. He had only the outline of a script, but spoke well, was appealing and sincere, looked pathetically thin in his ironed clothes, mentioned the necessity of sending frequent letters and parcels, talked about the loneliness, the waiting, the dreams of coming back home. The more people contributed, the better conditions would be for the forces. The appeal was a great success. The Department of Information decided that Peter was more useful speaking to people about the war effort than being in the front line. His leave was extended from week to week.

He was commandeered to speak on a platform erected in Martin Place, the heart of Sydney; large hoardings advertised a recruiting campaign. The traffic was diverted and people listened, argued, and shouted comments and insults. Once a woman gave him a sealed envelope, and on opening it he found a white feather. He enlightened my ignorance by explaining that it was a symbol of a coward, avoiding fighting during a war. I was upset: he pretended not to be, and tried to laugh it off. Then he did not call for a few days. It was unusual. I could not understand why. I walked to Martin Place, and there he was, on his platform, looking unkempt, his shirt and shorts in a disgusting state, his face puffed, his socks around his ankles. He saw me, looked embarrassed, stepped down, and said he had met a few of his mates and they had taken him drinking.

After this he started coming again. He attached himself to me, and we listened to open-air concerts amplified in the park around the Conservatorium, choosing Beethoven's *Pastoral Symphony* as our very own theme.

Late one afternoon, as we were walking in Pitt Street, the air-raid warning sirens sounded. I looked up at the sky unperturbed – it was inconceivable that Sydney should suffer an air raid; but Peter grabbed me by the hand and forced me to run for shelter. The sky was clear, nothing was to be seen – yet anyone in uniform was visibly agitated and my companion was seized by a panic that shook his whole body. When the all-clear sounded and I put my hand into his, he was still trembling. I knew again how much I cared for him. His ability to merge into any environment, identify with all people, was a very endearing quality. My few Russian friends loved him; he could talk to them about old Russia, Tolstoy, Turgenev and Chekhov and speak in broken English with a Russian accent that made them laugh and made it easier for them to understand him.

In the basement of our Phillip Street flat lived an old Russian violin maker, Ivan Ivanovich. He was eighty-five, looked like a skeleton, had no teeth, and sat all day at his table in the bay window, cutting, carving and gluing various woods. Occasionally, mysteriously, his bell rang, and a smart middle-aged woman would call for *soi-disant* violin lessons. The curtains would then be drawn, after which the *visiteuse* would emerge some two hours later, looking hot and flustered. Ivan Ivanovich would escort her gallantly to the tramcar stop, and return to open his curtains again. But in the evening, his smile to Peter and me was that of the cat who had swallowed a canary, and with a wink he would say, 'Me, very young tonight'.

We had a standing invitation to drink lemon tea with him. One evening, passing his door, we saw no light but heard great thumping noises. Fearing that he either had fallen or was being attacked, we rushed to the door and opened it. He was in the process of trying to kill a rat. Apparently it came every day and ate his glue. To catch it, he had placed the pot of glue in the centre of his room and surrounded it by clothes-horses covered with sheets, leaving one side open for the rat to get in. Then Ivan Ivanovich had crept up behind and thrown a sheet over the rat, and was now bashing it with a broom. He had not succeeded: we had disturbed him. He looked vicious, his few hairs standing on end, with his mouth stretched into a grimace and his eyes wild. He said he hadn't felt such hate since he had seen the Bolsheviks chasing people from their land after the Revolution.

This story became one in Peter's repertoire. He imitated Ivan Ivanovich perfectly: facial expression, accent and the smacking of the lips and twinkling of the eyes when speaking of '*la visiteuse*'.

I was teaching ballet as a guest teacher for advanced pupils in the biggest ballet school in Sydney. A large building full of studios was administered by two elderly sisters, the Misses Scully. They charged a large fee to the pupils whom I taught, but the class would be crammed to capacity with girls eager to get away from their routine lessons. I was paid only a pound an hour, but, not having a studio of my own, was glad of the money. Mama was working at home for a factory, cutting and stitching women's underwear. She could earn up to four pounds a week. We lived very frugally, but Mama never complained about Peter's constant presence and sharing of our meals.

At her factory she was advised where she could buy disposal materials cheaply. One Saturday, she took me to Paddy's Market, a sort of flea market where one could buy anything from a bicycle to a leg of lamb. We found a stall that sold faulty nylon parachutes, and bought one for fifteen shillings. It seemed a lot of money, but Mama had been assured that it was a good buy. It was packed tightly and did not seem very large, but unfolding it at home we found at least one hundred yards of thin nylon material sewn in the shape of sunray strips, wide at the edge, narrow in the middle.

Mama's first idea was to make Peter some underpants. She was used to working 'in bulk' now, so she cut six pairs at once. They fitted perfectly. The next day Peter came to say that he had kept the pair he had on, but his mates had asked him for the others. He had given them away and would be grateful if Mama could make some more. She did: twenty-eight pairs.

Marriage on a shoe-string

I knew in my heart how much he meant to me. Apart from the overpowering physical attraction, I loved his lively mind, his insatiable interest in everything that surrounded him. I had found a man whose every thought was in unison with mine, and with a love of languages, books, people, music, films. He was developing my interests and feeding my mind, which was avid for European memories, continental authors and foreign experiences.

He explained to me many Australian attributes, qualities that are often misunderstood: brusquerie, matiness, sarcastic honesty, bragging. Foreigners like me found it hard to fit into their pattern. Peter's help was the bridge that I crossed to appreciate Australia, her people and her language. He was obviously fascinated by my background, by the fact that I had met and worked with great musicians and artists, that I had been brought up in a traditional art in the theatre. He had a great respect for the 'proper' theatre, as he called it. He loved hearing about the countries I had danced in, the famous orchestras that played for the ballet, and the choreographers whose art was the continuation of the *commedia dell'arte*.

Listening to the stories of his childhood filled my heart with emotion. It produced great waves of pity and anger in me. I could not understand, with my strong Russian family ties, my romanticism, my sense of loyalty, how both his parents could have abandoned him. His mother, Betty Staveley-Hill, was an English socialite who remarried when Peter was three. His father, George Ingle Finch, took the child away from her, and then left him to be brought up by an aunt while he pursued his career. He was a clever scientist, experimenting with oxygen masks, a mountaineer involved in an expedition on Mount Everest that made world headlines, but he believed that Peter was not his son, and certainly he had no fatherly care for the child. He took him away as a revenge against the mother, but did not look after him.

Peter was buffeted between relatives, none of whom could bring him up. It was decided finally that his paternal grandfather would take charge of the young boy's education. Grandfather was eighty and lived in Sydney, retired from his duties as chairman of the Land Board. While sailing to the Southern Hemisphere, the boy was taken off the ship and made to stay with his grandmother, an eccentric who, separated from her husband, now lived in India and had dedicated her life to religion. She was a theosophist, a disciple of Krishnamurti, and lived near a temple on the outskirts of Madras.

Peter was thrust into the Buddhist faith. His head was shaved and he wore a saffron-coloured robe. He was made to go, with other monks, from door to door begging for food. These monks lived entirely on the charity of devoted people. They carried a small bowl into which a little rice was deposited at each house.

The small boy's predicament, which, incidentally, he enjoyed because no one took much notice of his actions, aroused the concern of visitors to the temple. One of them, an actress theosophist called Enid Lorimer, was shocked to see this European boy begging for food, and told her ship's captain. The upshot was that Peter resumed his interrupted journey and finally reached his grandfather in Australia.

Grandfather now lived frugally on his pension. He was strict, with a Victorian attitude to life, and was at a loss to know how to cope with the problems of a growing boy who had lived without proper schooling or discipline. The demands on young Peter were great: routine, school, timekeeping, homework, no wild roaming, good manners, cleanliness and correct behaviour. He ran away from home several times but was brought back. It was only much later, when Grandfather died, that Peter understood his kindness, his human feelings, his concern for the boy, and the inability of age to communicate with youth.

Peter's was a tragic childhood. He thought that no one really cared. He rebelled, hated school but always loved his books, and used his grandfather's library well. When the old man and his sister both died, Peter's care was delegated to a maiden aunt called Betty. She, in her resentment at having to look after him unaided and short of money, suffered from occasional rages and once attacked him with a knife. She slashed his thigh out of sheer temper because he had disobeyed her orders, and Peter carried the scar all his life. He left her care for good at age sixteen and took a job delivering newspapers.

He told me these stories simply, naturally, undramatically, not asking for pity or sympathy, telling them as if they depicted a normal state of affairs. He explained to me the mysticism of Buddhists, and admired Gandhi's non-resistance policy. Non-violence was his motto. What about the war, I asked, as he had joined up as a volunteer? Yes, but he was drunk when he did it. He had never regretted it, but he hated, hated what it did to people, the bestiality it brought out. Above all, the hungry people of Lebanon haunted him.

He talked about the war, the poor 'buggers' whether they were allies or enemies, ignorant, fed by promises of glory and propaganda as to who was right or wrong. If it depended on him, the world would be at peace and people, whatever their religion, would never take up arms and fight. But as the war was unavoidable and the Nazis and Japanese were so cruel, there was no other way but to be a soldier.

He had heard stories about Field Marshal Rommel's behaviour and gallantry in the desert campaign. On taking Australians and New Zealanders prisoner, Rommel had ordered some of their own captured beer to be given to them – a simple gesture that endeared him to the prisoners and won their respect. They were treated humanely in the desert campaign that he commanded.

We talked a lot about faith and religion. I told him about my struggles as a child in the Catholic faith, of my childhood with my wonderful grandfather. I told him how I had always missed my own father, and admitted that up to the age of eighteen I still prayed for my father to come back to us; it became a habit, until I realised I was only acting out of superstition, thinking that if I stopped, God would become angry, perhaps on the very day that He was prepared to send Father back.

We now spoke a mixture of French and English. He was receiving many scripts to read, and offers to perform in radio shows. Every script was brought to me and I was consulted. The radio too became part of my life. I had discovered plays and serials; I was thrilled that I had broken this difficult language barrier. I was now thinking in English, and found pleasure in reading scripts. Dialogue was so much easier than descriptions in novels.

Peter had filled my life, and I could not imagine it without him. This ability of his to empathise with the people he chose was extraordinary. He had become a Russo-French-literary-artistic-romantic-full-of-ideals-anti-violence soldier. To me he seemed also lonely, in need of care and feeding, in need of a woman to love him. Men had always looked after me, and now I felt I wanted to look after him. He let himself be looked after. His charm, his relaxed attitude, his ability to accept everything naturally: all appealed to me, as if we were already part of one another.

I confided in Dorothy de Luce, a friend who had been loyal to me during all my ups and downs in Australia. She said that before the war he was known as a promising young actor, but also as a heavy drinker. I had no fear of excessive drinking. My uncle's behaviour had turned my mother into a teetotaller, but I never objected to drinking. I could have a couple of glasses of wine, or not.

Peter's occasional disappearances continued. Monty, a mate of his, was in Sydney; Bulla, another, was on leave; or it was pay day; or he had been kept back at barracks; or he had missed a train into town. Life appeared empty to me then, and the anxiety of not knowing how long his absence would last disappeared when he made his apologetic excuses. I felt again that the poor shell-shocked soldier with no money in his pockets was ready for a bowl of soup.

I still had no idea of his outstanding talent. He had not seen me dance either, although my ballet appearances in Sydney had been rather spectacular. The war was on and newspapers looked for escapism, so the ballet drew many articles, comments, pictures about fashions, and articles about dancing, practising, making-up and so on. The ballet was a big fish in a small pond.

Amongst the people interested in ballet, I was a well-known ballerina, and I often heard disapproving opinions expressed. What was I doing with this untidy soldier – not even an officer – who was not fighting while all the men were away at war and the Japanese on our doorstep?

His proposal of marriage was neither dramatic nor romantic. He simply said, 'We ought to get married.' I even doubted that he meant it. He said he had thought about it for some time. He had told me long ago that he loved me, but now he knew that he could not go away without knowing that I would be waiting for him. He wanted to get married without delay, as his recall to active service was pending. I asked for a few days to think about it, knowing full well that I had never wanted to marry anyone as much as Peter.

I was impatient the next day to announce my acceptance; I imagined his happiness on hearing my decision. He arrived with a new script under his arm and plunged into reading it, eulogising about the quality of the play. When I dramatically announced that I had something to tell him, he said, without looking at me, 'What is it?' I said, 'I decided to marry you.' His reply was, 'I knew you would. It's inevitable, we're made for one another.'

We spent some very happy days planning what we had to do: get a small flat for a short while, book the ceremony, get witnesses. He had no money, but Mama, who had adopted Peter as her son, gave us the last twenty pounds in our kitty. We found a flat for exactly that sum, one month's rent paid in advance. It was, by our standards, a luxurious flat in Bellevue Hills, spacious, chic and modern, but we could not afford it for longer than a month. I would look for something cheaper.

Mama earned another couple of pounds by doing extra sewing. A couple more private lessons for the big studio gave me a little more.

We consulted the vicar of the nearby St Stephen's Church. He took us into the vestry and spoke of the solemnity of the marriage vows. I giggled nervously; the vicar told me that it was a very serious matter and that he hoped I realised the importance of it. Mama had found time to make me a new blue dress that would be useful beyond the marriage ceremony. I made myself a small Georgian-looking pillbox hat with a tiny shoulder-length veil.

On the day, Peter was incredibly nervous. His hand shook in mine during the exchange of vows. We had been asked if we wanted the church organ to play a bridal march as we were leaving the church. Because the fee for that was a further pound added to the initial three pounds, we decided we would save that.

We came out of the church in silence and walked back to the flat with our few guests. The best man, Alec MacDonald, had arranged for some beer to be delivered, and Mama had made some Russian sandwiches.

My luggage had been taken to the flat the previous day. Peter had moved in on the morning of the wedding ceremony. His luggage consisted of a big, dirty rucksack that contained a worn toothbrush, a soup-spoon and a billycan.

Life with Peter – or the buffeted ballerina: 1943–45

Life with Peter was living to the full, whether it was laughing or worrying. I felt I was alive, receptive and responding. He opened up new horizons for me, unveiled new dimensions, established new interests. He had a tremendous sense of humour. He was a raconteur par excellence. His explicit repertoire, requested at every gathering, consisted mainly of acting different characters in improvised postures and impossible situations, talking mostly in juicy adjectives. His acting talent unfolded to the full.

There was a legendary story about an Australian cane cutter who, having sweated away twenty-five years up north and with his pockets bulging in more ways than one, comes to the big city for a bit of pleasure. A prostitute gives it to him, and clears his pockets on the first night. The cane cutter's reaction: Easy come, easy go.

There was the silent mime story, of a dipsomaniac going to the bar and trying to sum up enough courage to ask for another drink. Unable to enunciate his request, he goes back to the door, and starts again many times. Finally, pronouncing quickly and resolutely 'Brandy and soda', he collapses in a faint, flat on his back, exhausted by his superhuman effort.

There was the story of Hippy Hipwell, a shearer of eighty who had a leg-of-mutton stump for a leg, lost in a drunken brawl. When drunk on rum, he became aggressive and fought everyone. His best mate, also roaring drunk, grabbed a saw, shouting, 'You'll never walk again, you bastard!' as he sawed off his wooden leg.

There was the story of the homosexual camel tentatively trying his luck with another camel. After all this time, the punchline evades me, but Peter mimicked the camel's behaviour very amusingly.

There was the story of drunken Cecil Perry, an alcoholic actor, who persuaded George Wallace, a beloved comedian, to come out on stage at a charity function at the town hall, in a kitchen sketch where he held a silver tray on his lap on which lay his extraordinarily large penis, garnished with parsley, celery and cucumber slices. It was done for a bet that no one would notice. No one did. Peter acted both Perry drunk and Wallace hesitating.

There were many stories about Russians, told with a perfect accent. Peter imitated some stubborn old Russians who told him that they were disappointed that a common soldier had married their ballerina.

There was a wonderful anecdote about one of Mama's suitors, who always carried a briefcase everywhere he went, filled with sandwiches packed around a revolver in case the Bolsheviks tried to shoot him. Peter told it beautifully.

Life with him was wonderful because one could not even quarrel. He drove me mad at times: he would laugh and any serious approach to life would end as a joke. He expected and got complete devotion from me. We were as one. For me, everything else dimmed and his wellbeing, his interests and his career became more important than my own. It wasn't only that I was in love and loved: I had found a man with whom I had an affinity. He was like a loveable child, naughty, relying completely on me to make decisions, carried away by wild schemes, influenced by anybody, by anything he read.

We indulged in luxury living for a month in our superb flat in Bellevue Hill. On one occasion I was cooking a leg of lamb and went shopping, leaving Peter and an army mate reminiscing about the Middle East war. They slipped into a pub 'for a quick one' and got sozzled. On creeping back home before my arrival, they discovered that they had slammed the front door and had no key. Peter's dilemma, knowing that the leg of lamb was cooking, was to get back into the flat so that my dinner wasn't ruined. Between the two of them, they found a fireman's axe and demolished a milk-hatch door. When I came back, Peter, the slimmer of the two, was stuck midway, in a diving position, his hips, legs and feet off the ground. We pushed and heaved and peed ourselves laughing, but nothing doing – he was stuck. The porter had to be retrieved from the pub to provide a spare key, and Peter was pulled from one end and pushed in the other. The bill for axing the milk door represented two weeks of army pay. But how could I be mad when he had done it all for me, to save my leg of lamb? We moved, covering our traces should any more bills arrive.

Peter had developed an interest in fossils, stones and rocks, and had infected me with his enthusiasm; we went on splitting and collecting rocks. Our luggage contained no clothes for Peter, three or four home-made dresses of mine, one case of books and two large fibro-suitcases full of stones. I carried these into our second flat, at the top of King's Cross, above a Chinese restaurant. The flat was permanently invaded by fearless rats, who looked me in the eye and used the opportunity of my paralysed fear to wander wherever they pleased.

When I announced hysterically to Peter that we were moving again, he clutched his head: 'Not now, darling, I don't feel well', and collapsed on the floor covered in sweat. It was my first real crisis. No telephone, no known doctor, Peter shaking and sweating, and a juicy rat helping himself in my kitchen. Peter was having an attack of dengue fever. I did not know he suffered from it – it recurs at intervals, like malaria. There was nothing to be done but wait for the crisis to be over; my night-and-day vigil did not help, because the fever just had to pass. Many wet sheets later, a weakened Peter, recuperating, said, 'Oh yes. I'd forgotten to tell you – I do get these fevers.'

We moved again, with me carrying the rocks, into another tiny flat above a shoe shop at the top of William Street. It had a bed and nothing else. Peter, on sick leave, went to an auction to buy furniture, and brought back a glass box, the size and shape of a coffin on legs, the top part of which was removable, revealing a shelf covered in purple velvet.

'What is it for, darling?'

'To exhibit war medals and such.'

'What war medals?'

'You can put anything in it – guns, sabres...'

'What guns and sabres?'

'Well, it was only 25 shillings, and before I knew it, I'd bid for it.'

He painted our bathtub a violent green colour that never dried. One took one's life in one's hands having a bath. The heater coughed, trembled and occasionally exploded, and one ended up with a green posterior. When the paint had to be stripped, it wouldn't come off.

Mama, having again saved a little, asked us to choose a wedding present. Peter, familiar with all the second-hand shops and pawnbrokers in Sydney, said he wanted the complete works of Tolstoy, which he had seen for sale. Mama was delighted. So now our nest consisted of iron springs for a bed; two cases of sedimentary rocks with fossils; one case of assorted books, mostly about the Roman Empire and French poetry; one glass coffin for medals; and the complete works of Tolstoy.

The flat became a landing point for the Cross, Sydney's bohemian hub. Soldiers, sailors, actors, tramps, all visited us. Two o'clock in the morning, soldier: 'I've got nowhere to sleep.' Five o'clock in the morning, bum: 'It's cold outside.' Seven o'clock in the morning, army friend: 'May I have a wash before parade in camp?' Three o'clock in the morning, actor: 'My wife has just slapped my face and left me. I feel miserable, can I stay with you?' Midnight, radio producer: 'I've just read this wonderful script, you ought to have a look at it.' Half-past midnight, Chips Rafferty: 'I'm bloody fed up with life – let's go and have a Chinese meal.'

We listened, we went, we offered our floor and our bathroom, we read scripts, we commiserated: life was busy. But there was also the total frustration of having no money, with dreary service days in the nearby camp dragging into months and years.

From active service, Peter was transferred to an entertainment unit, and often did not have enough sense to control his drinking. I could see the struggle that he had. It was not that he wanted or needed those drinks; it was that, in Australia, amongst men, particularly in the army, a man was considered a sissy, a coward, a fairy, if he didn't get 'pissed'. I understood every now and again the need for release, for drinks with friends; but great bouts of sloshing it down, reducing oneself to a state of incapacity, idiocy and paralytic stupor, and then being ill for a couple of days, was beyond my understanding. I tried, although I always considered it a waste of time, personality and life. Peter was of the same opinion, he said: it wasn't that he was an alcoholic – he didn't need the drink. I would have recognised it as an illness if he had done so, and sought a cure; but it was a habit. It was unthinkable to meet a friend without drinking, unthinkable to just have a few, one had to go on and on. Peter had many friends, and a few of these, such as Alec MacDonald, would sneer and point at me, would say, 'You're not going to let her stop you? What are you, a man or a mouse?' and proceed to drag him out.

There was no chivalry, as in Europe, where men share their evenings with their wives or girlfriends. It was a masculine world: they would go to pubs, clubs, dens, all mates together, and return home, if not waylaid yet further, in a state of stupor. I had often heard these friends comment, 'Who is this foreigner who thinks she can reform him? He's a man's man, our Peter, he'll never change.'

His love, his explanations, his charm, his complete devotion to me after these bouts, always persuaded me that he wasn't doing it because he didn't love me enough. It was his weakness, his habits, his roaming nature, his friends, his environment, his frustration as an actor. When he was with me alone, he seemed completely happy and satisfied, so I knew that I should get him away, to help him find himself and channel his talent. I understood the wasted time in the army, the aggravation of it, the state of nerves he was in. I was patient and loving. We always came to the same conclusion in our analysis. He loved me desperately. I was his only anchor. He could not live without me. He would stop. He was an idiot, and he loved me, loved me, loved me...

It was impossible to have a good row when the man admitted his guilt, collapsed in a heap of remorse, sobbed like a child, and reduced me to a wreck, feeling guilty about having remonstrated. He would try. I could count on it, never again... etc... etc... I felt minced. We always ended up in bed. Life would be happy again – fishing expeditions with the Chips Raffertys, the two men having lost their oars in the middle of the harbour, stuck, waiting for a tow, Chips abusing Peter, no fish caught, and Quentin and I, on shore, killing ourselves laughing. Weekends riding, at night lighting fires, with Peter stubbornly rubbing sticks on damp leaves as the aborigines do, but being urged, 'Use a match, mate, we're hungry!' Chops grilled on eucalyptus twigs, the haunting smell of which stirs memories in the soul of every Australian.

Circumstances changed Peter magically. He was offered the chance to act at the Minerva Theatre, and the army agreed to let him do it. The play was *The Night of January the 16th*, a murder trial. It was the first time I saw him act on stage. His enormous potential showed in the play, but he was as yet unsure, moving badly, often not knowing what to do with his hands or arms, his voice dropping at the end of his sentences. Nevertheless, he succeeded, but I knew he could do better. What I loved was that he had become absorbed in what he was doing, studying in front of the mirror, exercising his intonations, rehearsing his timing with me. I had seen a lot of French theatre and considered that Australian voices were nasal and monotonous: lip-lazy, I thought. Peter had the advantage of a superb voice modulated by good radio performances, where nuances have to be perfect. But his posture was static.

In the second play, Terence Rattigan's *While the Sun Shines*, things were much better. He had been helped in the production by a good comedian called Barry. An American actor, Ron Randell, played a sailor. Ron oozed larrikin confidence, but Peter's hesitations, his innocent portrayal of the Earl, balanced the play superbly. Peter knew what to do by instinct. I became very ambitious for him, arguing that he should do more and more theatre, to learn and to unfold his great talent.

I could picture him in Chekhov, in Molière, in Shakespeare: in romantic roles, in character roles, as a crotchety young man, as an old man, as a foreigner, as a Jew, playing a man of any nationality with ease. He was being considered for the role of Kingsford Smith, the Australian aviator and explorer, in a big production film, but Ron Randell got the part. I felt hurt for his sake. and he was the one consoling me. He seemed not to be taking life so intensely. If either of us was ambitious about his career, it was I, not him. Perhaps he was used to disappointments, and was an optimist as self-protection. Besides, he said we had all our lives in front of us.

Charles Chauvel cast him in the film *Rats of Tobruk*. Peter was mastering the technique of the cinema quickly. In close-up, his sensitive face and expressive eyes talked volumes. But the theatre was both his love and mine; he could, I knew, become one of those rare actors who mature as the years go by.

I was mad about my Peter; I was going to help him become the greatest actor in the world. But the army would not release him. Back to camp, back to the mates, back to shedding all the responsibilities of life. Back to excuses, back to wasting one's life. I, too, was under strain, waiting in the daytime while he was in camp, waiting in the evenings when his mates claimed him. I was going to do something with my life. I was bored, fed up, desperate. I decided to become an actress. I would join the Minerva Theatre Drama School, and one day be able to act with Peter.

I plunged into Shakespeare – but found the language incomprehensible, with words all arranged back to front. I had no memory for the spoken word and could not make sense of it. In a dramatic scene in *Julius Caesar* I was told I moved about too much: to keep still, to keep my arms down by my sides – the very thing I hated to see actors do.

Did I understand the line, 'The torrent roared, we did buffet it'? 'Of course! The word *buffet* is a French one, the torrent is water; it means we ate our lunch near the river.' The whole class burst out laughing. I knew I'd never make an actress. I would go back to my own career. We could do with the extra money.

Boro

My impulses to write unplanned letters on the spur of the moment have often changed the course of my life. In times of frustration, rage or despair, writing has helped me relieve my feelings. I never think at the time that a few written lines may have such a powerful effect.

This time my despair was about Peter's drinking, and my letter was to Edouard Borovansky, a colleague of mine from Ballets Russes days. Peter had been transferred to an entertainment unit stationed at Pagewood, a Sydney suburb. His superior officer was a Major Jim Davidson. Being an ex-bandleader with a flair for show business, Davidson had seen the need and the opportunity for an entertainment unit, and knew Peter from the days when radio shows were all-powerful, gaining the attention of the nation.

Davidson gathered into his unit professional actors, writers and musicians, and made them write, rehearse and perform sketches and plays and build complete performances that would entertain the troops. He was efficient, but dictatorial, partly because he had to try to keep order and discipline amongst a hot-headed, frustrated unit, whose sole ambition was to get out of the army and get on with their artistic pursuits.

According to Peter and his drinking buddies, Davidson was a dictator, a monster, cracking his whip constantly and making everyone's lives a misery. Peter and many others were allowed to live in their own homes as long as they were ready for parade in camp at 7.30 in the morning. Office hours were kept, and they were free to go home at five. They would scramble, like children out of school, in a rush to the nearest pub to down pints and pints of beer, an eye on the clock. Before six o'clock the landlord would often bodily throw the last customers out, enforcing the strict Australian law.

Jim Davidson's serfs, light-headed and weak-kneed, looked around desperately for more beer and company, and inevitably chose the Phillip Street Journalists' Club, open all night to feed and wine those writers and journalists of Sydney society considered to be the wisest, wittiest, cleverest and most avant-garde. They probably were, although quite a few of the members wore blinkers as far as anywhere but Australia was concerned, argued aggressively and were there only for the beer.

Nevertheless, Peter, easily influenced, was convinced by them that his profession of actor was inferior to anything they could produce. Under their influence he was sure that he wanted to be a writer. He wrote a few articles, which were published in a weekly radio magazine as short stories, and swore that he was through with that idiotic acting business, which was only re-creative.

Peter would bring home friends from the unit, all complaining about life in camp, discussing nothing but Jim Davidson and how they hated him, swilling beer till the early morning when it was time to go back to camp. I liked a few of his friends – I suppose the more civilised ones, such as Tom Rothfiel, an intelligent writer and not part of the beer brigade. He was full of ideas, and a good and interesting conversationalist. Or Red Phillips, another writer, a self-centred wit, with a caustic sense of humour. Or Chips Rafferty, a tall, clumsy, sensitive, easily hurt man, with a big heart and an affectionate manner, jokingly feeling my breasts, coarsely swearing. He had a wife whom he adored, and understood the togetherness wives require.

At least these people noticed my presence. I loved them. But oh – the others...

From the day Peter and I married, Alec MacDonald tried to put a wedge in our marriage by ridiculing love, loyalty, consideration for others, and above all women. His own wife was a martyr, good enough to cook and wash, but not to be included in general conversation. He was instrumental in waylaying Peter on many nights, by mocking and criticising him, saying that women can contribute nothing spiritually – 'Let's have another drink'. Night after night, alone in bed, I would listen to the ticking of the clock, aware of every sound of our lift door. I told myself that I must understand, that all men in Australia drink to excess.

Army wives lead a boring life if they don't get drunk themselves. After a few drinks I would have a headache, a stomach pain and no feeling of euphoria. When I was invited to the Journalists' Club for a meal, soapbox orators, thumping tables and wanting total communism in Australia, drove me to frantic arguments in my fractured English. Strangely enough, although they laughed at my language, they seemed to consider my opinions more after these encounters. Sometimes I would refuse to go there for a meal, being sick of clever puns made out of my name... Tomorrow and Tomorrow from *Macbeth*, or Tomato, or Toheroa or whatever: stuff that these wits would have hated had it been made with their names.

I used to pray during my waiting evenings for an offer of a radio play for Peter, knowing that Jim Davidson would give him time off.

It was during one of these hopeless periods that I wrote my letter to Borovansky, who ran a ballet school and had that year established a ballet company to dance in Australia and New Zealand. My letter just said, 'Wishing you great success. If you ever need a dancer, think of me.' Nothing more.

Borovansky sent a cable to the J.C. Williamson office in Sydney, saying, 'Essential engage Tchinarova, immediately'. By some incredible coincidence, at my precise moment of distress, Laurel Martyn, his ballerina, had injured a foot on the New Zealand tour and was out of action.

Before I could think about what I had done, I was on a seaplane to Wellington, leaving behind a bewildered Peter. Destiny had taken the upper hand.

Boro, as he was called affectionately even by those who hated him, having created a first-class professional company, was as successful with it as the Ballets Russes had been. It was a totally Australian group, reinforced by his experienced, talented, musical leading dancers, two of whom had performed overseas. Laurel Martyn, a ballerina and a choreographer, had danced with the Sadler's Wells Ballet; Dorothy Stevenson, trained in the Russian tradition, danced superbly with a great musical sense and a flair for choreography. The purely local young talent was marvellously represented by Martin Rubinstein, full of life, personality and technique; Edna Busse, a neat, conscientious, responsible dancer, brilliant in witty comedy roles; Vassilie Trunoff, tall and good-looking, strong, only fifteen years old and therefore too young for the army; and last but not least, Serge Bousloff, who had also left the Ballets Russes to settle in Australia and a new life. He was a true *danseur noble*, a good partner with a fine classical line, looking superb in tights and with a good ability to disguise his weaker technical points.

Borovansky himself was the backbone of the company. Not only a strong character dancer, he was also a great mime. During his career with Pavlova and the Monte Carlo ballet, he created many great roles. Whenever an eccentric was needed, such as the cuckold in *Tricorne*, the strong man in *Danube*, the Eunuch in *Scheherazade*, King Dodon in *Le Coq d'or* or Pierrot in *Carnaval*, Boro was the master. I remember him in *Petrushka*, making a feature of just an old soldier on guard with a spear, falling asleep. In the long first act, where nothing much is happening except for the crowd walking from stall to stall at the fair, Boro held the audience in stitches just by acting the sleepy guard.

His wife Xenia was an excellent teacher, with a strict, no-nonsense, critical eye. Her comments were realistic, sometimes crushing, in their assessment of any weak point. She gave the ensemble style and helped soloists to find their own. She was of enormous help to me later, when I joined the company and had to replace Dorothy Stevenson in a Spanish-style ballet; Xenia made me swing my skirt, arch my back and put some real feeling into a seguidilla that in turn portrayed in sight and castanet sounds the softness of seduction and the provocative temperament of a fiery Spanish girl.

Xenia was respected and liked. Boro was effusive, rude, a hard taskmaster who would often reduce his dancers to tears and certainly give them all bleeding toes. Not only did he model himself on the great maestros who ruled by fear, but it was also his belief that Australians, although talented, were lazy and undisciplined, with no tradition of ballet, and that no professional company could survive without bullying. The dancers respected him and worked very hard. Some of them – the ones who understood him less – hated his guts. I had always liked him from the Monte Carlo ballet days, when as an endearment he would nickname girls affectionately by emphasising their worst points. I was 'the long-nosed one'. When I joined his company I was promoted: he called me 'the long-nosed beauty'. The tone was as sarcastic as it had been when I was a child.

Under the hard, superficial crust, under his coarse exterior and unpleasant manner, he really had a heart of gold, and was himself vulnerable if criticised. His sense of responsibility to his dancers was infinite. His insults only masked a tremendous inferiority complex, and after having abused everyone at rehearsal he would wonder why no one made a friendly gesture towards him. He felt hurt and lonely. But work hard we all did. It is my belief that without Boro, Xenia his wife and the hard basic work put into the initial foundation, there would be no Australian ballet.

Once the company became professional, Boro's demands for better conditions from the Williamsons never ceased. He was always arguing for increased salaries, more issues of ballet shoes and tights, or not having salaries docked for travelling overnight in sleeping cars, and he got concessions for his dancers long before Actors' Equity stepped in.

It was Boro who put Australia's national ballet on its feet. The audiences were receptive, knowing quality when they saw it, and compared it favourably with previous overseas companies. They took Boro's ballet to their hearts, were proud of its achievements, supported it wholeheartedly and flocked *en masse* to see it in every city. The performances shone with liveliness and vitality. Boro was a good painter and artist and spent hours lighting sets with my old friend Bill Constable, the scenic designer, confessing to me later that he had had no previous knowledge of how to do so. He used his terror tactics on dancers to ensure clean shoes, clean tights, not a hair out of place, no safety pin showing. In other words, the ballet was a fully professional one.

I later heard that he had been very pleased to receive my letter. He announced at rehearsal, 'I promise you something out of the ordinary: a very strong dancer is joining our company. She will really show you how to dance.' It wasn't exactly a remark that would endear me to a group of people who had danced successfully for four years. At my first rehearsal I could sense an antagonism mixed with curiosity. No one knew that I hadn't danced for over a year, had occasionally practised half-heartedly, had lost all interest in ballet, had concentrated utterly on my husband, and possessed only one pair of ballet slippers, which were too small for me.

I was given the part of the Gay Lady in *Capriccio Italien*, replacing the injured ballerina. After one day's rehearsal my muscles were stiff, painful and wooden, my knees were wobbly, Laurel's costume was too short and too tight for me and my shoes were slipping off my heels. I had no confidence at all and was unnerved by the whole company watching and crowding in the wings. Feeling sick, my heart beating fast but with a big frozen smile, I marched in, trying to capture the difficult rhythm of the entrance. Boro said to me after the curtain came down, 'It isn't like Laurel: she does it delicately, you're marching down like a gladiator, and what's the bloody matter with your shoes?' I screamed back at him with tears in my eyes, 'Well, I'm not Laurel – give the part to someone else if you don't like me!' The dancers were stunned. They could not understand our Russian shouting, but they knew that I could and did shout back.

I was in despair; I wanted to go home to Peter, and knew I was risking my marriage. I had made the wrong decision to leave him behind and, what was worse, I couldn't dance any more. Obviously no one was impressed. Boro had to eat his words. He gave me another role, the Queen of the Wilis in *Giselle*. I tried to adapt myself to a role that wasn't me, an ethereal being, floating softly, gliding in and out of a dimly lit forest.

Dorothy Stevenson's dancing in *Giselle* was so beautifully fluid that I decided to make a contrast and dance the Queen of the Spirits in a powerful way, making my gestures big, supreme, menacing and definite. It worked well, and little by little, because the dancers saw that I was trying hard and not playing the *grande dame*, they became friendly. Martin Rubinstein, who watched every performance of mine from the wings, approached me one day shyly and said, 'Excuse me, madam, but may I tell you something?' Having never been called 'madam' before, I thought he was addressing someone behind me, and looked around. But he was talking to me. It appeared that in the finale of *Giselle* everyone was doing a *jeté battu*, a more complicated step than mine: I was doing a simple *jeté*. I put a stop to this 'madam' nonsense, did a *jeté battu*, and thanked him for telling me. From then on I became accepted.

The New Zealand tour was as gruelling as any tour with the Russians. I felt privileged to be part of this excellent pioneering ballet. The friends made there have remained my lifelong friends. There were no jealousies, no intrigues amongst us principal dancers; our styles were each different and did not infringe on one another's territory. We got on very well.

My worry was Peter. According to his letters and Mother's, he had become a changed man. He wrote saying that his life was ruined, and he had lost the only anchor in his life; he was depressed, he was never going to drink again. He had found what was the real meaning of life, and it was me and our life together. He wrote me innumerable love letters and poems.

Instead of spending his nights at the Journalists' Club, he went to my mother's. Mother cooked for him and washed his clothes, and wrote to me that he was lonely, lost, pining for me, counting the days to my return. They succeeded in making me feel wretched. Distressed, I regretted my decision, realised again that ballet was not worthwhile, that I had been selfish in going away and abandoning him, and that the sooner I was back, the better.

But I had not counted on Boro relying on me as much as he did. The Williamson management, encouraged by a most brilliant tour all over Australia and New Zealand, were planning a new season. They wanted revivals of the Ballet Russes's classical repertoire. Boro said he remembered them all. He didn't: he remembered the roles he had danced, but hardly anything else. The programme was to be *Carnaval*, *Schéhérazade* and *Le beau Danube*. I had danced in all these ballets and knew all the leading roles.

Boro begged me to help him reproduce these ballets. When we returned to Sydney, he explained to Peter how essential it was for me to continue to dance, and made a tear-jerking speech, reinforced by wine, about a young country in need of culture while I, fully trained, armed with tradition and knowledge, was being wasted when I could contribute so much. Peter was in tears, and so was Boro, the old devil. A deal was made, for the magnificent sum of £10 for each ballet I was to revive. Boro gave me the leading role of Zobeide in *Scheherazade*. I had witnessed the wonderful, statuesque Tchernicheva carrying the tradition straight from the Diaghilev days. I was very happy in that role, in spite of a back injury I had received years before when diving from the highest swimming springboard in Miami.

Boro involved me in rehearsals, supervising the whole company. He also gave me the leading role of the Street Dancer in *Danube*, and Chiarina in *Carnaval*. I had admired the finesse and chic of Danilova's Street Dancer for years. Never expecting to equal her, at least I had the example of her perfection. Her image gave me an inferiority complex, though, and in spite of Boro's encouragement and the success achieved, I was often physically sick coming off the stage and was advised to have a bowl in the wings rather than being sick over the scenery.

Eventually these roles became my favourites, and I felt the exhilaration of confidence, of success, of knowing that the audience is looking forward to a performance, and the satisfaction of knowing that we will hear thunderous applause at the end of a well-performed ballet.

Boro involved Peter too. He admitted him to rehearsals, consulted him and taught him a lot about lighting, and they experimented together with the moonlight in *Sylphides* and the exotic warm shades of *Scheherazade's* erotic atmosphere. Peter now became part of the ballet set-up and got away more and more from his unhappiness in the army. The theatre gave him satisfaction and Boro made him feel at home. I, of course, was hooked by ballet again. I found I could remember the ballets well.

The rehearsals and production of *Carnaval*, *Scheherazade* and *Danube* took place in Sydney. The season was a complete success and the faithful audiences were very pleased that their own company was capable of dancing the classics.

Inevitably a Melbourne season followed. It was impossible to get away from my commitments; Peter understood and did not discourage me. He accepted the situation of my being away a month here, a month there; I could not leave the ballet. Now, with the new programmes, my responsibility was great. I was leading the two most-performed ballets in the first opening programme, and I had regained my technique. I was also giving additional classes to the solo dancers at their request.

The regular morning classes were given by an excellent teacher, Leon Kellaway. I attended these, but in the evenings a small group seemed pleased to work with me, using my Balanchine experience and incorporating his method in the *enchaînements*, thus varying the barre work. They were interested in my approach. The classes grew daily, and they worked hard for me. I was part of the core of the company now, having assimilated my roles, basking in *Scheherazade*, being partnered by Martin Rubinstein, who was a perfect Golden Slave: sensuous, savage, soft as a panther. I know we danced well together, and when *Coppélia* was produced Borovansky paired us together again for the Mazurka and the Czardas. Our temperaments sparked off from one another, and he was an ideal partner for me. I could feel the whole of my body dancingly respond when we heard the welcoming applause of the faithful gallery resound as he dragged me on stage in the opening bars of the Mazurka.

Life again was full: nine to five, classes and rehearsals; six to eleven, classes and performances.

On *Danube* opening night in Sydney, Peter came into my dressing room and conjured an angry scene apropos of nothing. I would not cooperate, as I did not want a row: I was tingling with nerves. It was a full house, with many bouquets awaiting us in the wings. Agitated about my performance, I did not want to listen to his quarrel. I expected him either to stand in the wings – as he was allowed to – or to use the little door letting him into the auditorium. He had seen the revival, the rehearsals, the dress rehearsal, the lighting of the set when I was in my costume, and the warm-up in the interval before the ballet. He said that now all he wanted to do was to go out drinking, not to see me dance, nor wait for me at the end of the show, nor be home when I came back. I was crestfallen, and my concentration suffered. One part of my mind said: Go, and bloody well do what you want to do. The other was worried, blaming myself for having rejoined the ballet, acknowledging his reaction, but powerless to change circumstances. I understood his envy, his disappointment, his despair at wasting his time in the Army's entertainment unit, his anger at being kept from doing what he really wanted to do: be an actor.

Those nights, rushing back home alone in the hope that he would be there, and then staring at the four walls, were a sad anticlimax. I would unwind the wires of my bouquets, and go to bed listening to the clicking of the lift door. At about two in the morning the iron door of the lift cage would crash and Peter would come staggering home, often with a mate – a drunken soldier, or worst of all, my *bête noire*, the soldier and actor Cecil Perry, who would take up residence on our floor. They would clumsily tiptoe into the kitchen and bathroom whispering loudly, shush one another not to wake me, clang the pans, prepare a meal, look for more bottles and fall asleep heavily around four in the morning.

The alarm clock was set for six to take them back for the camp parade. They had to be shaken, their heads put under the tap. They would leave quietly, apologetically, to start it all again the next night. My call was at 8.30. I would look into the messy kitchen, try to tidy up a bit, pull the bed together, air the stale-beer stench from the room, and take refuge in ballet classes, rehearsals and the world that took my thoughts away and demanded all my concentration.

It was during these days that I realised Peter's dual personality. He could be happy and considerate, sharing his thoughts, be totally absorbed and lose himself in a radio play or a theatre project. He worked for days perfecting his adopted identity, living and becoming the character he was playing for a broadcast, reading books, discussing every move and intonation and making me feel part of him. He attended our rehearsals and absorbed our discipline and methods of work. Or his other side prevailed: he would become unreliable, drink too much, get involved at the Journalists' Club and come home disillusioned with the theatre and acting.

He could be loving and attentive to me, taking over menial jobs in the kitchen, cooking and tidying, understanding my efforts and my difficulties. Or he could be irresponsible, unreasonable, unlistening: underrating other people's efforts, making fun of application and dedication. He then would find people amongst his drinking companions who would support his theories. He would also pick people at random, in a pub, on the street, and make them feel they were his friends for life. I would be confronted with an odd, boring character, taking it for granted that he was Peter's best friend, when Peter by now had become completely uninterested in him.

My days and half-nights were spent dancing, and the rest of the nights often spent discussing ways of getting out of the army now that the war was over, or planning theatrical projects that had no chance of getting off the floor because of lack of money and practical possibility.

Peter and I decided that I should go on dancing so as to start saving money to enable us to go overseas and pursue his career. I was getting £17 a week and work was assured for a year in advance. Boro promised that, should I want to leave, he would arrange it. But his tactics were subtle. He gave me power, good roles and supervision over many rehearsals. He made Peter his friend and confidant, practically his collaborator. When Peter was in Melbourne on leave, he and Boro were inseparable. Whenever I was away, I was counting the weeks and days before our next meeting, and Peter's letters tore my heart. City after city; the love letters came every day.

Then we worked out a scheme. I was to write to an army commander, telling him that I would leave my husband and sue for divorce if he were not demobilised, as we could not bear the separation any longer; that we were both suffering from nervous breakdowns; that the war had been over for some time and it was only the dogmatic persistence of Peter's major that was still keeping him in the army. Alas, we lost our nerve at the thought of carrying it through.

Peter was finally demobilised in 1947 after a long illness that was as much psychological as physical, leaving him thin and neurotic. I suggested he joined our ballet company to recuperate and have a holiday – we were touring Tasmania. It was ideal, like a honeymoon but much better. He was greeted as a friend. Boro, to show his affection, gave me a lot of free time during the day, but never missed an occasion, during dress rehearsals, to remark that ballerinas should preserve their strength for ballet and not knock themselves out lovemaking.

In Tasmania I had to play my cards right and manipulate my husband wisely. Each day I gently bolstered Peter with propaganda: that he belonged to the theatre and with hard work and some luck would become a great actor. When he was with me, he wanted nothing else but the theatre. My worry was the influence of the Journalists' Club: the drinking, the magnetism of the printed word, the writers' flattery and the encouragement of poets such as John Thompson and Kenneth Slessor. Even exciting the envy of Alec MacDonald used to satisfy Peter, although Alec never thought much of Peter's writing, and mocked his lack of education and his atrocious spelling.

In order not to undermine Peter's respect and admiration for writers, I thought up a scheme that would feed that creative interest and combine writing and the theatre: to compile a book about the history of theatre in Australia. What first gave me the idea was the eerie atmosphere of the Hobart Theatre, which had a legend attached to explain it: the presence of a ghost, sometimes seen and often felt. It was said to be that of an actor whose dreams of performing had just been realised when he suffered a violent death, stabbed by another actor. A grey figure was supposed to appear at the back of the dress circle when it liked the spectacle on stage. We were told that it did so for us. It particularly enjoyed the artistic *Sylphides*, with its misty, bluey-green wood and ethereal white costumes. In the middle of the ballet, during the Prelude, the dress circle audience felt a chilly draught that made them cover their shoulders with their wraps, and a misty form distracted them. A whisper would run through the dress circle, lights would begin to flicker, and a disturbed audience would lose their concentration.

The story fascinated us. I suggested to Peter that he should look into the archives and find the real story about the ghost. He did, and the book's research was started. What fun we had; dusty archives were searched, old vaudeville actors interviewed, material classified. The picture that emerged had convicts, the army, the gold rush, the many plays performed. For the next year, no town visited escaped our eager, interested eyes. Peter and I were mesmerised by this research, and our little flat became a classified archive, with all information typed and tidily put away.

Tasmania's magic helped Peter make a complete recovery. We were very much in love in Launceston. On free days we picnicked by the rocky shores of a tidal river, and one afternoon as the water was receding we saw a mother eel frantically trying to save her brood of baby eels, by pushing them to safety back into the flow of the fast-disappearing river, keeping them individually in small pools of water in the holes of the rocks, swimming around them, protecting them from the sun, nuzzling, pushing them into the deeper water. In moments like this, never to be forgotten, I loved my husband very much. An actual physically tender feeling overwhelmed me; I knew that nothing and no one on earth was dearer to me than he. We were one in body, spirit and thought. Nothing else mattered. Being away for performances was forgotten, the army was forgotten, the drinking didn't matter, the doubts about not being akin disappeared; nothing mattered but our love for each other.

When we came back to Sydney, the Williamson management decided that the ballet had to have a rest. London musical-comedy successes were in fashion, and we were to take part in Ivor Novello's *The Dancing Years*. This was a production on a gigantic scale, with crinolines, chandeliers, ballroom scenes, mountain yokels, moving scenery, and vanishing sets that required timing, practice and able scene shifters. It was to be a production to outdo all productions. Our producer came over from London: Max Oldaker, a matinee idol who was also starring, as was the delightful Viola Tait. The ballet was not really needed, but it was included thanks to the persistence of Borovansky, who wanted to keep his company intact and working. Each of us ballerinas had one insignificant, boring number to dance, but were guaranteed full employment for months to come and some salary. But we had nothing to do between interminable acts of singing, confined in our dressing rooms knitting endless pullovers, with the amplifier going full blast, waiting for the blessed finale when all and sundry had to appear and mime singing, before the heavy curtains came down on 140 people with extended arms and open mouths.

On the first night the show finished at a quarter to one in the morning. Thereafter we learned to cheat; we took off our make-up and wore our street clothes under our crinolines in the finale, and *presto*, with the last curtain call we were on our way home.

Die Fledermaus, now called *Gay Rosalinda*, was next. Boro introduced a French cancan in the ballroom scene, and once again for months it was money in the bank.

In the meantime, Peter, full of the enthusiasm of professional ballet, was encouraged by me and by John Kay, a dedicated German-Jewish-Peruvian-Australian friend (a professional musician but a producer of plays at heart), to start a theatrical venture. Peter put all his deferred army pay into it and, with John, three other directors and a newly recruited small company of keen actors and actresses, created the Mercury Theatre, named after Orson Welles's first theatrical steps. I supported the company with money, and Mama made all costumes free of charge. It proved to be a worthwhile experiment and, in time, Peter's next step towards a meteoric career.

The first programme contained three short plays: Gogol's *The Gamblers*, a Lope de Vega comedy and *The Broken Pitcher* by Klaust. I was happy that I had led Peter back into serious acting; there was to be no more writing, apart from an occasional poem, no more considering his profession inferior. He was an excellent actor; he wasn't making any money, but I was, and our needs were small. What mattered was that he would continue to grow and learn and have the example of ballet dedication to inspire him. He saw his future clearly now: it was the theatre, the classical theatre, where he could contribute a fresh approach, not influenced or contaminated by previous experiences. He used his intelligence, his instinct, his flair, his God-given talents. When he lectured and taught, he was revered by young actors, dedicated people eager to learn, prepared to perform and not be paid, to rehearse at all hours just to be part of this fresh new venture: full of hope, excited at a good notice and the praise lavished on them.

It was convenient for me to continue dancing. No rehearsals were needed for my job, so I helped Mama to make costumes. She was a magician. She transformed her chosen materials into glorious robes, spending hours sewing ornaments cut out of felt and painted over to look like gold or silver. By now in the flat in Phillip Street that I had abandoned in order to move in with Peter, she organised a theatrical *Maison Tchinarova*. She had made close on 200 costumes for the Kirsova ballet: clothes for every dancing recital they ever performed in Sydney. She supplied the whole of the de Vries Opera with costumes, including for *Cavalleria Rusticana* and *I Pagliacci*. She made over a thousand tutus for ballet examinations for the dancing academy, and ballet tights for seemingly everyone in the Southern Hemisphere – New Zealanders found her address and she despatched tights there.

She was earning a lot of money, and when on Fridays I used to bank my money she would always add something, saying, 'For you and for Peter's theatre'. In my spare time I took to helping her machine her tutus. It was a real factory in Phillip Street; at one time she had as many as six Russian ladies all sewing away.

But difficulties arose again; another ballet tour was being prepared. Dottie Stevenson was ill and I agreed to dance some of her roles. During one Sydney season I was being overworked – when extra matinees were added, I would be dancing eight ballets a day. One newspaper wrote, 'We see a lot of Tchinarova; she insists on dancing roles in which she is superb and others that do not suit her.' I was furious, wounded, and told Boro to get someone else. I suggested Kathleen Gorham, a beautiful dancer, very young, with perfect technique, whose brilliant personality shone through her dancing. She had been a pupil of the Scully sisters, the finest teachers in Sydney, and I had noticed her talent when I gave some lessons there.

Boro did listen to me. He looked at Kathy, whose work was so good that she made everything look easy. He was thrilled. We both noticed, though, that she was not very disciplined. Her shoes would be dirty on stage, her coiffure would fly off, her straps come undone. Boro descended on her like a vulture, but she could answer back, or walk away and show that she did not care. Eventually she listened, and worked hard. She was soon groomed to dance leading roles, starting with a ballet arranged for her, *Terra Australis*.

I was ready to leave the ballet, because once again staying would mean months in New Zealand; but Boro would not let me go, and demanded that my salary be doubled to make the tour attractive. Boro promised that I could choreograph a ballet when we came back to Sydney. I was told that the tour could not go on without me, and I was letting the whole company down. I was begged, I was blackmailed, my feelings of comradeship were called upon, my loyalty was appealed to. Peter was approached to let me go.

I went. The time was short, the money was good, and I had made up my mind that this was definitely my last tour. The money would be useful. Peter still was not earning much; an occasional play for radio would bring in ten pounds, which would go into his Mercury Theatre fund. I was going to save; I was going to take us both to London, where his talent and his *raison d'être* would come to fruition. I could not go on in ballet with its touring, its long hours, its exhausting work. I loved my husband. I did not enjoy seeing him frustrated by my success, upset by my travels, and annoyed that our performances took place in proper theatres with a full orchestra, professional stage hands, proper decor and scenery. I was still the victim of his feelings of insecurity, and knew that the only way to combat them was to abandon ballet, which was *me*, and dedicate myself to his art, which was *him*.

Peter's absorption in the theatre became total. So did my happiness. At the time, I found the theatre, even on a small scale, infinitely more exciting than the ballet. I had danced every role I could. Nothing could satisfy me any more; I felt I could try to improve what I was doing, but I had no guidance. Boro was preoccupied with the ensemble and never helped me. What I was doing now was a repetition of previous effort. Every artist needs guidance, in ballet probably even more than in any other art.

Boro's promise of letting me do some choreography made me do some work on Scriabin's *Le Poème de l'extase* that appealed to my Russian soul. I wanted to portray the vision of Dante's *Inferno* and *Paradiso*. Gustave Doré's illustrations for the poem in a book I owned had impressed me particularly, and I felt inspired by the breathtaking groups he had drawn. Boro was enthusiastic and so was Peter, but my lack of confidence stood in the way. I wanted to do it but was nervous, and I wanted more to abandon ballet and be completely involved in Peter's work. So I handed in my resignation. They were prepared for it, as it was the end of a season. There was no fuss, no farewell performance. As I lay on the ground on the stage in Wellington after having killed myself as Zobeide, through my mind went the thought, 'This is the last time I will dance that.' I had no time to indulge in tears or regrets. The interval was fifteen minutes long. I had to wash myself from head to toe, having been covered in brown make-up after my passionate scenes with a sweating, painted slave. I had to do a complete change of make-up, put my hair up in curls, pin flowers in my hair, put on tights, ballet shoes, dress, have enough time for a few *échappés* – an exercise to make my points warm and ankles supple – and then come out sparkling as the Street Dancer in *Danube*.

The show folded without fanfare or farewell speeches. There was only one bouquet, from a faithful Russian friend. The sets and costumes had to be packed away fast to be delivered to the docks, with the ship leaving next morning. I drummed into my head, 'That's it, the very last time you dance, the very last time you hear applause that was meant for you alone.' I did not feel any relief, I did not feel any regret. I could not believe I was abandoning what I had been doing for twenty years, from the age of nine. I told myself that I could now live for my husband alone, totally and completely. I had saved a thousand pounds to cover fares to England. We were going to be happy, and never separated again.

Acting up

Eureka Stockade

Peter's early days as a film actor were half a world away from Hollywood in more ways than one. In 1947–48 he was cast in a small part in the film *Eureka Stockade*, directed in Australia by Harry Watt under great difficulties: rains, floods, temperamental actors, an overdrawn budget. Every known and unknown actor on the continent was employed – a great bonanza period for them all. Enormous chunks of the countryside were taken over near the town of Singleton, where a whole new film town was built. Singleton prospered; its two hotels, two pubs and two general stores had never known such riches. As well as importing English principal actors (the leading lady having her own mobile loo), Harry had brought down a hundred or so aborigines from a reserve in the Northern Territory. These were lodged in corrugated iron huts near the location. Although Peter's acting role was small, he also helped with the casting, assisted in the second-unit filming, and, because of a previous expedition amongst the aborigines, was made their welfare supervisor. He was Mr Peter Boss; I was Mrs Peter Boss, looking after the ladies.

One of our duties on Thursday evenings was to pay their wages. Men, women and children lined up by a table, while Peter dished out eight pounds into each outstretched hand. I ticked off their names in a ledger. Then the lot of them, clutching their treasures, promptly rushed towards the two general stores, whose shelves were immediately emptied of goods. Big parcels were taken back into the corrugated huts to be hidden away. Next, *en masse*, some with babies in arms, they hurried into town, to occupy the front seats of the only open-air cinema in Singleton. This they did nightly, looking at the same film again and again.

By Saturday morning, Peter and I would be woken up early by a loud knock on the hotel bedroom door. 'Mr Boss, Mrs Boss, can we borrow some money from you till next Thursday?' 'What did you do with your money, Bella? Jo-Jo?' 'Spent it, Mrs Boss, I bought soap.' 'Soap only costs 3d, Bella.' 'I take all soap.' After the same excuse on four Saturday mornings, I followed fat Bella to her hut. She had bought a wooden trunk that was filled to the top with Lux toilet soap. She loved the smell of it, but never used it. Jo-Jo, her husband, was spending his wages on beer, and when full of it was fighting mad, swearing at everyone and hitting her. She wasn't going to let him have her money; she had to spend it. Our accounts department was always in deficit. We soon knew that the lending had to come from our own pockets.

Singleton, invaded by three hundred bearded actors and their entourage, took on the look of a gold rush town in the 1890s. Shooting of the film had to stop when the whole valley and town became flooded. Water came up to our first-floor balcony. We were marooned. The producers and directors bit their nails in anxiety. The actors, the extras and their friends sat on the top floors of hotels enjoying it all. The longer the stoppage, the larger the pay. The beer supply never ran out.

On a weekend when most of the population was drunk, when the water receded and slush was at its deepest, the local sheep-shearers had a contest: who could take his horse up the steep town hall steps? They put sharp spurs on their boots, they flicked their whips, they pulled the reins, they shouted, they pushed, they terrified the horses.

I was watching from my balcony facing the town hall. I became wild with fury looking at the horses' sharply jerking heads, their petrified bulging eyes and attempts at bucking. I shouted to the men to stop, but they did not listen. I could not contain myself. I ran down and pulled at a shearer's coat to get him away from his horse, and shouted at him all the 'bloodies' I could muster. He shouted back that it was none of my bloody business. Then, suddenly, they stopped their racket and turned their backs to me. I thought from then on I was going to be ostracised, 'a bloody foreigner' with no sense of fun, but decided to face the shearers when they asked Peter next day to call me into the saloon bar. The leader of the shearer group stepped forward in his long muddy overcoat and worn-out boots, their toes pointing to the sky. He held a hand behind his back. I stood facing him, head high, knees a little weak, ready for the whip. He shifted from one foot to the other, cleared his throat and said, 'Ma'am, we live in a world of men, not goats. We like you; you're a man, you're one of us.' He produced from behind his back a bunch of squashed grapes in a wet paper bag: 'This is for you, Ma'am, from all of us.'

Harry Watt and Peter were friends. Harry said he wished that Peter was playing the lead in *Eureka Stockade*, but the studio wanted an established name and Chips Rafferty had become a star while Peter was unknown. Harry was able to grant a version of his own wish later, though – when we moved to London he gave Peter the main role in *Train of Events* (1949).

Prelude

In January 1977 Peter Finch died famous. A couple of months later, his name resounded all over the show business world. He was the first film star to be awarded an Oscar posthumously. I was nowhere near to bask in the glory. His third wife spectacularly collected the award in Hollywood.

On the night of his death, a London broadcasting station first announced that he had suffered a massive heart attack that very morning in a Beverley

Hills hotel. He was waiting to be interviewed for an American nationwide broadcast. I switched the BBC TV news on, hoping for more information, only to hear that he had died. The impact of his death sunk in slowly during the night, as I listened every hour to news bulletins on the World Service of the BBC. Memories stirred of our hopes and plans together, of the decisions we took, of our arrival in London in November 1948. We were wide-eyed, eager young people, ready to face anything, confident, starting a new life with the safe security of a thousand pounds in a joint bank account.

Further back, we had memories of Laurence Olivier and Vivien Leigh during the Old Vic's tour in Australia. They had wanted to see local talent perform: Where were the straight actors? The only shows in Australia at the time were revivals of musical comedies and ballets. It gave John Kay an idea. He invited them to a lunchtime performance of Molière's *Le Malade imaginaire* at the O'Brien's glass factory. The Oliviers, whether out of interest or duty, went, arriving well before time to see the actors clearing a section of the factory floor, setting the proscenium frame, securing the curtain, putting up the furniture, fixing the spotlights, and being ready when the bell rang for the lunch hour break. It looked more like a troupe of strolling players giving a village square performance.

This appealed to Olivier enormously. The audience gathered quickly, either sitting on the floor or on hard benches, munching their sandwiches, and the curtain went up on Peter, aged 31 in life, wrapped in my mama's dressing gown, playing a crotchety old man of 70, sitting next to a table laden with potions and pills. The pampered *malade* still had a twinkle in his eye for a pretty girl who, to preserve her chastity, had to avoid his eager, busy hand. The role of Argan is usually played by older actors. Peter had not seen anyone perform it, but had been inspired by his affinity with French actors whose performances he had watched so avidly on the screen. He grumbled, chuckled, fussed about, and always had this inner understanding, the light irony in the deep satire that Molière conveys so well.

The Oliviers were visibly enthralled. They laughed and applauded, and after the last curtain was down, promptly stepped behind it to congratulate the actors. Olivier said to Peter, 'If you ever come to London, look us up.' Poor John Kay; in promoting his show, he had invited the royalty of the theatre, not suspecting that their remarks would change Peter's life and, through Peter's withdrawal from the venture, eventually destroy the core of John's own project.

Later during the Old Vic season, Peter was chosen to introduce the Oliviers in an ABC programme. We were both invited to visit them backstage after their performances. Peter went into Olivier's dressing room, I into Vivien's. She had been playing Lady Teazle in *The School for Scandal*. She was limping and in pain from some knee rheumatism she had felt while dancing a gavotte on stage. She asked me how dancers coped when they feel pain. And without listening to my reply, said, 'You bring that clever husband of yours to London. You must promise.'

Vivien did not have to make me promise – my mind was made up even before she had set foot in Australia. That remark was merely reinforcement to my ideas, and encouragement of course. Australians, in my estimation, have never appreciated their home-grown talent. One has to conquer England or America to be considered good; if the artist returns home to stay, the suspicion arises: 'Is he finished overseas? Can't he earn his living there any more? He wouldn't come back to stay if he could.' But let someone go away for ever, then the Australian blames the artist and considers them too grand to return.

Peter had to go away. Others had also encouraged him, including the film directors Ralph Smart and Harry Watt and the producer Leslie Norman.

When we sailed to Britain, I knew in my heart that the move would be final. I was distressed at leaving my mother alone, so far away. I was aware of the sacrifices I was making, not only in leaving dancing – that was accepted now – but in leaving my mother. My darling Mama would be four weeks' journey away from me and I would miss her dearly. There was a hope in my heart that she would eventually come to live in England, but to try to displace her at that time was unwise. Friends came to see us off, throwing paper streamers from shore to ship. I clutched on to mine, held on shore by a bravely smiling Mama; as the ship sailed away, my throat contracted and my tears flowed. Our hopes were that in England Peter would find a family, his mother, his father, even if each was now remarried. Surely they would be overjoyed to find him again?

Peter's cousin Betty had given us an old bundle of letters dated 1919–20, a correspondence between Peter's father George, and Charles, the grandfather who looked after Peter in childhood. We read them avidly as soon as we reached our cabin. They were confusing. Charles wrote reproaching George for abandoning Peter; George replied that he suspected the child was not his. In that case, Charles said, why did George take Peter away?

There was another child of the marriage, a younger son, Michael. There was a mystery somewhere. Peter and I would disentangle it all.

London

In London we felt a mixture of elation and sadness: elation at how much there was to see, to do and to explore; sadness at the damage done during the war, the devastation around St Paul's Cathedral, and the blocks and blocks in ruins. But there was also the gaiety and wit of the Cockneys, the bus conductors, the barrow-boys and shopkeepers. There was the Christmas tree in Trafalgar Square, where the carols sung that year on Christmas Eve sounded particularly moving. Peter recorded them for a programme of impressions he sent back to be broadcast in Sydney.

Our second week in London's Regent Palace Hotel was memorable because I found a flat that looked spacious and clean and because we managed to contact Peter's father, Professor George Ingle Finch. We made an appointment for tea in the hotel lounge at three. The professor arrived at 2.30 and was ushered upstairs into our small bedroom, which contained a double bed and one chair. I jumped off the bed in my stockinged feet expecting a big emotional reunion – but nothing like that happened. We shook hands, he talked about the weather, said December was a bad time to land in England, asked us about the length of our stay – and said he was looking forward to his tea. He was a tall, slim, dry, very distinguished-looking man wearing a monocle. As we passed by one of the windows in the lobby displaying cheap jewellery, he looked at it, lifted his eyebrows, dropped his monocle and said 'Trash' – a tone and gesture that Peter tucked away into his repertoire of stories.

The tea table was cramped, the room was noisy, the sandwiches were dry and curling at the edges, the cakes hard and the conversation dead. I could not understand his cold attitude, and his indifference upset me. He said he had another appointment. Our meeting lasted no longer than three-quarters of an hour, and the professor's final words were, 'Contacts have been broken; you must try and trace your mother.' We asked how. He suggested a firm who held a trust in Peter's mother's name. And he was gone, not even shaking hands...

Peter had an ability to dismiss anything unpleasant from his mind, albeit only on the surface. I know he suffered from this encounter, as I did. I had noted the name of the trustees, but Peter didn't want to pursue the enquiry.

We moved into our flat to discover that it was too big and cold, and were told it was in the wrong district for an up-and-coming actor. We didn't care – we had fun. On Saturdays the Portobello Road was in full swing. There were lots of cheap vegetables, and slabs of whale meat to compensate for the meat rationing; we tasted it and hated it. The market became colourful before Christmas when the stalls sold what they called 'monster novelties' – any kind of cheap wooden toy, rag dolls, inflated animals, paper chains and sparklers.

Peter decided to record the witty cries of the barrow-boys. He had on loan a powerful tape recorder. He plugged it into the same socket in a pub that also supplied lighting for the whole line of barrows. There was a flash and a bang and Portobello Road was in pitch darkness. I was left with the machine, surrounded by angry barrow-boys, while Peter ran to buy all the hurricane lamps and candles he could find. That night I learned many new swear-words.

With my ballet days over, our plan was to have a child. With full and joyous cooperation from Peter, within a couple of months I was pregnant.

Our first few weeks in Britain, freezing in a dark, damp flat, eating whale meat and meatless sausages, were spent mostly in bed, with Peter making quick dashes to his agent to reassure himself that they remembered him, and me dashing to the bathroom to be sick. Friends and acquaintances were informed of the miracle of my future production.

Harry Watt, who was a friend indeed, introduced Peter to Michael Balcon of Ealing Studios and helped him to get his first part in a British film, *Train of Events*. He played the role of an actor who murders his wife and keeps her body in a wicker basket. Mary Morris played the wife. Even in these first weeks in England, Peter had not been idle: he had read a report about meat from the market on the BBC Home Service at 6 a.m., compered a New Year's Eve programme, written his weekly letter to an Australian magazine and made his infernal recordings of places and sounds.

But there was no trace of the Oliviers; they were in America. When finally an invitation came for a sherry party, it was an appalling anti-climax. It lasted half an hour, and the exchange of conversation was, 'You're all right, dear boy? Good. Do keep in touch.' Nothing more. What we did not know at the time was that Olivier was planning to produce a James Bridie play, *Daphne Laureola*, and meant to give Peter the role of the young Polish student Ernest Piaste. But before that, Peter had to audition for the famous, marvellous actress Dame Edith Evans, who was playing the leading role. The script was delivered to us by Cecil Tennant, who glanced at our flat and did the equivalent of dropping a monocle by saying, 'You cannot live here, dear boy.'

Peter set to work. The days spent preparing for that audition were the most anxious I had experienced in our life together. He never slept, he didn't eat, he lost weight, he shook continuously. He made me read aloud, repeatedly, every line of his script, making notes, registering the sounds of my Russian accent. He repeated after me every word I said, to get the Slav intonations. He went to the audition in a dream, facing a darkened auditorium, and read a scene with Diana Graves. After a few minutes that seemed eternity to him, he heard a well-known voice say from the audience, 'You don't know me, my name is Edith Evans. I will see you at rehearsal on Tuesday...'

Many articles have been written about Peter's phenomenal success in *Daphne Laureola*, of the 'star overnight' kind. He was thirty-two and had worked in show business since he was sixteen; there wasn't an angle of acting he had not explored. Radio had perfected his voice. His debut on the West End stage had been engineered by Olivier; but if he hadn't been capable of acting that part, he would not have got it. I knew too that without me, without my driving force, there would not have been a Peter Finch there. I was deliriously happy; all my dreams had come true. He needed love, guidance, the security of a relationship and to know that someone, me, was caring desperately.

The prospective father's protective instincts developed, and in the spring we found a better and more central flat, adjoining Wyndham's Theatre, where *Daphne Laureola* was playing. A glorious sunny summer followed. Peter worked, while I and Lyn Foster, a loyal friend and godmother-to-be, saw every West

End show, revelling in the magic and art of the English theatre. Peter was acting with Edith Evans, promoted by Olivier. I was carrying Peter's child. Life couldn't have been better.

Peter's curiosity about his mother returned. We went to the trustee's office handling her affairs and stood facing a conservative-looking gentleman, who refused to give us her current name and address, but pushed unobtrusively into our hands a slip of paper with that information on it. Her name was Staveley-Hill, her address Carbis Bay, Cornwall.

Peter telephoned her and was invited to visit on Sunday. The only suitable train was at 11 p.m. on Saturday, changing lines at dawn. There was no one to meet us at the station. Half an hour later, a taxi brought an elegant woman, in perfectly cut slacks, blonde hair flowing, wearing large dark spectacles, accompanied by a stocky teenager: Peter's mother, and his half-sister Flavia.

There were no hugs or kisses. A simple 'Hello' and 'Call me Betty, I can never be on time, I'm sorry.'

In the cottage overlooking Carbis Bay, traditional afternoon tea was served, during which I found balancing tea-cups rather uncomfortable in my advanced stage of pregnancy. The conversation was incredibly shallow: the weather, the seagulls, how they flew close to be fed. The next half-hour was spent throwing stale bread into the air. Flavia brought in her pet rabbit, and its antics occupied more time. A cyclist who had lost his way rang the bell and was asked to stay for tea. There was more vacuous talk, and not the slightest reference to the mysterious past, the unbelievable present, the joy of the reunion.

My polite restraint lasted. I was in England. I was learning although not understanding, trying to compare this to scenes in Chekhov's plays: undercurrents with a smooth surface. Before bed, snatching a moment with Betty, my intensity exploded. I asked:

'What was your impression when you saw your son?'

'Oh God! He wears a signet ring on the wrong finger.'

'Had you ever wondered what had happened to him?'

'No, I had to eliminate him from my life.'

'Had you heard of his West End success?'

'Yes, I saw a photograph in a paper and was sure it was him.'

'When was that?'

'A few months ago.'

I shall never understand, I thought. Peter was wearing a signet ring for the stage to hide his embedded wedding ring. If a son of mine had come back into my life after thirty years wearing a ring through his nose, I still would show more love and emotion.

My body was preparing to give birth soon and my nerves were taut. I couldn't get over the indifference shown that weekend.

Later, Betty became a burden to us, and Peter supported her for many years. It was only after his third marriage that Peter began to sever all ties with his old friends and relations. Later, Betty became destitute and unkempt in her old age. Her other children were unwilling to help. She lived in a small house, with a leaking roof, unpainted walls, and stained carpets from dogs and cats. I felt sorry for her, but grew tired of buying and carrying endless parcels of groceries for her. I wrote to Peter and his third wife in Hollywood, and a cheque arrived soon after to settle Betty's debts again.

Our daughter Anita was born during the year's run of *Daphne Laureola*. When she was a few weeks old, Dame Edith Evans took her in her arms, and we heard that sublime voice sing, as she was cuddling her, 'A child, a child, what a miracle... how I would have loved a child.' Lyn Foster and Vivien Leigh became Anita's godmothers.

Peter was a very proud and loving father. He could stop her crying and could amuse her; he helped her to take her first steps, to form her first words – but he disregarded her hours of sleep. She would be lifted out of bed in the middle of the night when he came back from the theatre, and be made to stay up and be amused, and so be thoroughly awake when it was time for all of us to sleep. I was battling either for him to be quiet, because she should sleep, or for her to be quiet because he needed to sleep in the daytime.

With her birth it was as if my heart had expanded with protectiveness, concern, devotion and love towards the little one. She couldn't be left alone; she needed her food, her sleep, her routine, her comforts. The demands on my time increased. Between a successful young actor living at night and a baby's needs, life was busy. We both adored her; she was taken in a carry-cot to dinners and parties, peacefully asleep. The only difference in our attitudes to her was that my care was constant, his spasmodic. He often showed his jealousy of my divided attention.

Peter did four plays consecutively for Laurence Olivier Productions. My life revolved around him and around Anita. We entertained a lot, as Peter made friends easily. The John Mills dined with us, as did the Michael Redgraves, and many other actors and actresses gathered in our Dolphin Square flat – a posher flat this time – and many bottles of wine were opened late at night, probably to the despair of our neighbour Harold Hobson, the theatre ctritic, and his charming wife, who never, but never, complained.

When Anita was three, my mother wound up her lucrative business in Australia and came to live in London. Unable to live idly and unwilling to be a burden financially, she invested all she had in a guest house, but was a doting grandmother always willing to help with her beloved charge. Peter's mother Betty, who had by then moved to London and was residing in Dolphin Square as our guest, loved to join in the social side of our life but was a dead loss as a traditional grandmother. She never took the child out, never babysat, never gave her anything and never showed any interest, affection or love.

My greatest wish was for Peter to continue his theatre work. The occasional film, yes, to reinforce our deflated budget; but theatre, theatre always. The Old Vic season of which he was part was highly praised by the critics. It brought Ken Tynan to his knees before Claire Bloom's Juliet. Peter played a magnificent Mercutio. He had guts, was manly and agile, and spoke the poetry with a divine voice that conjured up the romantic aspect of the character: an elegant, mischievous Mercutio whose death brought about the tragedy and gloom of the play. When he died, it was like a flame extinguished.

I knew it was essential for Peter to act in the classics, and asked his agent, Olive Harding, to arrange a Stratford season for him. She promised she would, but it never happened – a pity, for I knew the unlimited possibilities of Peter's talent. I always advised him to keep to the theatre; but having led him there, my powers diminished. He now had an advisory council, a strong agency, an experienced panel that knew how to plan a career. It was out of my hands. Films were considered essential, and the money was good.

Looking back from 1977, I did not want to think any more – Peter was dead. My other memories were buried deeper. Peter had died famous, probably more so than if he had stuck to the theatre. He had a superb quality on the screen too. His eyes registered emotion and conveyed his thoughts more than many lines of dialogue. He was a cameraman's joy.

This is how his Hollywood career started.

Night visitor

On a frosty January night in 1953, when we were warm and snug in bed, the phone rang. I glanced at the clock: 2 a.m. Unable to let it ring without answering it, and knowing that Peter never would, I dashed into the living room to do so. A determined voice named herself as Vivien Leigh and announced that she was coming round to Dolphin Square to see us. She wanted to talk. She was on her way and would be there shortly.

I ran back to the bedroom with the message. Peter jumped out of bed. She had never called on us before. Surprised and alarmed, we began frantically tidying up the flat, left in a semi-chaotic state after the departure of close friends – noisy, animated, boisterous actors who had joined us for supper, to eat, drink and unwind after a performance at the Old Vic. We emptied ashtrays, gathered glasses and stacked newspapers out of the way.

Anita, woken by the phone, wanted to know what was happening. 'Your godmother is coming to visit, but you must stay in bed...' Anita decided that it must be Lyn Foster, her other godmother, who was coming; she adored Lyn, so she would get up. Explanations, persuasion and menaces only succeeded in keeping her in her room with the door open.

A few minutes later, we heard the lift door click outside our flat, and our door bell ring – it was Vivien. It had been snowing and her hair was wet; she was wearing a mink coat, but on discarding it she had very little underneath, just a clinging, sleeveless dress that looked more like an underslip. She handed Peter the script she was carrying, and demanded that he read the part of the tea planter immediately.

She said the flat was smoky and airless, and rushed to open the windows, which we normally opened only in summer, because of the gales that blew from the river during cold weather. Then she said she was cold, and ran her hand over the radiators, which never functioned properly because we were on the ninth floor. She announced she was hungry, and rushed to the fridge, whose door wouldn't open because a table was blocking it. When I tidied up and was able to open the door, Vivien found that my food reserves consisted only of the remains of a roast, shrivelled and close to the bone. She wanted it, then didn't, said it looked disgusting, and proceeded to polish a small round table with her handkerchief, telling me, 'You should be careful and put place mats under your glasses – rings from wet glasses ruin furniture.' I remember thinking that obviously she didn't know how little we had spent on our furniture, bought from a second-hand shop around the corner, nor in what state we found it before I polished it to make it slightly presentable.

Peter was amused by her activities and came to my rescue with an explanation, but was promptly told off and ordered to continue reading the script. Vivien had decided that he was to play the leading role opposite her in her next Hollywood film. Larry had let her down, she said, after promising to play it. She was going to show him that she didn't need him.

'What about a screen test?' asked Peter.

'There's no need for one. I have the right to approve my leading man, it's in my contract, and I've chosen you.'

She had received an Oscar for her performance in *A Streetcar Named Desire* and the studio was begging her to make another picture. They would agree to anything. Peter, flattered, overwhelmed, was avidly reading, skipping passages, not referring to his role, instantly snapping into the part, reading some lines aloud. Vivien interrupted, saying that the film, *Elephant Walk*, was going to be the biggest production that Paramount Studios had done for some time. She considered it a wonderful story, and was angry that Larry did not want to play it, as she had chosen it as a vehicle for them both.

She became impatient when Peter took too long to read the script.

'I know what's best for your career. To advance it, you should now star in a big Hollywood film. I've seen you as Mercutio in the Old Vic. You're wonderful, you can return to the theatre after filming. You're wasting your time in small roles like the one in *An Italian Straw Hat*. There is no question of you asking anyone else's advice. That's what you're going to do.'

Peter tried to keep up an appearance of dignity, wanting to read the script to the end.

'That won't be necessary', was the impatient remark.

Anita's calls of 'Mummy' became more and more pressing. Vivien marched into her room, and turning to me said, 'The child does not want to sleep. She was born under the sign of Scorpio, like me – if she chooses not to sleep, she should be allowed to get up.' My weak protest about it being 3 a.m. was dismissed.

She inspected our flat in every detail, opening drawers, noticing that not everything inside was folded. Curtain linings were condemned as 'badly home-made'. The view on the river she admired, and she was romantic about ships' sirens on foggy nights. But then she criticised the central heating and told me off for not complaining to the management and blasting them for their inefficiency.

Then as suddenly as she appeared, she announced she was leaving and wanted to walk along the Embankment to her home in Chelsea. As it was 4 a.m., Peter insisted on seeing her home. In a flash they were gone, leaving me with mixed feelings of elation and alarm, trying to pacify an over-excited child.

Hollywood

Quick decisions

The efficient office of Laurence Olivier Productions, associated with the Music Corporation of America and headed in London by Cecil Tennant, went into action. Olive Harding, the backbone of the establishment who arranged contracts and salaries, booked passages and had the ability to smooth out all difficulties, acted fast.

In a few days Peter was released from his contract at the Old Vic, the Hollywood papers were signed, the handsome sum of £9,000 plus expenses was agreed upon, and Peter, clean shirts and all, was packed off on the plane with Vivien on his way to Ceylon. Peter had no option but to accept the part of the tea planter, with Vivien playing his wife.

The story, set in a tea plantation, concerned a megalomaniac tea planter who had built himself a bungalow the size of a palace across the path usually taken by a herd of wild elephants when travelling to water. The shooting location was to be in Ceylon, as the film required a real tea plantation. The inside and outside of the huge bungalow were reconstructed at Paramount Studios in Hollywood. The location shoot was a short one, and the interior scenes at Paramount were scheduled to take eight weeks' work.

I asked Olive Harding, always a most helpful advisor, whether she thought I should go to Hollywood. I wanted to follow Peter, of course, but I would understand if I were told to stay in England. It was his first film there, and I had a small child to look after. There would be all th complications of accommodation, nannies and the paraphernalia of a child. I would have to pay my own fare and I did not have the clothes for Hollywood's glamorous social life. Olive insisted that I should go, and take Anita with me. It was essential that I should be there, she said. I was very glad that she urged me to do what I wanted to do anyway.

The office booked my passage in a cheap tourist-class cabin on the *Queen Elizabeth*, due to sail in a few days' time. I dashed off to buy the essentials. Glamorous clothes were hard to find. With no money to go to the couturiers, I decided that Los Angeles would be a better place for shopping. I bought a couple of utility suits to travel in, and risked a permanent wave that turned frizzy. Anita's wardrobe consisted of a very warm tweed coat with velvet collar and leggings. We were far from looking like the wife and child of a prosperous actor.

The voyage was rough and Anita was seasick. I had crossed the Atlantic several times and sailed across the Indian Ocean, but on this crossing passengers were flung from one side of the deck to another, crockery was swept off the tables and went crashing across the floor, and chairs had to be fastened down.

The smooth entry into New York Harbour brought hundreds of passengers on deck for the first time, looking like us: pale, drawn and with shaky legs. I tried to distract Anita, showing her the Statue of Liberty and the skyscrapers, but her only question was, 'Mummy, when do we get off?'

People travelling first class disembarked first. It was five hours before we were let off the ship. An agent from MCA, the American agency, was waiting for us and was surprised and annoyed that we had travelled tourist class – clearly something that stars' wives were not in the habit of doing.

In New York a car was there to meet us. It was early evening and our plane to Los Angeles was leaving next morning at dawn. I had informed my ballet friends, Galina Razoumova and Yurek Lazowski, now married, that I would be passing through New York, and we spent the night with them. Galina had been my best friend during my childhood and adolescence, and I had been emotionally involved with Yurek in my young days. I had not seen them in thirteen years; they now had two daughters aged three and five.

Early next morning we were driven to the airport. Before the coming of jet planes, the journey to the West Coast used to be a slow and tedious flight. To keep Anita occupied I had armed myself with plenty of coloured pencils, plasticine, paper for drawing and little story books. I was embarrassed when she kept asking me loudly why the man sitting in front of her had no hair. She was mesmerised by this shiny flesh. She behaved perfectly when I explained that some people have less hair than others, that it was becoming to their faces. I thought I had succeeded in keeping her entertained during the eleven hours of the flight when, just before landing, the bald-headed man pressed the button of his reclining seat and collapsed it very low in front of Anita. With the speed of lightning, she seized a cushion and, holding it firmly by two corners, with a mighty blow struck him squarely on the head. I was mortified, and by this time so tired that it took all my self-control not to burst out laughing.

The airport in Los Angeles shone with coloured lights; the happy relief of a smooth landing, and the knowledge that we had arrived and that my tribulations were over, filled my heart with joyful expectation. Another young agent from MCA greeted us and ushered us towards a black, luxurious, chauffeur-driven limousine while apologising for my husband's absence, explaining that he was still working at the studio and would be at the house to meet us. By 6.30 we were deposited in the driveway of a very large and handsome house and led past a big swimming pool, around which were set some twenty tables covered with tablecloths in a deep shade of pink, each table decorated with the same shade of pink roses elaborately arranged in cascading pyramids.

We entered the house to be met by a black maid, who informed us that she was on the permanent staff, as were a Filipino cook, who was busy at the moment, and a chauffeur, who was still at the studio. I saw seven or eight men hovering around the tables. I could not understand: was it a hotel? There was no reception hall. A guest house? There were no other guests. A private house? Why would we be staying there?

Inside, a wide, luxurious staircase led to two parts of the house. The maid guided us to the right-hand side and showed us into a large living room, then into a double bedroom en suite with an enormous bathroom, en suite again with a smaller bedroom. I was told that this was my apartment. I said there must be some mistake, as this bedroom was full of women's clothes that were not mine. The twin beds were stacked with glamorous underwear, negligees, lacy nightgowns, rich silk dressing gowns and smart high-heeled slippers. The maid said there was no mistake: this was my bedroom. She led us into the smaller bedroom and opened a cupboard to reveal a complete wardrobe of dresses in Anita's size, the smartest wardrobe of clothes for a child I had ever seen, one that only American fashions were capable of producing.

I knew we would have to smarten up, and this made life easier. How thoughtful of Peter. I did not want to ask questions about the house. As Peter's wife I felt I should have known the answers, that it was somehow humiliating to have to ask. But I felt like Rebecca on arrival at Manderley, too overcome by its splendour.

Alone with Anita's chatter and her questions of 'Where's daddy?', it was hard to gather my thoughts. Obviously these clothes were for us, yet I felt uneasy. Usually Peter and I chose things together, and more often than not he had had to be reminded of the bare necessities. Why was he suddenly so thoughtful and so generous in an almost exaggerated way? I blamed myself for being Russian and suspicious. It was lovely and loving of him. He was showing his pleasure at our arrival, surprising us with his gifts, projecting us into the glossy world of Hollywood like two Cinderellas. I felt even more like one, with my frizzy hair and my utility suit.

Fiddle-de-dee

My first thought was for a bath for both of us after the exhausting journey. I stripped Anita. While I was bathing her, the doors flew open and Peter, followed by Vivien, rushed in and embraced me warmly, then, lifting Anita from her bath, wet and covered in suds, and enveloping her in a towel, kissed her and played with her, throwing her up in the air and hugging her. Vivien, impatiently, cuttingly, said there was no time for that: in half an hour the guests were arriving. She told me to leave Anita with the maid and get myself ready.

'What guests, Vivien?' I asked.

She replied she had planned a welcome party especially for me; she had asked all her famous friends. Seventy guests would soon be here to meet me. Half an hour: I gasped in distress. 'But I must put Anita to bed!' No, she had to be left to the servant.

'She doesn't know the woman.'

'She'll have to get used to her.'

I looked at Peter, who stood in the background shrugging his shoulders, shaking his head and signalling that I had better do as I was told. He was powerless to interfere. I stood my ground and decided quickly to try to settle my child.

Anita pleaded, 'I don't want to go to sleep, I want to be with my daddy.'

Vivien shouted, 'Shut up and do as you are told.' Turning to me, 'You've brought up your daughter very badly – ignore her and get into a sari. The party I have planned for you has a Ceylonese motif. We will be both in saris.'

I had the choice of two saris, spread out on the bed: a pale blue one with a border of gold thread, and a bright emerald-green one. I chose the bright green one, not knowing that Peter had selected that for me while Vivien had chosen the pale one. Vivien, displeased, said the colour was vulgar. She took over to show me how to drape the sari as it was done in Ceylon, but she could not manage it on me. I said that I knew how to do it, having had quite a few of them and having worn them during the war as evening dresses at dances. Peter said that, wearing this colour and looking so exotic, I reminded him of *Scheherazade*, in which I used to dance the favourite slave. At this Vivien brusquely ran out of our bedroom and vanished.

It was then that I discovered that Peter and Vivien were sharing the house for the duration of the filming. Until then I had thought that Vivien was here because of the party. I protested at the lack of privacy if Vivien was going to be here all the time, in and out of our flat. He said it was quite all right: there were two separate sides to the house. Vivien had been strained and sometimes difficult, and he thought that she was close to a breakdown. He was happy that I had arrived, as she had to be looked after, and Peter was relying on me to do that.

The head waiter came up to announce that the guests were arriving, and I went down anxiously to greet them. Peter went to Vivien's part of the house to hurry her up. I descended the staircase as in a spectacular Hollywood film, noticing at once that no woman among the dozen guests was wearing a sari. I was the only one in what looked like fancy dress. I felt foolish, and had to master my stage presence and some false aplomb not to run in panic to my bedroom. I could see faces that looked familiar because I had seen them on the screen: David Niven, Stewart Granger, Jean Simmons, Dana Andrews and many others that I remembered seeing but in my bewilderment could not put a name to.

People were arriving in groups. Elia Kazan, Irving Asher, the producer of *Elephant Walk*, whose name I knew and whose lovely wife was friendly and helpful. William Dieterle, the film's director. It was soon a sea of people, greeting me, talking, being curious and welcoming. I tried to appear natural and sophisticated, when in truth I was desperately waiting for Peter and Vivien to make an appearance.

Finally, Peter ran down and asked everyone to sit at tables, as dinner would now be served. The waiters, hovering around the tables, looked stony-faced and unconcerned, but a general feeling of discomfort was apparent. Where was Vivien? Peter looked harassed. Should we wait any longer? No, Vivien had told me upstairs that I was the hostess. David Niven and his wife Hjordis, having met me only that evening, were reassuring and friendly and looked after me. Peter disappeared again. Niven led me to a table for four, sat between his wife and me, kept the other place for Peter and joked and talked as if nothing was unusual. I felt reassured and relaxed in their company; they understood my complex situation.

Peter kept running to and fro with bulletins on Vivien's state. She couldn't come down, she was waiting for a phone call from Larry. Larry was on the island of Ischia; she had tried to phone him, but he could not be found anywhere. The phone operators in Italy were stupid, the connections were unclear. Suddenly, screams, shouts and loud sobs pierced the conversation, and all heads turned towards the portico. Peter's panic-stricken running steps reverberated in the stunned silence. He shouted to David Niven to come up, he needed some help. 'Can I do anything?' I asked. No, I was to stay down with my guests. After a while Stewart Granger's help was requested. Jean Simmons, Granger's wife, came to join our table. There was a general feeling of uncertainty; the guests did not know what to do, but were aware of a major drama happening. People came to me to say that they were happy I had arrived, and that now everything (what? I thought) would be all right.

Little by little the guests left, most of them soon after dinner, pleading an early morning call as an excuse. The close British colony of Hollywood actors stayed, loyal, worried, sensing that they had to lend moral support. Among them were Noel Drayton, who played the part of a tea planter in the film, and Abraham Sofaer, another leading actor. They were friendly, and I was grateful to them for making me feel at ease and for doing what was possible to make the situation appear normal.

The major drama happening upstairs involved us all when Vivien began to rush down the stairs screaming, crying and fighting, restrained by Niven and

Granger, then forcibly taken upstairs again, shouting 'Larry, Larry, I want Larry!' Peter stopped me rushing upstairs, assuring me that she only wanted the comfort of her old friends.

The waiters calmly started to clear the tables, pretending to be deaf and dumb. Although they were used to Hollywood dramas, this one was on a major scale.

Finally, the noise appeared to stop. After a while the friends came down and everyone left, saying again how good it was that I was there. I withdrew into our part of the house, peering quietly at Anita, blissfully asleep. I tried to walk on tiptoes so as not to disturb the blessed silence. Eventually, Peter joined me and calmed my fears and questions of 'Is she mad?'

'No, she's strained, lonely, worried, not hearing from Larry.'

'But this is not normal behaviour,' I said.

'You don't understand,' was his reply. 'You are logical, balanced. She is close to a nervous breakdown, she has to rest; please look after her, help her. She loves you very much,' he continued. 'She thought of nothing but your arrival, she bought all of Anita's clothes, she ordered the party, the food, the special flower arrangement. Let's discuss it all tomorrow; let's go to bed.'

This was what I wanted above all too.

Peter was very pleased that I loved the fabulous underwear he had bought for me. He told me that he was being given $500 a week by the studio just for expenses. The house and the food cost nothing, as Vivien was taking care of this. He wanted me to use the money on luxuries for myself and Anita. He produced a golden bracelet, set with precious stones, that he had bought for Anita in Ceylon and said that he had also bought a lovely ring for me; but so as to not pay duty on it, on Vivien's advice he had let her wear it. Unfortunately she had left it in the ladies' loo at an airport.

'Couldn't it be claimed or the authorities informed?' Peter had tried, but Vivien didn't remember exactly where she left it, and she had been so nervous about flying and so distressed at having lost the ring that he had decided not to pursue the subject.

My head was whirling with contradictory thoughts: damn the ring; but the presents, the drama, the party, my tiredness, the flight, the arrival, the guests, all crowded in my head. All I wanted was bed and the love and affection of my very passionate husband, who had given me many indications that this was what he wanted above all too. The two single beds had been put together and our reunion was, as usual, a loving encounter, a pleasure well satisfied, a habit, the comfort of knowing one another well, limbs somehow fitting into each other, searching for, and finding, particularly loved gestures and then, the tender relaxed sleep of Peter, in his favourite position, one leg bent right across my thighs and his head on my breasts. I felt at last that all was well. I was loved and secure.

While I was in that euphoric state, in between being awake and sleeping, our bedroom door flew open and a demented-looking Vivien, her light robe open and disclosing her naked body, rushed to our bed and with tremendous energy and screaming obscenities tore off the bedclothes. On discovering us naked, she threw herself on Peter in great passionate embraces. He pushed her away and she collapsed at the foot of the bed sobbing, shouting, 'You haven't told her, you haven't told her! How could you be sleeping with her, you monster? You're my lover!'

The thunderbolt effect produced by this scene turned me into stone. I was stunned. Peter, who had quickly grabbed a robe, was shaking with anger – I had never seen him in such a wild rage before. He tried to get Vivien to her feet, but she was clinging to his legs. He got her up, but she still clung to his head and pressed her lips to his. He unfastened himself from her grip, pushed her back, pinned her arms against the wall and shouted, 'We'd agreed to keep Larry and Tamara out of this, last night – we'd agreed to keep it secret, not to hurt anyone, and to finish it all.' She sobbed, abused him, screamed that she could not bear to see him and me together being so happy. That my arrival, so keenly awaited by Peter, was misery to her. That he was hers, and that he should tell me that the marriage was over. He shouted back that they had discussed it all the night before. He had told her that his marriage was not over; it was their affair that was over.

She was screaming that he was hurting her. He released her, and she then menacingly, forcefully, pushed him and started fighting, calling him every dirty word, forcing him to make a choice between us. He shouted that it had been agreed that they both would remain married. He yelled at her, overpowered her again, dragged her to her part of the house, then, leaving her there sobbing, shut all the doors in between her and us.

An unbelievable silence followed. I felt paralysed. My brain was numb. I was cold, shaking uncontrollably. I was speechless. I just sat on the edge of the bed in my flimsy, pretty negligee. I did not know what I wanted from Peter. An explanation? There was no need. A gesture of affection? I would consider that false. A row? I was incapable. I didn't even feel the hurt. I had turned into stone. I just sat and sat. It was for Peter to make a move.

In our greatest moments of drama, pain, conflict, emotion or disagreement, Peter had always escaped, mostly into sleep. Now he did not say a word, but just curled up on the bed and went to sleep. I sat telling myself that it should hurt, that I must have known all along what was happening. I suppose I had, but did not want to admit it. What should I do? Make scenes? Fight Vivien? Make her nervous breakdown worse? It would affect the filming. Pack up and leave? That would arouse the curiosity of the press. Announce their affair to the world? Could I do that to Olivier, Peter's benefactor? Should I disappear discreetly, pretend I was visiting friends? I was exhausted, too tired even to enter a fight or to announce to all that I was walking out.

I stared into space until dawn, realising that I was set against the world's most beautiful and powerful woman: a celebrity, intelligent, witty, capricious, spoilt, cultured, loved and... wealthy. In life, when she had set her charms upon Larry Olivier, she took him away from his wife and child. In her profession, she always got what she wanted. She not only played Scarlett O'Hara in *Gone with the Wind*, after two hundred other actresses were considered and discarded, but got an Oscar for it too. Her charm was unbelievable, and her friends and acquaintances adored her. Her marriage to Olivier was considered one of the most romantic in the world. They were the royalty of show business.

What could I do? Break it up? Announce the drama? Destroy the legend? The decision should come from Peter; he had told me he wanted to break it off with her. Let him do it. He would have to be firm, and face it. It was his doing entirely. How could he be so disloyal to Larry? I was powerless. What could one do, if one's opponent was one of the greatest beauties in the world?

As the sun was rising, I heard a light knock on our bedroom door. I thought I must be imagining it, but opened the door anyway. It was Vivien. She was dressed in a buttoned-up gown, and tears were rolling down her face. My first instinct was to shut the door on her. I dreaded another scene. My sense of responsibility, raising its silly head, told me that Peter needed his rest, as the studio car would be calling for him in an hour and a half. I did not want more confrontations, more truths. I was tired and couldn't take any more emotions. I tried a lame excuse to avoid a scene. 'It's too early,' I said. I pretended I had been asleep. Vivien's arms embraced me, her head on my shoulder. She asked me to follow her into her suite. She was subdued and upset; she calmly cried and begged me to listen to what she wanted to say. She didn't want to speak to Peter, but only wanted me.

Transfixed, I followed her. I was cold, calm and silent. In moments of crisis, an unnatural detachment takes me over. I can observe coldly what is happening, as if it is not my concern at all. Much later, emotion overcomes me.

Vivien got into her bed and asked me to come close. I chose a chair with my back to the window. She cried, imploring my forgiveness for what she had done, begging for my friendship, my affection, my love. She looked distressed and said she needed to be cuddled like a child. It made her unhappy, she said, that I was looking at her coldly. She wrung her hands, tried to arouse my sympathy, told me stories about her childhood: how, when the family lived in India, she had walked into a room when her parents were making love. It had given her the impression that her father was violating her mother. Since then she had deeply resented men, their selfishness, their superiority, their authority.

But they were weak and they were fools. Women were much better creatures, finer, more sensitive. Deep down she wanted to avenge all women, wanted men to suffer for what they were doing to women. 'I have found a way,' she said. I immediately thought that she had borrowed a speech from some film or play, but she looked sincere; it was a much more convincing performance than many she had given on stage or screen. She wanted to be friends with me. We could join together, make men miserable. 'Please, please,' she said, 'don't shut me out.'

She understood the closeness that Peter and I had, and she did not really love Peter; it was only Larry she loved, but he was slipping away. He was busy, he had his own career to be concerned about. He had not phoned last night; she was resentful of Larry's indifference, and that had made her beastly to Peter. She was desperately sorry, she loved me, she loved Anita, she was jealous, she wanted a child from Larry. She never wanted to hurt me.

Her complicated explanations made me want to shout that she had played with my husband – what did I care if Larry had become indifferent to her? What about me? Then I heard the burr of the car that had come to take them to the studio. I went back to our flat and woke Peter up. Within five minutes he had jumped out of bed, rinsed his face and dipped his head in water, put on a pair of slacks and a shirt and was ready. Vivien had asked me to tell the driver that she would call him to take her to the studio later.

With a smile and a wave and a cheery 'Goodbye!' Peter was off, saying, 'Look after her, will you? See you tonight.' I envied Vivien and her power through her vulnerability. Oh, to be a helpless woman whom everyone protects and looks after, to be the concern of all around you, in contrast to me. There I was, deeply wounded, with a child to look after, tired, worried, my marriage on the verge of being shattered, lonely and losing my confidence, and it was somehow expected that I would cope.

Columbines

My first thoughts were for Anita. I did not want her to be in the house all day and to witness the ugly emotional scenes that I was certain would recur. I had been given the phone number of the wife of the MCA agent who had met us and who had said that I could phone her if there was anything I wanted. I knew from experience that Americans were very helpful and hospitable. I decided to ask her to help to find out if Anita could be entered into a kindergarten school that would occupy her at least part of the day. My request was met with friendliness.

An hour later, a charming woman arrived in her car and said she was at our disposal. She had the address of a little school nearby and had already phoned it, and Anita had been accepted. I was grateful for the speed, efficiency and friendliness. Anita looked sweet in one of her new smart dresses, and we were both driven to the little school, which cared for about twenty girls and boys whose ages ranged from three to five.

We were shown the premises, an airy, brightly painted classroom, furnished with tiny wooden desks and chairs, children's books on shelves, blackboards, coloured crayons. The dining room was clean and colourful, each place with a child's name written in large letters on the back of the chair. Anita's name was amongst them, newly painted. We were shown a dormitory with tiny wooden beds, and on each pillow a black mask without holes for the eyes. I asked, 'Why black masks?' I was told that after lunch the children took an hour and a half's rest. They put the masks on to keep the light out so that, blindfolded, they did not play around and prevent one another from sleeping.

Anita, to whom I returned after my inspection, had already found a friend, Jo Ann, a pretty, smiling girl of her own age. They were holding hands, and Jo Ann was taking Anita to show her the swings. I left quite happy; she was safe and being looked after. I smiled inwardly, imagining twenty children lying on their beds in masks, little Columbines and Harlequins, all trying to sleep, while Anita, who had never slept in the afternoons, would be disturbing the peace with her endless questions.

I would be free every day from 9 until 4.30. Clothes were my next concern. My American friend was interested and full of advice. We drove up Wilshire Boulevard and looked into shops. It was exactly what I needed to forget my troubles for a while. We went to Orbach's, a friendly store full of attractive clothes, a lot of them at bargain prices. With my $500, I bought slacks, casual Hawaiian shirts for lounging around the swimming pool, cotton dresses, cocktail dresses, an evening dress – all pretty and smart, to make me look more like the American women I saw.

I decided to have my hair chopped off to get rid of all the frizzy bits, and chose a short and casual style, such as Gina Lollobrigida and Ava Gardner were wearing then. I bought some costume jewellery and some elegant shoes. I had never gone on such a spree before. I knew it was an escape, a disguise, like Columbine hiding behind a mask.

I didn't even know then that inwardly I had decided to stay in Hollywood, to face the situation, to establish my rights as a wife, to cope – and, above all, to try desperately to compete with the glamorous, cunning, skilful, charming, devastating Vivien Leigh.

Ten days that shook my world

When I returned to the house, laden with parcels and with my chattering daughter repeating 'OK' with different intonations, I found that Vivien had not gone to the studio. She said she had sent a message that she felt unwell, and they could shoot some scenes that did not include her, such as a revolting one in which the planters were all drunk and riding bicycles. She inspected all my purchases, disapproved of most of them, said that it wouldn't be what she would wear, and succeeded again in chipping away at my already crumbling confidence.

'When Peter comes back from the studio, we're all going to a party.'

'I thought you were unwell, Vivien.'

'I'm perfectly all right.'

'But your work, your health?'

'I just didn't want to be filming today. Anyway, mind your own business.'

On Peter's return, he was rushed into changing, the chauffeur told to wait, Anita sent to bed, and I ordered to put on a cocktail dress. Peter loved my hairstyle, and said it made me look like an Italian model and showed off my bone structure. Vivien said I had been a fool not to have had it done before; it had looked dowdy.

We were off to someone's house in Santa Monica. The familiar faces of the British actors greeted us. I remember being fascinated by the different ways in which food was presented at these Hollywood parties. This one's motif was tropical. The huge table near a swimming pool was laden with sliced red watermelons arranged in patterns. Mountains of cooked lobsters were piled on beds of crushed ice, salad bowls the size of babies' baths were filled with tropical fruit. The palm leaves mixed with huge red hothouse flowers added an exotic note to the spectacular display.

Peter kept close to me, and Vivien close to him. He drew a friend's attention to my new look. Vivien pulled him by the arm and said she was going home and, as she had dismissed the chauffeur, was going to drive herself. She said she was suffering from a violent headache and could not stand parties. We could see that her determination was unshakeable, but we could not let her go alone. We felt responsible for her. We had only been at the party for ten minutes, and she was the guest of honour. We made our excuses and followed her, sensing that she was in one of her dangerous moods.

She sat at the wheel of the car and impatiently told me to sit next to her so that I could take over the driving if her headache got worse. I protested that I couldn't drive. She turned to me angrily and said I was as stupid as Peter, who couldn't drive either. How could I come to the USA without being able to drive? Did I expect that I would always have a chauffeur on hand? She insisted that I sat in front and Peter in the back. We rode in silence, feeling like two powerless idiots, incapable even of getting ourselves home. Vivien was impatient, strained; she drove fast and very ably.

On arrival, she rang for food and ordered avocado salads for us all. The Filipino cook apologised: there were no avocados in the house, she hadn't ordered them that morning. 'Get some,' was the irate command. 'In future, keep the fridge full of them.' The car was despatched for avocados. When they were finally served, it was not the way Vivien liked them, the cook was a fool who had taken too long, she didn't want them any more.

She then decided to invite guests for the evening, but none of the people she rang were available. She felt let down; everyone was having a good time except her. No one loved her, and we were a couple of bores. She seemed to have tremendous energy, was constantly tidying, placing and replacing vases and ornaments, dusting them, until it became a compulsion. Verbally, she was brilliant; her intelligence and her wit sparkled. She would either speak in clever epigrams, proving that she had a unique mind, or be sharp, humiliating and insulting. Peter and I bore the brunt of her insults or were contorted with laughter at her humour. It was exhausting to keep up with her plans, her schemes and her energy. She never wanted to rest, and when at two in the morning we at last managed to get away and go to bed, when all was quiet, we heard the sound of a motor downstairs in the large living room. Vivien was vacuuming.

She had prepared a huge bowl of avocado salad and was expecting us to join her; she told us off sharply for wasting our time sleeping. We tried to enjoy her speciality drenched in lime juice, while she switched on a TV channel that had closed but showed bands of lines continuously rolling along. She sat transfixed, as if hypnotised by them.

After a while, as though it had produced an effect on her mind, her speech became speeded up, continuous, monotonous, like a chorus out of a Greek tragedy. She spoke of suffering people, of treachery, of self-destruction, of children sacrificed, of male egos, of the loneliness of souls searching for one another, of reincarnation of cats with the spirit of people long dead in them, and of people who had been cats long ago in Egyptian dynastic times.

She stood posing with magnificent gestures; she wrung her hands; she looked domineering and vulnerable in turn, always very moving, but worryingly so. I could recognise passages from plays she had acted in, but I could not believe that it was all acting. Was she insane? Yet she was so logical at times, so articulate, so brilliant, reciting great chunks of poetry or Shakespeare.

When she collapsed in a heap sobbing, we carried her to her bed, and suddenly she seemed normal again. I was torn between intolerance and great pity. She had a great capacity for drawing compassion, but she exhausted people and made them act against their better judgement. I wanted to help her, to protect her, yet I was angry, tired and fed up with the dramas.

In our own quarters I said to Peter that I was sure a psychiatrist should be consulted. He told me not to worry, that a doctor would be seeing her tomorrow. We were naïve and inexperienced: neither of us had come across mood changes of this sort.

Action in *Les Présages*, Ballets Russes de Monte Carlo, 1937

In the title role of *Thamar*, Ballets Russes de Monte Carlo, 1937

The Borovansky Ballet, Dorothy Stevenson (sitting), Jonet Wilkie (putting on shoe), Tamara (far right), Laurel Martin (standing), 1944-48

Mama at her sewing machine, 1940

Scheherazade. The Borovansky
Ballet, with Martin Rubinstein
as the Golden Slave

Capriccio Italien,
The Borovansky Ballet, 1944

Myrthe in *Giselle*,
The Borovansky Ballet.

With Peter Finch,
our wedding photograph, 1943

With Peter and baby Anita, December 1949   With Peter in London

Peter, William Dieterle, and Elizabeth Taylor in Hollywood, 1953

The young Vivien Leigh

Interpreting for visiting Russians, E. H.Underwood of UK (right) and Nikolai Bezryadin, editor of *Soviet Siberia*, 1967

Interpreting for Anthony Dowell at the end of the Royal Ballet's tour, Kirov Theatre, 1987

Mama with Anita
at her graduation,
Bristol 1970

Anita with her
husband Val
Harrison

With Irina
Baronova,
my oldest
and dearest
friend

It was dawn and studio time again. Peter was driven off without Vivien. I felt uneasy. After taking Anita to school, I came back to the house to find Vivien sunning herself by the pool, eating avocados again. She was friendly and charming, looking devastatingly beautiful and absolutely normal. She announced that we would be speaking French all that day. That suited me, so we did. Her French was very good, and I was under the impression that she was testing mine. Had she chosen German, which I believe she spoke, I would have been lost, but French was my very own language.

As we discussed the French cinema, her fluency deteriorated. She looked depressed, said she could see why Peter loved me, and started crying. She asked if I could swim. I was no Olympic champion, but, yes, I could keep my head above water.

'Let's have a contest.'

'No, Vivien,' I said, 'the water is still cold for me – I like it really warm.'

She plunged in and swam well, but then as I walked back to the house, I heard splashing and gulping sounds and looked back. She was at the deep end of the pool, her head submerged, beating the water with her arms, pushing herself upwards, choking and gasping. I jumped in and pulled her to the shallow end. She fought me, crying, 'Let me drown, I want to die!' The maid ran out of the house and we took Vivien upstairs.

She was trembling, crying and visibly ill. She would not let me go, saying that I had saved her life, and why had I, as no one loved her anymore? I had become a focal point to her, sometimes of love, sometimes of extreme irritation; but whatever state she was in, it was as though she couldn't do without me, either to pick on or to express her love to.

The telephone rang non-stop, mostly reporters who had heard that the film was in trouble. I didn't know what explanation to give about Vivien's health, but I knew that I could not tell the truth. The studio phoned at regular intervals, and then I was summoned by the management of Paramount to meet the big boss, who wanted to talk to me.

A large, luxurious car swept me through Paramount's main gates. I was ushered into the commissary, the main restaurant of the studio, my attention immediately focusing on a huge painting of Victor Mature as Samson. Peter was there, presiding over a table of actors – planters from the film. With a great display of affection, he introduced me to his colleagues. Lunch, which I did not want, had been ordered – more gushy salads with pink mayonnaise. I could not face food.

At three o'clock I was escorted to a splendid office, the like of which I had seen only in films. A very important-looking man in a superbly tailored suit extended his hand to me, and told me warmly how very pleased he was to meet me and how I could be of tremendous assistance to him, to the film and to the whole of Paramount Studios.

The producer and director would wait for a couple of days for Vivien to get better, and would shoot scenes in which she did not appear. In the meantime, the press were going to be very curious about her, and would phone the house. I said that they had done so already. If the telephone was not answered or was cut off, rumours would start that would be detrimental to the film. I was the only one who could keep the whole of the American press at bay. I would be doing a great job, and would be saving the reputation of a film that was the biggest and most costly that Paramount had undertaken for some time. He would have me shown round the huge studio, where I would see that, where normally six films were being shot, the planters' bungalow was occupying the space of at least four sets.

I was dazed. What could *I* do to save the great Paramount Studios? It was like an unreal dream. I could not believe that these words were being spoken to me by one of the heads of Paramount, that all the front pages of the US newspapers were waiting for me to utter something.

'What should I do?' I asked.

'Answer the phone sweetly, with an unconcerned voice. Say you're Peter Finch's wife, a good friend of Vivien's, and that she is suffering from bronchitis and will be all right in a couple of days.'

He was counting on me, he said, and knew I would do it well, for Paramount and for Vivien Leigh. I thought he would add 'for the Stars and Stripes and for England'.

I was lavishly treated, like a star, and shown the sumptuous set: a giant house built in a tropical setting, the artificial sun drenching its luxurious gardens. On the shaded terraces, dozens of actors, their faces painted in various shades of brown, played the servants in attendance. I was shown the mechanical, life-size head and trunk of an elephant, looking very real but made of rubber. In the film it would be used in close-up to show an elephant lifting a man with his trunk and crushing him.

Although I was taking some details in, my mind was occupied with Vivien. A scene was being set and Peter was busy, so I asked to be driven back to the house. There I found doctors in consultation. I was not taken into their confidence about the diagnosis, although questioned at length about Vivien's behaviour. They asked whether a relative could take the responsibility of having her specially treated. I asked what that meant. They just said that it was 'special treatment' and that papers authorising it could only be signed by a relative – in this case, her husband. In the meantime, I was to do what I could and she was not to be left alone. The best thing, they advised, would be to comply with her every request and not to aggravate her.

Towards evening, her friends called: Niven, who was soothing, and Granger and Simmons, added normality to a very delicate situation. Peter was late returning from the studio. Vivien constantly asked for him, saying that he must be drinking too much again. I felt she should not blame him so much: she herself drank a lot. He, at least, was not missing filming days.

She became tearful again, saying she was tired and needed her rest. Her friends went away. I returned to my flat, but she came to me and started telling me again in detail what a monster Peter was with his drinking. The weekend before I arrived, Vivien had driven Peter to Palm Springs, conscious that circumstances might change because of my arrival. She wanted Peter to spend a happy, loving night with her, away from everyone, but all he did was drink and tell her what a shit he was. On his conscience were 'poor Larry' and 'poor Tamara'. Vivien felt disgusted. Hadn't he realised that their love affair was meant to be, was unavoidable, was written in Heaven? One could not battle with one's destiny. Peter was hers and it was idiotic of him to drink so much that he became incapable of returning all the love she had for him.

His reaction had been to say, 'Bullshit. I shouldn't have done it. I can't face the pain I'm inflicting, I can't live with myself, having betrayed Larry's trust. I want to turn the clock back and to forget that anything has happened between us.'

I tried not to appear annoyed at her details and confessions. My temperament was changing. I did not want to aggravate her, as I was afraid of her reactions. I was sometimes convinced that she was mentally disturbed, at other times that she was acting or deliberately telling me all that just to hurt me. If it were illness, I blamed everyone in London for not having warned Peter. Surely Cecil Tennant knew, Olive Harding knew, Olivier himself? Was it because mental illness was considered shameful, or would prevent her from continuing her career? Or, worse thought of all, had she lost her sanity because of her affair with Peter?

She needed her closest relatives with her, not servants, cooks, chauffeurs and maids; she needed someone loving and understanding. Over the next few days it was Peter and me. Peter took refuge in drinking and stayed out as late as he could. I became changeable too. I wanted to help, but had a heartache about my marriage that was eating into me. It gave me a physical pain in the pit of my stomach, and turned me off food completely. I was exhausted. I was keeping routine hours for Anita's sake, but was always available for Vivien's whims. I was there to meet her friends and guests, there waiting for Peter to arrive sozzled from a bar after a day's work at the studio, and there to get him out of bed in time at dawn. I was supervising meals, pacifying a worried, troublesome cook who never knew what to prepare and became a bundle of nerves before he finally left. Above all, I had to answer the phone non-stop to very curious, very persistent reporters who never gave us any peace.

The next few days were complete chaos, as several doctors came and went. A nurse was called, who physically manipulated Vivien. Vivien hated her and became difficult, very abusive and frightening. She could not be stopped from coming into our quarters. Then she would calm down, became dependent, loving and very generous. She repeatedly asked me to go to bed with her, saying that two women together was the most pleasurable lovemaking. I said, '*C'est pas pour moi*'.

The difficulty was to guess what she wanted next, and this was when people close to her were more acceptable to her than strangers coming to treat her, until she turned on her loved ones and behaved with unbelievable cruelty.

I was getting jittery. I was battling with a compulsion to help her while knowing that the more I did so, the more dependent on me she would be. I was afraid of her outbursts. She was angry about Peter, wanted to destroy his masculinity, criticised his appearance, abused him for losing a Cartier watch that, unknown to me, she had given him. She wanted to have me on her side, nagging him about his unpunctuality, his clothes, his drinking. He escaped as often as he could, worried and harassed, the studio continuing to demand his services.

We had many invitations, which always included Vivien. One evening, the Nivens gave a dinner party. Peter persuaded me to go with him. Vivien had been better – more her sweet, charming, witty self. She wanted to rest and stay home. After putting Anita to bed, I had switched on the TV for the resident maid to babysit in our quarters, and made her promise that she would not leave the flat for any reason until we came back before midnight.

Peter and I went to Pacific Palisades, a good forty minutes' drive. I felt uneasy: it was a long way, would take hours, then drinks, dinner, the drive back... My stomach turned into a knot again. I had not realised how neurotic I had become. We arrived at our destination, where Hjordis Niven, devastatingly beautiful, greeted us warmly. I snatched one martini, then said to Peter that I was going back. In spite of all his assurances, I felt I had to rush home. Peter followed but was annoyed, having to cope with another neurotic woman whom he had thought was well balanced.

I urged the driver to hurry. Perspiration was running off my body. I was shaking with a feeling of impending disaster. As the car approached the house, we heard screams from our quarters. I recognised Anita's piercing voice when she was in a rage. Vivien was standing over her, in the middle of the room, pushing her down by the shoulders, shaking her, shouting at her, forcing her to sit on a pot, while Anita, angry and petrified, was screaming her head off wanting to go back to bed. I rushed to separate them, to retrieve my child. Vivien's furious voice shouted, 'Thank God you're here! I would have killed her if you hadn't arrived in another minute, I can't bear screaming and disobedient children. She didn't want to do what she had to do, and I was going to make her.'

I took Anita, shaken by sobs, to her bed, ordered Vivien out; then, when all was calmer, asked for an explanation.

Subdued, Vivien said, 'I have dismissed the maid.'

'But she was to stay till we returned.'

'I want to look after my goddaughter.'

'Another time, Vivien.'

'It's nine o'clock, she has to sit on the pot, or she'll soil her bed.'

'She has never soiled her bed in her little life.'

'I am a mother and I know about children.'

'I would have dealt with her on my return,' I said.

Vivien wouldn't listen. 'Anita's stubbornness is driving me crazy,' and then ordering, 'Keep her out of my sight.'

This experience proved to me that I had to be on guard day and night, and should not listen to anyone but should follow my instinct about the danger of Vivien's changing moods. I shook for days after when I thought of Vivien alone with Anita in the menacing situation in which I had found them.

The next day, when I came to collect Anita from school, my child was in disgrace, separated from the other children. The principal teacher told me that she had bitten her best friend Jo Ann on the arm. I was shown the bruise, a blue circle surrounded by teeth marks on the upper arm. Jo Ann, after crying, had forgiven her, but Anita was sullen, irritable and did not want to go back to our house.

A friend of Vivien's, John Buckmaster, moved in with her. All the doors were closed. The smell of incense pervaded the house and Indian music could be heard day and night. Peter was summoned in, but soon came out. They were chanting, practising strange rituals, cleansing their minds of evil thoughts, Vivien had said. They were going back to nature, dancing naked, purifying their bodies.

The doctor's visit put a stop to that. There was nothing worse for her than extremes in behaviour. Vivien possessed a tremendous drive and hardly slept, as though her illness gave her unlimited energy. It was draining me and everyone else concerned with her, but emotionally I could not let go of helping her. I felt Peter was partly responsible for her breakdown, and Sir Laurence was not making an appearance despite the urgent phone calls and telegrams being sent to him.

After the soul-cleansing episode, even the maid deserted. She said it was weird staying in the house and she was too frightened. During nights and long parts of the day, in between nurses' visits, Vivien had to be looked after. Once, on returning from school, I found my flat in terrible disorder, all the drawers emptied onto the floor. All my underwear, my nighties, my lovely negligees had been shredded with scissors. Nothing was left except the clothes I stood in. I didn't even protest, just looked in dismay, afraid for my own sanity.

Vivien was being treated, but it was as if the treatment made her worse, certainly more violent. A very strong nurse came regularly and many times prevented her from injuring herself. The nurse was present when Vivien rushed in to attack me, brandishing a knife. She was expertly restrained, and then, quick as a flash, ran towards the window and tried to jump. The nurse and I grabbed her by the arms; there was a struggle, then tears. I knew now that these moods came in cycles. After a crisis there was usually a calm, a lull, and I prayed that this particular crisis was truly over. We assumed then that she would rest, sedated and exhausted, and I was left alone again in the house with her. But, sedated or not, Vivien could not sleep. She fidgeted, made herself busy cleaning and cleansing herself.

I heard her drawing bath water. My senses were tuned, and I listened alertly to every sound. The bath water ran for a long time, then I heard my name being called, first gently, then more urgently. The water wasn't being turned off. I dashed in, alarmed. Vivien was submerged in an overflowing bath, her head completely under water, her legs rigid, sticking out, her eyes open, her hair flowing. It was like a frightening shot out of the film *Repulsion*. I hurriedly pushed her feet down, lifted her head. She was foaming at the mouth. I saw an empty bottle of pills by the side of the bath and assumed she had swallowed them. I fought to get her out of the bath: she pushing her head back under water, I trying to keep her head out, pulling the plug and emptying the bath.

She was not unconscious. I asked her how many pills she had swallowed and what they were, urging her to push her fingers into her mouth to make herself sick. She did, then started sobbing. She was like a child, frightened and obedient, making herself throw up, and then she finally allowed me to get her out of the bath. Some distant memory made me quickly fetch some salt, mix it with warm water and make her drink it. She did that, was sick again, and clung to me. She looked like a poor, miserable, drowning kitten, her beautiful eyes begging for help.

My hand was on the phone to summon help, although I knew the danger had passed. She begged me not to. She did not want doctors and nurses. There was only one doctor she trusted and he was in London. She was pining for Larry: why wasn't he here? A week had gone by since she had asked for him. She only wanted to be with me and ask for my forgiveness for having been so beastly to me.

I was again completely convinced by her sincerity, and as days passed I tried to forget the threat to my life and hers. But I desperately wanted someone to take charge. Finally, one afternoon, I saw the tall, confident figure of Cecil Tennant arrive. He was the Oliviers's good friend, agent and business associate – a man of the world, used to dealing with any difficult situation, firm and reliable in a crisis. Cecil hugged me and together we cried. I had never thought it possible to see cool, tranquil, unflappable Cecil cry.

Sir Laurence arrived too. After consulting the doctors, and with tears in his eyes, he thanked me for my help. He looked tortured, dazed, but still nothing was said about the reason for Vivien's illness.

I was confused by the lack of explanations. I was full of guilty feelings about Peter's misdeed. I still thought that the affair was responsible for the breakdown. I was amazed that Olivier took it so calmly. Now that he was in Hollywood and taking full responsibility, Peter and I were advised to move into a flat of our own. Our presence, although soothing Vivien occasionally, was aggravating her more often now.

The move was made quickly. While Peter was at the studio, an efficient MCA man arrived in a car and helped me pack. A two-bedroom flat for us was found in Wilshire Boulevard. I thought I was going to have some peace at last. But Vivien demanded my phone number and called me incessantly.

I spent my first night in the new flat alone. Peter did not come home. I even suspected that he hadn't been given my new address and phone number. He must have gone to talk to Olivier. How would Olivier react? What would Peter feel? What would Vivien do? These thoughts tortured me, and as usual when I really needed my husband more than ever, he was away, out or drunk. Not even a phone call. I was bitter, worried, wanted to go back to England. Let them all stew in their own mess.

Yet I felt sorry for Peter, too. He had never been morally strong. I had asked him how the affair started. He told me Vivien had started it; she had come into his bed. I found it hard to believe; but a few days after my arrival in Hollywood, at a cocktail party, I overheard Dana Andrews, who had been with the film unit in Ceylon, telling a friend about the night in Ceylon when Vivien undressed and came to Dana. He was convinced that she was mentally ill, as her general behaviour was most peculiar. When Dana refused to let her stay, she went to Peter. That confirmed Peter's story.

The next day, as I was trying to regain some sort of balance, I was phoned by Sylvia Fine, Danny Kaye's wife. She was the only one who had a thought for me in that emotional time when all thoughts were for Vivien, Larry, Peter, Paramount and keeping it all out of the press. Mrs Kaye spoke to me quietly and in a very friendly manner, inviting Anita to meet her daughter Dena. She told me not to worry, that Vivien was a diagnosed manic depressive, and that this was not the first time that it had happened; all her friends knew of her illness and covered up for her for the sake of Sir Laurence. Peter was not the first friend who had fallen victim to her mania. Sylvia said that Vivien was going into hospital in London, to her own doctors, and that I must try to resume a normal life, and be strong no matter what turmoil I felt. She was reassuring, understanding and kind and I was extremely grateful that she realised I was a victim too.

I sought a book on mental illnesses and found in it exact descriptions of the symptoms Vivien had: the manic state with loss of restraint, the tearing-off of clothes, excessive sexuality, elation, alcohol in moments of euphoria aggravating the patient's mental state, and precipitate speech, as if her mind was speeded up. In depression, the patient was clinging, frightened, suicidal, dependent. The mood changes, the loss of memory, the cruelty, the excessive generosity, the present-giving, the abuse of loved ones, the criticism, the humiliation of friends – it was all in the book, as in a revelation from Heaven.

I was stunned. All these symptoms had been known about, and classified in a simple medical book, describing exactly what I had gone through in the past ten days, and no one in London had warned us that it could happen. Did they perhaps think that an admission of her state of mind would make her illness worse, once she realised she was a manic depressive? How was she still able to perform, learn lines, appear continuously in plays and films? How was it that her marriage had not been damaged if she had had these attacks before? How terrible for Olivier to have to live with the constant fear that an attack could happen at any time. How was it that she had not died from one of her suicide attempts? How was it that the press did not get hold of a story?

Within a couple of days they did. Vivien was flown back to England in a heavily sedated state. The huge dose of sedatives given to her almost killed her, but did not keep her calm for long. She was taken aboard a plane on a stretcher, her arms strapped to the sides. The newspapers of the world published photographs of her tied-up wrists.

Changing planes in New York, she was sedated again but on her feet. She refused to get into the plane that was to fly her, Olivier, Tennant and her entourage to London. She was forcibly pulled from the car and pushed into the plane, screaming hysterically, sobbing wildly. The photographers had a field day. Our blood ran cold seeing these pictures. Poor Olivier – nothing could have been worse. Affairs, infidelity, all paled with the ordeal of his responsibility.

I had to try to do what Sylvia Fine told me, and introduce some kind of normality into our lives. I was tense and jittery; I had lost twenty pounds in weight and my clothes were falling off me. Peter was busy. The studio, which had closed for a while, reopened again, and filming restarted with Elizabeth Taylor replacing Vivien.

We bought daily newspapers, avid for news of London. Vivien had been admitted to hospital for electroconvulsive therapy. She was also packed in ice, another form of shock therapy, to reduce her body temperature. She had been isolated and no visitors were allowed. After a while, no more bulletins were issued. My ordeal was over too, I thought. It took me a while to readjust. I felt sorry for Vivien, but I could not forget her last phone call to me, just before her departure.

She had spoken at length, angrily, viciously, because I had moved out of the house. She abused me for abandoning her, laughed at my shortcomings, including the length of my nose. She said that no man had ever resisted her, that Peter was hers, although he was back with me for a time; that he was now a changed man, and she would get him in the end. She would break up our marriage if it was the last thing she did.

Years of waiting

The nightmare was over – temporarily – and the lustre of Hollywood worked its magic. A whirlwind of invitations and unlimited hospitality followed. Elizabeth Taylor's home became as our own. She was then married to Michael Wilding, and they had formed around them a British colony, all expatriates, enjoying the life there, but in spirit still in England. Their American friends adopted us warmly. Parties, parties galore. Rosemary Clooney sang, Danny Kaye clowned, Richard Burton frowned. Jose Ferrer performed amusing pantomimes. Michael Rennie dived into Elizabeth's pool beautifully. Lauren Bacall and Humphrey Bogart exuded glamour. Irving Asher gave us a tenth wedding-anniversary party with champagne, caviar and many presents for Anita. Dana Andrews, the proud owner of a slender, elegant yacht, took us all to Catalina Island. Food and booze were so abundant that, on the way back, no one could say for sure which were the lights of San Pedro, our port.

Next day, many swollen faces were seen at the studio. But this did not matter, as the final scenes of the film were to be shot, in which a herd of elephants would smash the set to smithereens. As a special favour, I had been invited to witness the spectacle. The set was prepared: big fires were tidily started in all corners, and the furniture had been sawn to break up easily and carefully put together again to look normal. At the touch of a finger it was to fall to pieces.

A dozen or so circus-trained elephants were kept in check ready to hurl themselves at the palatial bungalow. The cameras were prepared, set, and ... 'Action!'. The keeper prodded his elephants. They marched forward obediently and, unexpectedly, managed to tiptoe their way across the living room of the bungalow without touching anything at all. The cameras were reset and the fires rebuilt, while the director told the keeper to shout at the elephants and make them seem angry. The keeper promised. He had rehearsed them: some were to lift the piano legs and drop them again, another had to wrench the chandelier off. Orders were given again. The elephants looked more and more restless, shifting their weight from one side to another; and when the now-enraged keeper screamed at them, they all formed a circle in the middle of the living room, joined trunks to tails and performed a daisy chain. Guests were asked to leave the set, and bigger fires were built. At last the first sign of anger came, when the lead elephant started banging his trunk on the ground in repeated rhythm and charged. The herd followed him, and a satisfying stampede swept through the set.

The film's schedule extended to five months. Peter was hoping for more work, but the next film offered to him did not satisfy his agency. We took a very slow boat back to Europe. Peter was trying to avoid confrontations.

Endgame

We returned to Dolphin Square to find that Peter's mother and half-sister had incurred enormous debts in our absence. We indulgently paid them all and shifted the pair to another flat; and soon many of the people who entertained us so lavishly in Hollywood were coming to London.

Elizabeth Taylor was filming *Beau Brummel*, while her husband Michael was living in tax exile in Paris. In between weekend commutes, she made a habit of coming to us after studio hours, bringing her friends. The incident that convinced us we should look for a larger flat was when we were about to serve a special dinner cooked in our mini-kitchen for one of Michael Wilding's rare visits. I bought a large duck and looked up an Indonesian recipe. I prepared it painstakingly for eight o'clock, after which it could simmer – I knew that Elizabeth was always late and wouldn't be there before nine. I peered into my oven at five to eight. Suddenly there was a sizzling noise: the duck was aflame. My cries for help brought in a startled Peter. He rushed to the tap, filled a jug full of water and threw it on the duck in the oven. Black smoke poured out, filling the kitchen, and, as the front doorbell rang at eight sharp, I let the Wildings in, shouted 'Excuse me!' and ran back into the flat. They followed me into the smoky kitchen, where Peter and I were beating the duck with wet towels.

Peter was offered a seven-year Rank contract, and his office decided it was the right thing for him. I still wanted him to work more in the theatre, but I was overruled. The films he was offered were often trivial. A happy one was *Make Me an Offer*. Its director, Cyril Frankel, a sensitive, artistic man, became a friend. Wonderful evenings were spent planning, working, eating, drinking, sharing thoughts. I felt loved again, wanted, needed and fulfilled, and pushed the dramatic episode in Hollywood away from my mind.

However, Vivien's cruelty about my looks remained a niggling thought. I decided to have plastic surgery on my nose. The experience was ghastly. The surgeon did not believe in general anaesthetic; too much blood was involved, he said, better to keep the patient conscious. He gave two injections of local anaesthetic, one into the depth of each nostril, then after a while took a cutting instrument and proceeded to detach flesh from the base of the nose to the bridge, from inside. He stretched the skin forward until I felt I had an elephant trunk. He then took a hook with a sharp edge, pushed it up to between my eyes and, with a series of sharp jerks, scraped the bone to get rid of my little Roman bump. The sound of the bone breaking reverberated in my head. The blood poured out, the nurse replacing full vessels with fresh ones. The operation lasted an hour and a half, during which time the surgeon kept talking about football, cricket and chess. He said afterwards he did it to keep my mind active.

At home, I recovered quickly, and once the bandages were removed I admired myself in profile, seeing a new woman on the threshold of a new life. The first shadow cast on my euphoria came from Vivien. Six months had gone by since her illness. She had obviously recovered as, with a great amount of publicity, she was preparing to star in a Terence Rattigan play, *South Sea Bubble*. I felt it was better to send a formal telegram of good wishes and stay away.

An invitation came to us for the premiere. Peter said it would be unfriendly not to go, and that it would be even more strange not to go backstage. Peter assured me that everything was in the past, forgotten and forgiven; but his hand shook in mine as we entered Vivien's dressing room. Crowds of her illustrious friends came in too, worldly, sophisticated, warmly embracing her, praising the play and the production. More flowers arrived, more telegrams were stuck around the mirror. Vivien, putting her hands on my shoulders, addressed the crowded room and in a loud voice said, 'I want you all to meet the most courageous girl I know. She has just had an operation on her nose to try and look more glamorous. I think she is wonderful.' She went on to ask minute details about the operation. I made my answers light, hoping I was being amusing, observing that her friends were even more embarrassed than I was. Peter hugged me. From then on, Vivien ignored us completely. Once again she had made me feel unworthy of her company.

But the next day she telephoned and we were invited to the Oliviers' country retreat, Notley Abbey. It was as if by royal command. We went. I was apprehensive, but Peter pointed out that it would offend Olivier to show any reluctance. Vivien must have recovered, or she wouldn't be on stage. Her marriage was sacred. 'What about ours?' I asked. Peter said he had made it clear he loved me and always would.

Notley, an ancient but modernised abbey, combined gracious living, chic comfort, extreme formality and complete relaxation. The antique decor was superb. The dinner ceremony was most precise, but the mornings were relaxed, sipping delicious drinks in tall, cool glasses. Sitting with Noël Coward, Robert Helpmann and other fascinating guests, it was hard to believe that Vivien had been ill at all. The only signs of aloofness came from Olivier, but then he had always appeared distant, his eyelids half-closed, his thoughts impenetrable. He was courteous, remote, and probably plotting his great performances.

Vivien shone as a hostess: everyone's comfort was of prime importance, glasses were refilled and exquisite flowers arranged in bedrooms, as if nothing on earth mattered but the well-being of her dear guests.

In that summer and spring of 1955, the Oliviers were acting in Shakespeare at Stratford, playing *Twelfth Night, Macbeth* and *Titus Andronicus*. Vivien had bad notices. The flamboyant critic Ken Tynan said, 'Vivien Leigh's Lady Macbeth is more niminy-piminy than thundery-blundery, more viper than anaconda'. Olivier's performances were unanimously praised by all.

Vivien, more and more, called for Peter. Invitations for me to visit Notley ceased – in fact, secret arrangements were made so as to exclude me. A car came to collect Peter, and occasionally waited for him for hours. He assured me that he was only helping. Helping, I thought! Helping... I couldn't imagine that with Olivier there Vivien and Peter were still 'carrying on'. Peter's behaviour was becoming erratic; he drank to excess, and disappeared for whole days and nights.

When he came back, he was all for buying a house, moving into more suitable premises. I found the ideal place and borrowed a thousand pounds from Mama for a deposit on it. Olive Harding, Peter's agent, was in favour of an investment, as Peter could not hold on to any money. Mama, with her business acumen, had advised me to buy a large house, with additional flats let to tenants. At least this could be a guarantee of financial security. Olive arranged for a mortgage, and we moved in with our few sparse sticks of broken furniture.

Peter, harassed by Vivien, was working on a film with Kay Kendall. I read in a morning paper that my marriage was finished. I confronted Peter, who said Vivien had spoken to a pressman. As demanding as ever, she was exhausting Peter. Olivier was filming *The Prince and the Showgirl* with Marilyn Monroe. Although Vivien was busy acting (in *South Sea Bubble*), she was upset not to be in the film in the part she had originally created in the Rattigan play, *The Sleeping Prince*, on which it was based. She had met Marilyn on her arrival and disliked her.

Vivien's latest news – confidential, Peter said – was that she was pregnant, and he, Peter, possibly the father. When the announcement of her pregnancy made headlines, there was no reference to Peter. I was on tenterhooks once again. What was it to be – divorces, babies, scandals, press, the pressure all over again? The reporters, ever astute, were phoning us, and offering me money for a story. There were tears, scenes, me demanding that decisions be taken, Peter as usual with his head in the sand. The calming influence of good friends made me bide my time and wait. The warm presence of my daughter prevented me from committing suicide. She came into my bed, afraid of a stormy night, saw me crying and said, 'You always cry when daddy comes home. He mustn't come here any more. I will tell him that.' My heart broke to hear the child's reasoning. How could I kill myself when I loved her so much?

Peter, feeling guilty, little by little withdrew from home. He had found refuge on his mother's sofa. Some time before, his mother's three children had agreed to forsake the inheritance of a trust in their names to buy Betty a cottage in Chelsea. She was happy when Peter transferred his drinking there, brought his friends and paid the bills.

During our separation, Betty was positively destructive to our relationship, and I realised how like her he could be: unconcerned, self-centred, promising exciting outings to Anita, not turning up at the appointed time, leaving her staring out of the window in expectation. My heart bled for her. I was angry too. It was one thing to abandon a wife, quite another to let a child down. His unexpected visits – drunk, remorseful, crying – did not help their relationship. Lively and logical, she dared to question him. He hated fashioning answers, became unpleasant, felt guilty and reverted to the superficial attitude of his mother.

Vivien found Betty's cottage convenient for meetings. She was ill again; she said she had had a miscarriage, and was after Peter again. Poor Peter: torn by loyalty to Olivier, fascinated by Vivien and ashamed of his neglect of Anita and me. The more guilty he felt, the worse he became.

Our joint bank account was reduced to nothing. I borrowed shillings from Mama to pay the milk bill, and more and more for food. I went to his agent's office and suffered the humiliation of begging for money. Olive Harding promised to try, and she did the best she could. Peter was running up enormous nightclub bills, paying everyone else's tabs – running away from himself. Yet, when he returned to stay for weeks with me, he seemed to recover, to draw breath, to be grateful that all was normal again.

I was sorry for him, tortured by his appearances and disappearances. When he went away, he never took any of his clothes, books or souvenirs with him. In effect, he was using our home as a base for his gallivanting. In the middle of the night he would call in, often with Anthony Steel, each hardly managing to stand up. He would introduce me, his wife, as the only woman he had ever loved. They would drink some more, collapse, he in my bed, Anthony on a sofa, sleep it off and go away again.

I would read in the papers about his romances, all denied the next day. Once more I was worried about my own sanity, and fell into bouts of deep depression, full of sleepless nights waiting for the doorbell to ring; and when it did, I had to listen to what a monster he had been, how Vivien had affected him psychologically. His tears rolled down uncontrollably at the sight of Anita.

After Hollywood, Peter's career flourished – Olive Harding, ever his able agent, saw to that. Film after film were lined up; some he enjoyed, some he hated. He was always able to establish a rapport with his directors and the actors and actresses with whom he worked.

I repeatedly told myself I must accept that show business is both spectacular and cruel. Creative imagination and intense emotion are the enemies of conventional life. When successful show-people are constantly in the public eye, their behaviour, romances, affairs and marriages are reported in detail in the press. They cannot be seen in anyone's company without unleashing speculation about their private lives.

Most of the public loves the gossip and innuendoes, the preliminary 'know-all' of some columnists. It sells papers. Many actors and actresses lead private and happy lives, not promoting publicity. Others bask in the adulation and seek it; others still, cannot avoid the attention of the world. They wear disguises, dark glasses and fancy hats, to no avail.

The most difficult, almost impossible situation arises when a partner no longer in show business has been married for a long time to a handsome, talented actor who, as the years go by, improves in looks, increases in popularity, progresses in his career and, being gregarious, becomes the friend of hundreds of intelligent, handsome, rich, beautiful people, and collects numerous hangers-on on his way up. The actor is on call every minute of the day; his social life never stops. He is pampered, flattered, recognised everywhere and greeted with eagerness. He is usually absorbed in his work and feels deeply any situation required for his role. He forms a close association with the actors and actresses playing opposite him, and is often involved in passionate scenes in his films.

From acting in these scenes at work to involvement in ones similar in life is but a small step. He is emotionally tense, receptive, susceptible and open to any demands upon him, physical or mental. He cannot switch off and detach himself from the character he is playing.

Many actors and actresses in Hollywood go to psychiatrists to release the stress. It is an accepted state of affairs. Others drink to excess, many to try to forget that they are growing old or that their careers are fading, or to hide some inner disappointment in themselves. Still others drink out of habit.

A relationship of long duration is bound to suffer under such conditions, and it is invariably the husband or wife of the successful artist who is the victim. The fame and confidence gained by the one is a handicap for the other. The artist wants to burst out and form new and easier ties, free of questions, recriminations, demands and reproaches. There is a new and adoring person in their lives, whose demands are different, flattering, more urgent, more intense, more passionate, new and exciting. The new love is either younger or more glamorous, is free of commitments, and has no scruples about who gets hurt.

Peter and I had been married for more than ten years when the storm struck, tearing everything apart in its wake. How could one resist the charm, the beauty, the sophistication, the intelligence, the wit and the demands of Vivien Leigh? How could one escape being carried away by the tide of her moods and emotions, with characters out of her plays all jumbled up in her mind? How could one feel anything but a great pity for her, want to look after her in her distress, try to understand, try to forgive, make allowances? The deep scars left by her behaviour to me seemed skin-deep in comparison with her suffering. It was years after before those scars left their true mark.

I do not blame Peter at all for his affair with Vivien. It was in no way an act of treachery towards Laurence Olivier, his benefactor. It was impossible to resist her in her illness and her vulnerability. My suffering increased as time went by. The realisation that my marriage was beyond repair gradually sank in. My willingness to forgive made Peter feel more guilty. The worse he felt, the greater was his resistance to resuming a normal relationship. He would disappear, stay away – then come home, plan trips to the Continent with me, dream of buying a farm, of cultivating citrus fruit for the rest of his life, or of living on a desert island with me, or perhaps with Vivien, away from the scandal and the prying eyes.

We managed to stay together for another two comparatively happy years. He was working hard. Work was his escape – that and drink. It was impossible to get away from Vivien. No one ever got away from her. She told me that, when she saw my efforts to rebuild our life, she did her damnedest to continue the affair. He resisted, but not hard enough. His restlessness was terrible; newspapers eagerly printed stories about his search for justification, his women, his talk of his freedom from commitments, his new-found loves. Then he would come back to me to tell me about his adventures. I could no longer reason with him. After two more years of patient waiting, slowly – too slowly – I came to realise that nothing could be done. We had both been hurt too much. Too many words had been said in anger.

The most hurtful thing when a spouse has been abandoned is to read in the newspapers about the amorous adventures or intense love affair of one's famous partner. The attributes of the new love seem insults to the old. It erodes one's confidence; one wishes to disappear, not to be seen. One suffers from a sort of paranoia – 'Everyone knows me, they all know the situation, they all pity me.' Pride, a reluctance to arouse pity, stops one from enjoying the company of friends. One avoids going alone to a party and leaving alone or being driven home by a friend who, one suspects, feels sorry for one's loneliness. The only wish is to withdraw from the world.

There is an alternative to the withdrawal, and that is to splash one's thoughts and feelings over the headlines. The abandoned spouse should never be blamed for agreeing to do so. One feels a need for revenge, a wish to wound with a sharp phrase; the natural reaction is to fight back with all the anger that has accumulated.

I resisted this temptation. The people involved in my drama were too famous, too respected. This was particularly so with Laurence Olivier. I did not want to anger or hurt him by making public what had been kept from the papers but was common knowledge among his friends. What was I to gain by blasting it out? The money offered by a couple of alert magazines was of no interest to me. I never divulged the truth.

Now three biographies of Peter have been published, one of which, *Finch, Bloody Finch* by Elaine Dundy, is sensitively and perceptively written. It explains Peter's complicated personality, his need for constant attention, his wayward character and unfortunate childhood, all contributing to his behaviour. The memoir by Peter's second wife, Yolande, is very critical of him but is obviously sincere. The other, compiled in a hurry, emphasises hell-raising anecdotes, and the author claims a closer friendship with his subject than really existed.

Peter's liaison with Vivien is now public knowledge. Her illness, too, has been described in a biography by Anne Edwards. Barry Norman, on the BBC, has shown a balanced documentary of Peter's life. Seeing all this unveiled has eroded any feelings of unhappiness. It is like part of someone else's life.

But at the time, my misery was acute. I decided to cut myself off from all theatrical friends and, if I could make the effort, restart a completely new life. First of all, to detach myself sexually from my husband I needed a lover, and not just a passing affair, so easily gained and so unsatisfactory. I was in need of loving and being loved. I did not know it at the time, but there was a part of me that I was no longer able to surrender. I could never again make a total commitment. I had barriers; I was not going to be hurt again.

I found a good lover: attentive, demanding, inexhaustible, adaptable to my whims, constantly present, loving, possessive. Telephoning, writing messages, leaving little presents, he also worked hard at winning the affection of my child and succeeded fully. I was lucky to find him. He was strong, intelligent, handsome and sensitive – an artist, suffering at the time from a broken love affair, who assured me I was his inspiration. He said I put him back on his working path. He painted my portrait again and again. He drove my daughter and me into the wonderful English countryside, into an old dilapidated mansion with an overgrown garden. He chose a dog for us, a thoroughly unsuitable one for the city – a disobedient beagle.

When I met this man, my life became so busy again that I knew I was on the road to recovery. It was fulfilling my need and giving me confidence. He restored my bleeding soul, my wounded ego. He adored children and was a good father to Anita and a morale builder to me. The love affair was ideal, except that my lover was enormously jealous; he made himself ill with jealousy. Violent scenes would follow after Peter's visits.

I knew that I should be free and seek a divorce. Peter still had the ability to affect me, to hurt and wound. His personality had altered completely; he never laughed now, and had even stopped being articulate. His language had become worse than lavatorial; he was gross, he stank and he came to insult me. Why he kept coming is a mystery: why I still opened the door to him an even greater one. I suppose I was hoping for a glimmer of my old Peter. I suffered for Anita's sake and for inflicting on her a selfish, self-centred father. Once, at three in the morning, he asked her to play the piano. She played a child's piece. I saw his eyes fill with tears; he rushed to the bathroom, slammed the door on himself and wept. He then stumbled out into the night. The child, not understanding, looked at me nervously. What could I say? 'Daddy's upset.' 'Why, Mummy? Didn't I play well?'

I decided to build a wall around the two of us. I was going to ask for a divorce. By 1960 I had waited for three years, and there was nothing else I could do.

The divorce was a farce. I had a lover – not admitted in court – while Peter had many. To justify himself, he went wild. The cause of our split was Vivien, yet Peter had to spend a night in a hotel with a woman who specialised in being a co-respondent. She charged £50 and was in bed with the defendant in the morning when tea was delivered by a bell-boy, who would testify in court that the defendant was the man he saw. Peter swore to me afterwards that he never even touched the woman – they spent the night playing canasta. He hated playing cards. My opinion of the case was very low. The lawyers knew, the court knew. I did what I was told to do. My conscience was clear. I was free.

But that bit of paper saying 'In the Court of Justice etc... etc...' does not make any difference to one's feelings. Divorce is a ghastly experience. The heart is heavy, there is physical pain at the pit of the stomach, there is an ache in all one's body, and there is nothing but emptiness, the realisation of failure. Strangely enough, my lover and I decided that we were unsuited to one another. Our love could not mature into a total relationship that would include loyalty and companionship. The excitement of clandestine meetings wore off by the time the decree absolute was through. Having coped so well with dramas of real importance, I could not cope with his demands, his moods, self-centred attitude and frequent scenes. I could not feel anything any more. We had a heart-to-heart explanation, called one another selfish, and split up. He then met another woman who needed consoling.

I was alone, with the responsibility of looking after a house, parts of which I let, and a child. Most difficult of all, I had to make hard decisions. In a happy state of mind, climbing Everest seemed easy. But when I was unhappy, little things – a blocked-up sink, having to change a plug – reduced me to tears.

Peter remarried immediately, but never ceased his nocturnal demanding visits to me. He became a famous film star; in a few years his second divorce made headline news.

After Peter

So far I have described my life more or less chronologically, but after my divorce from Peter several aspects of my subsequent life overlapped; and anyway there are some things I should like to review in a less time-driven way. So each of the chapters that follow stands more or less on its own.

Tamara, help me

In life, as in death, Peter was lucky; he died of a massive heart attack. Four minutes and it was all over. One short, sharp, excruciating pain and then oblivion...

Mama, in her final years, suffered enormously, and her decline towards death, the torture of seeing someone I loved die slowly and painfully, threw me into the depth of misery.

I had noticed a change in Mama three years earlier, in 1976, when a very unpleasant incident occurred in her guest house. At two o'clock in the morning a woman ran down two flights of stairs screaming. She left behind her a trail of blood; the banister, the walls and carpet were covered in it. By the time Mama left her bed to investigate, she could only see a Spanish woman, an old tenant in the house, who excitedly described in Spanish what she had heard in an adjoining room: a noisy quarrel, screams, doors slamming and that frantic rush down the stairs. At four o'clock Mama phoned me to say that the police had called to make enquiries. They had asked for a spare key to Room 6 where the incident occurred and had locked it. They went away, but told her that they would be back at 8.30 that morning. Mama asked me to come round to her house.

I was there well before time. Two plain-clothes CID men arrived and started to interrogate Mama. They would not answer my questions as to what they knew. Mama, usually so definite in her answers on any subject, whether she was right or wrong, went into a haze, staring into space. To all their questions as to the name of the tenant in Room 6, how long he had been there, what nationality he was, Mama only stared blankly, repeating, 'I do not remember'. I took charge, and found her registration book, with the name of a Frenchman and the date of his arrival in the house. I explained to the police that I was supervising the guest house. I did not want to make it appear disorganised and the responsibility of an elderly lady with no memory.

Mama protested vigorously, saying, 'My daughter, not live here, house mine...' My instructions to her in Russian did not improve the situation. I saw the two CID men exchange glances. I was asked to accompany them upstairs to witness their search of Room 6. The window there was broken, and the net curtains were covered in blood. These were removed and taken away. There were signs of a struggle in the room: bottles overturned on a table, ashtrays spilled on the floor.

I stubbornly kept on asking the men what they knew, but they were reluctant to answer. I could make out that a woman, with her wrist heavily bandaged, had gone to the police station and charged a man with violent assault and attempted rape. Her story was that she met the man in a cafe. She had been lured to a party, and on arrival at Mama's house found herself alone in the room with the man, who attacked her. She had been so afraid and horrified that she tried to jump out of the window. He stopped her, so, rather than face rape, she slashed her wrist and ran away.

As the charge included an allegation of violence, the CID men had to investigate it. I saw that they were not fools. They could see a lot of women's clothes in Room 6. It was evident that the woman had been living there, and that the whole drama had been a lovers' quarrel after which she, in a vengeful fury, had gone to the police and accused the man of attempted rape and violence. That night the woman cruised the King's Road in Chelsea in a police car, and pointed out her alleged rapist sitting in an all-night cafe.

The young Frenchman was arrested, kept at the police station until dawn, and interrogated. He said he had been in London for three months as a tourist. He had met the woman in a cafe a week before. She told him she had nowhere to live and he put her up for one night. She had moved in and stayed. When he asked her to leave, she became violent, broke the window, slashed her wrist, and went to the police to accuse him of rape. He said, as far as she was concerned, there was no need for rape at all.

The young Frenchman was allowed to phone his people in France and was released. The same day, his older brother flew in, packed his bags and took him out of the country. The police let him go, obviously believing his story.

My dilemma was that I had noticed Mama's loss of memory. The next day, she denied that she had forgotten anything; but a week later, when I mentioned it and asked whether there had been any consequences after the Room 6 incident, she asked, 'What incident?' I tried to remind her. She took out her register and said, 'I have a Japanese man living there, and there's been no incident.' I could not believe it. The whole drama had been completely obliterated from her memory.

For twenty-five years Mama had been completely happy in her house. She spoke with pride of 'my house'. She had plunged into being a landlady with the same enthusiasm and determination with which she did anything she attempted. She had come to live in London at our request, but she was not going to be a burden to anyone. She had always been independent and now she wanted to run her own business. She wanted property. Grandfather always told her, 'Get some property and you'll be all right.' The opportunities in London in the early 1950s were immense. Full blocks of houses, streets of them, were empty. Mortgages were available for a small deposit. We had chosen a lovely large Victorian house at 18 Lower Sloane Street, near Sloane Square, well built, with large rooms, high ceilings, and a communal garden at the back. Mama decided there and then that it was ideal for letting rooms *meublé*, as the French would call it. Her money stretched to a deposit, solicitors' fees and stamp duties, and the bare minimum was left for furniture and carpets. Peter's contract with Laurence Olivier was used as guarantee for a mortgage loan. Olive Harding achieved another of her miracles there. We combed second-hand shops in Pimlico and found cheap treasures: five shillings for chairs, ten for tables, an armchair for fifteen. Her aim was to furnish one room at a time and then let it, and with the money earned proceed to do the next one. It was my turn to help her. With fifty pounds we furnished three rooms, bed linen and all.

With great impatience Mama marched to the corner newspaper shop and put a card in the window: one double and two single rooms to let. She accepted with joy the first three people who rang her bell. This was to have disastrous consequences. The first tenant, a man, lived in Room 7 for a month, paying no rent, and disappeared at night, leaving a pair of dirty socks and a letter telling her that she was inexperienced and he was teaching her some lessons: a) that she should always get paid in advance, and never believe tenants' hard-luck stories; b) that she should never give people new sheets that had not been laundered, as they were full of starch; and c) never to accept a tenant, like himself, without luggage, as obviously people without luggage were shady characters up to no good.

The double room was let to a mature woman, a Mrs Martin, who produced as a reference a scrapbook of a stately home with photographs of the owners, and a letter signed by a titled lady highly recommending her as a reliable housekeeper who had worked for them for some twenty years. Mama admired the photographs of the stately home, was impressed by the letter, and with great joy introduced me to Mrs Martin. My heart sank. Clearly the woman, with her peroxided hair, her skirt split to her thigh, with high heels that forced her to walk on tiptoe and bent knees, was not the housekeeper type. Mrs Martin then introduced me to a tiny, shifty-looking Chinese man, tightly clutching a fibre suitcase, who she said was her husband. The doorbell rang, and to our surprise in walked a young man, carrying a lot of photographic equipment: a camera on a tripod, spotlights, projectors, reflectors. Mrs Martin said he was her son, who was interested in photography. 'Good,' said Mama, 'I would like some photos of my lovely granddaughter.' I said nothing. My suspicion was overridden by Mama's goodwill.

The newly installed telephone rang non-stop for Mrs Martin, and the doorbell for Room 4 rang at regular intervals. We spied on the visitors. Her son would open the front door, letting in very proper-looking gentlemen, often in formal business suits and bowler hats. The son, smiling, told Mama that he was taking photographs on behalf of the companies they worked for. One man, on coming down the stairs, would meet another going up, regularly, on the half-hour.

Mama, watching the ins and outs, finally became suspicious. She confronted Mrs Martin, saying that, although the room was very large, it was let to two people, husband and wife, and was never meant to accommodate three and a studio. Mrs Martin appealed to Mama's soft heart and maintained that her son was not living there, but that she was giving him a chance in life to start on a fresh career. How could a mother refuse him that? These explanations were passed on to me, but I had no doubt at all that they were false.

At that time, in the 1950s, war had been declared on prostitution, and by law the owners of any premises plying this trade were prosecuted. Mama was worried. She had a rigid lease with the Cadogan Estate. Also, above all, she wanted a 'respectable' guest house. She became agitated and militant, and next time the phone rang, instead of pressing the button to call Room 4, she went up and opened the door of the room. She was left speechless by the spectacle that confronted her. Mrs Martin was lying down on a tiger skin wearing a bottomless and topless black corselette, with long suspenders, black stockings and her high-heeled spiky shoes, and was posing, displaying her assets. The so-called son had strategically placed his equipment, reflectors and all, and was taking pictures, while a gentleman in a pinstriped suit was sitting at the side with his trousers down, enjoying himself.

When Mama had recovered her speech, she shouted, 'What do you do here?' – as if she needed to be told – 'Everybody, I throw out!', and she flung a case of frilly accessories down the stairs, where it landed on the half-landing. She returned like a tornado and snatched the tiger skin. The gentleman escaped, clutching his umbrella. Mama then kept the front door chained. Once, as I was having lunch with her, a well-dressed visitor rang the bell. Mama shouted, within hearing of the long bus queue that was forever outside her door, 'I know why you go upstairs. I call police! You pornographist!', at which the well-dressed visitor, red in the face, fled without looking back.

The photographic equipment disappeared off the premises. Mrs Martin put on a twinset and pearls and went to the rent tribunal, complaining that she was being overcharged. Mama was summoned. Our lawyer said that, unfortunately, no charge of prostitution could be proved; Mama would have to go through a normal hearing of the rent tribunal. There was a three-month waiting list for hearings, and in the meantime Mrs Martin could not be moved.

Mama declared her own war inside the house. Day and night the door remained chained so that she could control everyone going in. She hardly slept. I had to go to Hollywood, leaving Mama in this unholy mess. Such was the unfairness of the law that the tribunal could not be told of the activities in Room 4. Mama in her eagerness impatiently interrupted her solicitor and said, 'Rent normal, woman prostitute, photos pornography, Chinaman sell drugs...' She was promptly shushed. The sole concern of the court was the rent charged. The rent was not reduced, but three months' grace was allowed to Mrs Martin, who went out looking for better pastures. With great glee, at the exact hour when the court order expired, Mama threw everything she could out of the room, and had the lock changed.

So Room 4 was empty again, and Room 7 had disappeared; Room 8 was now the problem. This had been let to a real titled lady who had gone to seed through drugs. The Chinaman had brought her into the house, and obviously was her supplier. Undrugged, she was generous, quiet and very gentle, but when drugged she was suicidal and hysterical and banged the walls with her fists and head. At first poor Mama did not understand what was happening. From being a sweet, well-spoken, beautiful woman, the lady was transformed into a doddering, crazy fury. She was asked to leave, but went of her own accord when the Chinaman left. We later learned through a newspaper which printed her photograph on the front page that she had committed suicide.

These first three cases would have discouraged many, but not Mama. She was going to run a respectable guest house. Within a few months, it became known in Australia within the dancing and acting world that there was a cosy place with a friendly landlady in England, and many actors and dancers, spurred on by Peter's success, used it as a base and sat by the phone waiting for their agents to call.

Mama lived for her house. Improvements were made, carpets bought, bathrooms added, curtains made, furniture painted. Mama never stopped working – for instance, in between times she made a full set of children's costumes for performances given by the ballet classes that I ran for a couple of years in the late 1960s, in the church hall of St Augustine's in South Kensington.

Then, aged 75, she decided that she was wasting her days. The house was running itself, but she had to remain active. She went into partnership with a tenant to make and sell scented candles. She was making them, he was selling them. The basement became a small factory; the business flourished. They decided to economise and buy in bulk. Wax, perfume, wick string, saucepans, packing boxes and fireproof glasses: the more one bought, the cheaper it was. The house smelled like a church perfumed with cheap soap. Their crowning glory was when Harrods bought their candles for its Christmas display.

There was a lull in orders in the spring, and by the following Christmas all the shops had similar candles made by other people who had copied the idea. Mama and her partner were left with tons of wax, miles of wick, hundreds of packing boxes, litres of perfume oil and a laboratory full of chemical dyes.

Her gambling activities were varied. Casinos at Cannes and Nice were familiar with her; in England she could pick winning horses with a pin; her football pool entries were always ready for posting by Wednesday; and her luck was incredible. When she was banking the cheque for £5,000 that she won on a Premium Bond, a bright young teller, beaming, asked her, 'How does it feel to win so much money?' She shrugged her shoulders: 'What's money at my age? I want nothing. It's only sport to win...'

Her activities wound down gradually. She became less interested in the general upkeep of the house, and less aware of the type of person to whom she was letting her rooms. I was keeping an eye on her, phoning, visiting daily, trying not to appear to be supervising. I did my shopping in Chelsea. By then, as I will relate later, I was working as an interpreter, which took me away for periods of time, and once, on getting back, an old French tenant said to me, 'This is the end – the house will be ruined. Your mother has made a terrible mistake. She has let in an Algerian, and, before you know it, the house will be overrun by Algerians; they bring their friends in, they are devious – they are thieves.' I could not believe that all Algerians were undesirable, but soon found that this particular one was. He persuaded Mama to let him have her large living room, next to her bedroom on the ground floor. The living room had a separate entrance and direct access to the hall and the street. He installed himself there and observed the comings and goings of the house. Twice I caught him creeping into Mama's room, because he had heard her go into the bathroom. He pretended he wanted some information. What he really wanted, and succeeded in doing, was to remove the spare keys from the board and gradually clear out all the valuables from each room. At the final reckoning he had stolen about £2,000. Pay packets disappeared from hard-working Japanese tenants, and my mother lost about £800 in rent money and two valuable rings.

We called the police, who questioned the Algerian. Pointing at Mama, he said, 'This old woman is mad – she doesn't remember anything. She lets anybody into the house; she should be in the madhouse.' The police did nothing. Because I changed all the locks and hid the spare keys, the Algerian became menacing. I did not want to leave Mama alone in the house, so I slept there. At night he let in dozens of people; they slept on his floor, used the room for their meetings, and vanished during the day. The old Frenchman said they were a gang of thieves who met at night to plan robberies. Their system was that two men would enter a shop and engage the attention of a salesman by trying on clothes, while two more would come in with a suitcase and clear the hangers of leather and suede coats. They became so efficient that they even robbed Harrods.

The French tenant knew this because he frequented an Algerian cafe and had overheard two of the customers say what a convenient place my mother's house was and how easy it was to steal in London. I kept watch on the Algerian and when he went out I sneaked into his room, where I saw plenty of evidence. The room was full of leather coats that were packed into a car the following Sunday and taken to France. This procedure was repeated often. The Algerian's girlfriend cleaned his shoes, worked, handed him her money and often nursed a black eye, and wore a very expensive coat with a huge fur collar.

I decided to move into Mama's house, as I was afraid for her safety. The Algerian realised I was aware of his activities, and swore he would kill me, and Mother too. He had once left a butcher's knife at the threshold to Mama's room. There was no spare bed, and I slept on Mama's floor, jumping up during the night at the sound of the front door opening, to stop the gang coming into the house. The Algerian abused me, shouted that he was a man, and that I, a mere female, could never outsmart him; the room was his, the house was not mine, I would be disposed of and the house set on fire; that I could prove nothing, because my mother was mad.

I went to the police again, but they did not want to have anything to do with the quarrel. They said that anything happening between people indoors was none of their business. I became a nervous wreck, shouting at the Algerian. He was furious. Our slanging matches at first were in English, with feeble results on his part, so he switched to French. From past memories I brought out all the French nastiness I knew, and to his '*sale Bolshevik!*' I answered '*sale pied noir!*'. The worst imaginable insults were screamed backwards and forwards. On one occasion Mama came out of her room and brought out a few French words too. On seeing us together, his rage knew no bounds. He pushed us into his room, locked the door, put the key into his pocket and, producing his large butcher's knife, said he was going to kill us both, there and then.

As I have said before, in moments of real danger, emotion or panic, I go quiet and am able to observe the scene from a distance, as if I were not concerned. I laughed. I knew that there could be nothing worse for him than to be laughed at. I marched calmly to his window, opened it, and announced to the bus queue that Mother and I were about to be assassinated. The people in the queue looked at me; then, in the time-honoured English manner, they looked away, pretending to be deaf. The Algerian panicked. He unlocked his door and ran out into the street. I knew that I was winning. I hired a lawyer, the best, a costly one who employed an even costlier counsel. They were unable to change the law, but served the Algerian with a twenty-eight-day notice to vacate. The tenant and his idiot girlfriend went to the Citizens Advice Bureau, claiming that they were being persecuted by a woman who was not even the owner of the house. They were told to go to the rent tribunal, and eventually a date was fixed for the hearing. All this meant waiting.

The Algerian, having found out all the rules of this stupid law, stopped paying rent, and told two other friends to do the same. They were convinced that I could do nothing. I lost a stone in weight worrying about the case, and was a bore to all my friends, being able to talk of nothing but the Algerian.

He continued his crooked activities. Mail was being intercepted, money orders removed, and a cheque for £10,000, which by mistake was sent to Mama's address, was found in a waste-paper basket – the Barclays Bank manager to whom I returned it could not believe his eyes. An Iraqi diplomatic passport was found hidden under the stair carpet.

With this passport in my hands, I went to the police again. They took away the passport for ten minutes then returned it, saying that they were powerless to act, as anything found in a house is not considered legally relevant. They suggested I mailed it to the Embassy, which I did.

The battle took its toll on me. What I was most worried about was retribution from the gang. I had been told that they damaged houses, broke windows, set houses on fire; that the easiest thing for them was to throw a bottle of petrol through the window and run away. I had to abandon work and set myself up as a round-the-clock vigilante.

Through all this, Mama behaved as if nothing was happening. She forgot things from hour to hour. I had consulted specialists when her memory started to fail. It was a (to them) routine case of atherosclerosis. What worried me more than the memory loss were the blackouts and dizzy spells she was having. I suggested that she sell her lease and come to live with me. Mama would not hear of it, and I couldn't do it over her head. Besides, how could one sell a house full of Algerians were using terrorist tactics?

The day of judgement arrived. In the morning the three magistrates visited the premises to resolve the dispute. I did not find them friendly. They inspected everything closely, asked a few questions, wrote a lot on official sheets of paper, and did not show any feelings at all. The Algerian dressed himself like a sheik of Araby; he had on a fabulously embroidered caftan and his hair was teased into a halo. His room for once was clean, tidy and not in its usual state with opened cans of beans and fish pushed under the bed. Mama had had a dizzy spell and was in bed. I felt the magistrates could have got the impression that Mama's illness was staged. I hated the Algerian and disliked the magistrates' clinical attitude.

In the afternoon, I went into the tribunal, shaking like a leaf in a gale, armed with doctors' certificates about Mother's health, my only valid reason for having the room vacated. I marched into that court determined to be calm, unemotional, articulate and as English as I could be. At my side was my solicitor, my counsel and his secretary. I was firmly told by the counsel that I was not allowed to mention anything about the Algerian's activities or threats. With murder and fear in my heart, and a smile on my face, I did as I was told. The tribunal has to protect the tenant. There he was, holding hands with his idiot girl, looking pathetic, claiming to be about to be thrown to the wolves, persecuted and with nowhere to go. And there was the law on his side, the right of a tenant being stronger than any other principle. I was gloomy, but still calm.

Suddenly my spirits rose. The magistrate asked him if he worked. The Algerian, with pride, said, no, he didn't have to work, his father was wealthy and was sending him money. But his fiancée did work in a boutique. In that case, said the magistrate, you are free during the daytime and can look for another room. The room's rent was assessed at four pounds more than we were charging. He was told to pay his arrears and given four weeks to vacate.

Having lost the case, the Algerian, a typical loud-mouthed coward, did a midnight flit, leaving his girlfriend to pay the arrears. She spent five days crying. A look of hope showed on her face when the police arrived in search of him. He was wanted for questioning about theft. My old Frenchman told me he was later sent to jail. His girlfriend waited for him; and as he was about to be deported, she married him.

By 1977 Mama was getting very lethargic. She slept long hours in the morning, fell asleep after meals, and hardly got out of her room. On going to hospital for a check-up, she was told to remain there, and at the end of a few days was diagnosed with diabetes. After a few weeks on a starvation diet, and once the level of insulin to be injected had been established, she was discharged. I was taught how to inject her every day, control her diet, make sure that she did not over-eat, and watch for signs of tiredness. The hospital gave me a little book of symptoms with descriptions of hypoglycaemia. I was warned she could go into a coma or develop gangrene of the feet. It worried me like hell. I moved her to her own house and installed myself there, with the intention of selling the short remaining lease.

But first I had to get rid of all the tenants, and then of twenty-four years of accumulated possessions and the rubbish left by previous tenants. Never in my life have I worked so hard. Mama had collected enough china, curtains, bed-linen, blankets, electrical equipment, brooms, old trunks, suitcases and theatrical costumes to fill this huge Victorian house chock-a-block. There were tambourines, umbrellas, old letters, books, lamps, vases, knick-knacks, clothes and the paraphernalia of the candle venture.

It took me three months to sort out, clear up and pack unwanted stuff into disposal bags, which Anita transported in her little Renault as jumble for church bazaars. Our faithful cleaner and friend Tilly was a tower of strength. She loved Mama, worried about her and helped me a great deal.

It was time to vacate the house. I went to the bank every day and withdrew hundreds of pounds, which I distributed like confetti. The two Japanese, the cleanest, quietest tenants of all, accepted two weeks' rent, bowed very low, said, 'Thank you very much' and left without a murmur. The Italian man did not believe that we were selling the lease; he thought we wanted to raise the rents after his departure, but finally he accepted a substantial sum. The old Frenchman, my spy, accepted a very large sum, and at the last minute extorted another hundred. But the Algerians, friends of my enemy, promised to go and then wouldn't. A definite date had been fixed for vacant possession. One Algerian demanded a full year's refunded rent – which he got – and as he left, at night, he stole the best blankets, eiderdowns and rugs from his room.

I was so happy to see the last of them that I didn't mind. Mama was in a permanent state of haze, and Anita and I didn't even tell her that her move into my house was final. Our fear was that one day she would charge down my road and go back to her own place. She could not be left alone for long. The insulin worked miracles, so she was looking very well, and maintained that there was nothing wrong with her. 'Why don't you let me go to "my house"? My tenants are waiting,' she would say.

My greatest battle now was to stop her eating. She had developed a monstrous appetite and was always hungry, but was only allowed the minimum of carbohydrates. My life revolved around her; my time was spent hiding food, locking doors, seeing that nothing was left in the fridge and cooking three small balanced meals a day. The greatest trouble occurred whenever I invited a few friends for dinner. Mama was very helpful in clearing and washing up, for which I was grateful, until I discovered that she was devouring all she could in the kitchen. When I remonstrated, she started hiding things. I found biscuits in her bed, nuts in her pockets, bits of cake hidden away. My vigilance never relaxed. She forgot that she was a diabetic, and every morning would ask me what the injections were for, and was angry at my controlling her food intake. She used to resent my helping her into a bus or a taxi: 'I am not an invalid!' she would say angrily.

We lived quite happily for a year. What saddened me most was that the times were gone when I could discuss a problem with her or exchange an opinion. She was absent in spirit and mind, and watched TV for hours without knowing what the programme was about. In 1979 she took to her bed with abdominal and chest pains. Pleurisy was diagnosed in one lung. Antibiotics helped, but the abdominal pains would not go. She endured an excruciating series of X-rays after a barium meal, during which I was allowed to stay with her on condition that I wore a heavy radiation-proof gown. She clung on to me like a baby. It was difficult to move her, as she was in great pain from colonic spasms. Her only worry was not to soil the couch. She was sent home to await the diagnosis; the hospitals were working on a semi-strike basis and very few patients were being admitted.

She was finally called in and I had a feeling that she would probably never come home again. Pathetically, she would not let go of my arm, asking me when she would be coming home. She had tests every day and the surgeons were adamant that she should have an operation to remove her cancerous colon. Being of independent spirit, she would never call a nurse to help her out of bed; in her hazy state she walked out of bed unaided and fell, gashing her shins badly. When I visited her, she had a frame around her bandaged legs and her feet had swollen to gigantic size. She refused to swallow any food, but because of her diabetes and the daily insulin injections, her carbohydrate intake had to be kept up. Because of the shortage of staff, I was asked to come every day at meal times and try to feed her. She never lost her memory to such an extent that she would not recognise me. She waited for me to appear, three times a day, either to ask to be sat up or moved down or to relieve herself. She never asked for painkillers, and was in constant pain that forced her to moan with every outgoing breath.

I was persuaded to agree to an operation for her, which would mean that either she would survive it, having a very strong heart, and have an additional few years of life, or she would die. The alternative would have been a complete blockage of the intestines, a perforation, and a few painful weeks of life.

When she was being bathed by two nurses in preparation for the operation, she slipped and fell in the bath. Two of her ribs were broken and her face and shoulders were bruised and black. I was very angry. I had bathed her for close to two years and had never dropped her. The operation had to be postponed. Her strength was fading, and her health deteriorated daily after that fall. She was in excruciating pain and started suffering from bedsores that had to be dressed every day. One lung filled with liquid, and the biggest needle I ever saw was introduced into her chest to withdraw the liquid. I was behind the curtain and heard her moans. The doctor asked me to be at hand, in case she asked for me. She never complained, but just moaned. She knew that she was amongst English people, so she answered questions in English. When the pain became unbearable, she turned to me and in a broken voice that I shall never forget, more a lament than a request, said, 'Tamara, help me'. This plea, from such an independent, proud, game woman, whose spirit was slowly breaking, tore my heart to pieces. She asked what was the matter with her, what could she do to get better, and please, please, please to help her…

For the last two weeks of her life, when the diarrhoea never ceased, when she had to be sat up so as not to fill her lungs with fluid, to be turned in bed or be forcibly fed, she took some liquid from me, because it was me and she trusted me and I told her to have some glucose. She vomited every day. She had been taken to the Royal Marsden Hospital for an additional scan, which revealed a secondary cancer, of the liver this time. She was being given heavier sedatives, and I was told that she would not have long to live. When the painkillers wore off she would clasp my hand, and repeat, 'Tamara, help me'. My visits to St Stephen's Hospital were non-stop; the agony I witnessed I shall never forget.

The doctors decided on injections of diamorphine. I knew that it was a killer, but death does not come easily. When she was moved into a private room, they must have increased the doses. Her eyes were rolling, her mouth was open, she was exhaling with a tremendous sound. I waited. She became conscious again, but the dreaded rupture was happening inside. The staff nurse insisted that she had to be lifted out of bed to relieve herself. She was weak and could not stand up, her body limp and heavy. I made a tremendous physical effort to lift her onto the commode. Her arms weighed tons around my shoulders, her head rested on my chest. I sat her down gently, while she embraced me and clung to me, asking why she had so much pain. Then when I had to wipe the blood away softly, she yelled and shuddered and seemed to faint for a moment. A nurse helped me put her back into bed. Mama clasped my hand and begged me for help again. Another nurse came in with more diamorphine. They tried to make her as comfortable as they could, and she calmed down for a while.

I had a long-standing date for dinner with Irina Baronova. I phoned to say I couldn't keep it, and gave my reasons. Irina rushed to hospital to see Mama, who was heavily sedated. We were told that she was still strong, that she would last till the morrow and longer. We kept a vigil, then went to my home and sat half the night talking. Irina helped me get through that night. I rang the hospital at midnight, and was told that Mama was sleeping peacefully. At six a.m. I had a call from the staff nurse to tell me that Mama had died at 5.30.

I was told she never regained consciousness, but at times, particularly in the silence of the night, terrible doubts assail me. I often dream of her, and on waking, think... had she become lucid before dying, looked around for me to say once more, 'Tamara help me', and saw that I wasn't there?

When I went to the hospital in the early hours of the morning, her body had been removed to the mortuary. A very pretty and compassionate nurse, who had looked after her, took me there. Mama was lying in a little chapel, her skin like yellow wax, her eye sockets sunk, her forehead like cold marble under my lips.

As I turned round, something in the nurse's looks and uniform reminded me of a faded photograph I had of Mama as a Red Cross sister during the First World War. I was gently led away by the nurse, who softly put her arm around my shoulders, and then I saw that her large blue eyes were full of tears.

Engineering English

I have always been hard-working. Nothing depresses me more than sitting at home day after day, mind unoccupied, wandering from living-room to kitchen and back again. I become gloomy and feel sorry for myself; I need to work.

Soon after my divorce, at a non-theatrical party, I learned that a large British Trade Fair was being planned in Moscow for the following year (1961), and that an agency was recruiting interpreters for various British engineering firms. I have always spoken Russian fluently, and both my parents were Russian, but a job as an interpreter could never have been further from my mind. I was not formally educated, and a ballet school provides a very limited education. But I went to the agency and put my name down. They said they were interested only in men and that their books were full.

Four weeks before the Trade Fair, the office called me. EMI Electronics were anxious to find an interpreter urgently. Their specialist, an electronics engineer they were planning to take to Moscow, had been refused a visa. I had an interview with him and an EMI executive. They asked me about discussing electronics in Russian. I laughed. Electronics? I don't even know how electricity works, except that it has two wires. We had a long talk; I did not conceal how ignorant I was on any technical subject. How could I work with all these clever, highly technical people, exchanging accurate information about closed-circuit colour TV?

The engineer turned to the executive and said, 'She doesn't propose to change any fuses, but she *is* fluent in Russian, is intelligent and has a pleasant manner.' I was amazed, but I was hired. There followed two weeks of frantic activity, when I hardly slept, worrying about the consequences and shaking at the prospect of going to the Soviet Union for the first time. I got a visa, and arranged to have my daughter looked after in my absence. I made a will, just in case... And before I knew it, I was on a plane to Moscow, surprised that everyone around me spoke Russian.

In fact, all went well. My job was made easy by the skill of the specialists of both countries, who understood one another's technology. There were many cameras on our stand pointed at its visitors, who were amused to see themselves in colour on a TV screen.

One of my tasks was to pick a friendly-looking child out of a crowd, sit her on my knee and let her see herself on a large screen while I interviewed her. The natural expressions of wonder made it into a magic show. I also presented and did the commentary of a fashion show staged by ICI with live models. I stayed in Moscow longer than the others, because we sold all our equipment to the Moscow TV Centre and they needed an interpreter while it was being installed.

On my return to Britain I hoped that 'with a little bit of luck' I could become a professional interpreter. But it was not an easy task. There were 599 others from that trade fair, all with the same idea. I had to specialise.

What subjects did I know well? Nothing technical. No one wanted ballet; it was science and technology that were required. Nevertheless I applied, and went for an interview with the British Council. A very able, efficient, severe woman asked me if I really knew what the job entailed. 'You will be nothing but a machine. Your opinion does not count, your personality does not exist. You are merely there to convey the thoughts of the people you are working for. At no time at all must you let anyone see what you feel. You must not change their intonations, their meanings, or alter anything said, even if they make mistakes; your job is to translate even if it is against your better judgement. Translating for industry is a most responsible job – a mistake could cost the country millions.'

I was crestfallen. Millions? Industry? I couldn't take the responsibility. It would worry me to death. I knew I had failed my test. Months went by. I had forgotten my ambitions, when I received a letter from the Foreign Office summoning me for an interview. A formidable-looking bearded Englishman, speaking fluent Russian, asked me what I knew of Professor Ingle Finch's work as a physicist. 'Nothing', I said. 'Good', was the reply. My life, obviously, had been investigated and I had been given a 'pass'.

The bearded man, testing my ability, made a long speech of welcome in English at an imaginary reception by a mayor, for a Russian Minister who had just visited a textile factory. I was to put the speech into Russian. I plunged in. It is amazing how fast the mind works. I knew I was stuck for the Russian word for 'textile'. Before the Revolution, many words had been borrowed from the French. I ventured 'texteel' and it happened to be right. I had passed again.

Two days later, the Foreign Office handed me a twenty-page itinerary. A delegation of specialists and directors of factories was visiting Britain. Their interest was in machine tools. A plant with a hundred thousand workers had been built in the Soviet Union, and a town created around it. Fiat of Milan was supplying machinery to manufacture motor cars. I was to be the delegation's official interpreter during their three weeks' inspection of machine-tool factories.

I couldn't believe it was happening. I looked up 'machine tools' in a dictionary and worked out that they were tools to cut metal, but that we would be looking at machines that made the tools to make the machines to cut the metal.

I spent two days crying, occasionally looking at my terrifying schedule: the Midlands, Scotland, Welsh steelworks, official receptions, nightly speeches. I repeated for days the unpronounceable Russian names, employees of some composite-word ministry, 'machino priborintorg'. My daughter gave me confidence. She is level-headed, cool and logical. In my moments of panic, which were to recur for the next twelve years during the life I was now beginning as a freelance interpreter, on seeing my tears she always said, 'Mummy, you can do it' – although, in the later years, it was more, 'Stop carrying on, you know you can do it!'

Our first stop was Newcastle. As I was asking a Geordie operator to explain about his machine for the fourth time, the Russian Minister turned to me and said, 'I know you speak Russian, but can you understand English?' He was right: I couldn't. To this day the Geordie's intonations are incomprehensible to me, although I got used to the Scots, the Welsh, the Mancunians and even the Jamaicans with a Birmingham accent.

I was quickly forced to become a specialist. With a sweet smile I would ask the Russian, 'What do you call this?', write it down on my pad and put the same question to the Englishman. At night I repeated the words parrot-fashion until automatically, as a sort of Pavlovian reflex, the right word came to me.

Many delegations visited Great Britain in the late 1960s and during the 1970s. I remember crying a lot before a group of scientific magazine editors landed, official guests of the Foreign Office. Me? Science? Anita firmly said, 'Mummy, get on with it'. She became fluent in Russian too, first studying it at the French Lycée in London and then at Bristol University.

The editors brought an interpreter with them, perhaps because they wanted all information double-checked. He translated material about black holes and quasars at the Royal Observatory and left the giant telescope to me. Machines and instruments were now old friends to me. He translated a lecture given in the Nuclear Enterprises establishment, while dealing with the Hunterston nuclear power station was my job. I was amused to find that a fish-farming research institute used the warm water from it to speed the growth of fish, who normally feed well and grow only during the warmer months.

My head was full of useless information now. The Imperial College of Science and Technology lecture was left for my Soviet colleague. The linear induction motor, a development of Professor Eric Laithwaite and demonstrated as a little model of a vehicle suspended on a rail, was mine.

I regained my confidence for oceanographic surveying equipment, and when we went to the House of Commons at Question Time, that too proved not in the least difficult. I withdrew again in the Department of Physics at Cambridge, but in Oxford was good at simultaneous translation of a scientific film about fleas.

Superstition prevented women from landing on a North Sea platform pumping oil for BP. My men, complete with helmets, boarded a helicopter in Grimsby, leaving me slightly disappointed but free to have my hair done and buy a new blouse.

The difficulties of electro-optic detectors and lasers were counterbalanced by the simplicity of audio-visual language courses, when a picture was shown on a screen and a word repeated. Computer specifications left my brain feeling woolly. By the end of the tour I had translated a speech by the leader of the group for a BBC radio interview, and from there, worried and panting, I rushed to Lancaster House for an official farewell reception, expecting to have to translate endless speeches, to find that many Foreign Office people spoke Russian. This group of visitors was exceptionally interesting. They spoke a lot about the performing arts in their country. Opera, ballet and music were familiar to all of them.

One evening in my room I listened to Tchaikovsky's second piano concerto, and my Russian soul stirred again. The curse of being a Russian, even a generation removed, is that there is inside one a reserve of joy and despair. It is released like a tidal wave at the sound of Russian music, and every other reasonable sensation is submerged in the flow. Songs and music bring out a deep sense of sadness or rapture, bring back memories to warm or chill the soul. They are the spring that releases the pent-up emotions that lie dormant, ready to be unleashed at the sound of a melody. Tchaikovsky conjures up for me the living past in Russia, his melodies often originating from folk songs.

I recalled the ballet, the operas, the pathetic refugee in Paris singing his tender songs, exposing his own tortured soul, his search for perfection, his despair. My deep feeling for Russian music and the performing arts have helped me greatly in assimilating the role of interpreter. It gave me a rapport with the Russians.

In spite of what the woman from the British Council said, a lot of the interpreter's time is spent in non-official activities. There's shopping and occasionally taking visitors to doctors, invitations to sample their food, and thousands of personal questions to be answered. But, above all, my new profession opened up a completely new world for me. On the long journeys between steelworks, I asked for songs. They sang in buses and on fishing trips, easily harmonising the music, and they knew all the lyrics. The British specialists enjoyed it too.

The variety of jobs I was offered kept my nose buried in dictionaries. Certain large contracts specified that part of the transaction was barter: Russian equipment was produced in part exchange for goods. One such piece of equipment was an electronic machine that, with the aid of a probe fitted with a miniature bulb and inserted into the urethra, used electronic impulses to crush stones in the bladder. No cutting of the body was necessary. The bladder was emptied and warm water pumped in; the surgeon located the stone and then crushed it into sand.

Two such operations were to be performed in England. I was to interpret the introductory lecture, explaining the theory, to some forty students, doctors and specialists assembled at Guy's Hospital. The Soviet surgeon had no licence to perform the operation in Britain, and the local surgeon was not familiar with the machine and needed direction.

I had to don a surgical cap, mask, shoe covers and long white gown, stand between the two surgeons in the theatre, facing the unconscious and spreadeagled patient, and translate: cotton wool, water, probe, impulses switched on, enema, basin, etc. With trepidation, I had made a list of all the organs concerned. My dictionaries did not include 'testicles'. The coarse Russian word used by all is the equivalent of 'balls'. Mama said the same. Anita searched in vain in her books. I called on my Russian doctor; she was out, but her receptionist, an old refugee from the Tzarist times, had been a nurse and said I could ask any question. I asked. She replied, 'Balls'. Eventually I found the proper translation in a medical dictionary. It had taken me two days to locate one word.

The operation at Guy's was most successful and interest was aroused. We went to the leading hospital in Norwich, which had the reputation of having the best urology department in England. We were scheduled to arrive at two p.m. but arrived soon after one. The Soviet surgeon, a handsome, lively Doctor Kildare type, asked to see the laboratory. Our host, the leading British surgeon, obliged. He took out of a refrigerator a plastic container similar to those used in delicatessens. Using a fork, he extracted some frozen white matter; his team was experimenting on freezing body parts to check for cancer cells. One of the Russians from the Trade Delegation, a non-medical chap, asked what the frozen matter was. He was told 'a penis'. He turned green and slipped to the floor in a dead faint. He was taken away on a stretcher and was not seen again that day.

My speciality was metallurgy. I spent years watching crankshafts being measured, camshafts being ground, springs for nuclear plants being produced, cylinders being transported on conveyors, tools being sharpened on carborundum wheels, presses coming down with mighty thumps; I saw electronic equipment being tested, emergency stops pulled, pressure valves checked, temperatures recorded, blueprints investigated and huge machinery secured and packed.

I climbed on top of high, curved vessels, went up twisted ladders and round gas containers, visited oil refineries, sewage works, fertiliser plants and gypsum quarries, and was in a barge dredging the bottom of some river. I wore masks, gloves and special clothing for working near toxic chemicals. But I also saw the best parts of England, Wales and Scotland. Every good restaurant was used for guests, every beauty spot visited – lakes, mountains, stately homes. I enjoyed it all and I liked the Russian people.

By now my vocabulary was growing by the day: plants, flowers, insects, wild animals. I kept a clear head. The friendlier the ambience, the more is drunk at receptions, and the more anecdotes, verses and proverbs emerge. An understanding of the character, habits and humour of each country is essential. The pride of the English in being good losers; the humiliation a Russian feels if he does not succeed. The pride of possession that Russians have because it is the reward of achievement; the reluctance of the English to say 'I have' or 'it costs'. The habit the Russians have, if they feel friendly, of asking personal, intimate questions; details being volunteered in England only after very long acquaintance. An interpreter should be a bit of a diplomat: unprejudiced, informative when asked, antagonising neither hosts nor visitors.

Some jobs, though, are livelier than others. One such, in 1970, involved the editing and dubbing of the film of *Waterloo* to be shown to royalty at a special gala performance. The producer, Dino de Laurentiis, was Italian, but a celebrated Soviet Union director, Sergei Bondarchuk, had been asked to direct because of his successful film of *War and Peace*. *Waterloo*, with an international cast and starring Rod Steiger as Napoleon, had been made in Russia but was being dubbed and edited in London.

By the time I was asked to interpret for the director, to whom foreign languages were a complete mystery, the film was going through a crisis. He had shot five-and-a-half hours of film and wanted to emphasise, in a twenty-five-minute final sequence, that after a war there are no victors: both sides are losers. He wanted Wellington on his horse inspecting the dead and wounded, fields of them, in a never-ending scene. The American distributors refused to show the film with a long, sombre final scene. The director's five-and-a-half hour film was cut to two-and-a-quarter hours, the final scene to a few minutes.

I was introduced to him – a strong-looking, bushy-browed, thick-necked man with a mane of unruly hair, brooding in a corner in frustration at not being able to tell everyone his thoughts. The editor was about to resign. The composer spoke in French and hated his composition being cut. I walked in on a row in three languages, English, French and Italian, and had to introduce Russian comments into the shouting.

I picked up the tempo, accelerating with each remark, volume amplified with each insult, speed and loudness increasing until I had to shout over everyone's voice to be heard, when the absurdity of it all struck me. I turned to the director and said, 'This one is resigning, that one is protesting, this one is threatening, and they are all abusing one another with unbelievable language.' At this point, Bondarchuk took me by the shoulders, pushed me into a corner, shook me like an apple tree and shouted, 'Your country is ruled by capitalism, producers are nervous of introducing new ideas, distributors are only keen on showing what they think is wanted, you are all ruled by money and greed, you produce rubbish to please an ignorant public. I am a respected director in my country; my work is never mutilated, pennies are not counted. If I want dozens of helicopters for a scene, I tell the government and they provide them promptly. When I make a film, it is shown. Here, my baby, my creation has been taken away from me, cut to pieces, altered unrecognisably. And you say your system is better than ours.'

My arms hurt under his grip. I defended myself timidly. 'I am only an interpreter, not a politician.' He buried his head in his hands and said 'Never again, never, never again.'

The Royal Film Performance was a grand affair. The producer, his wife Sylvana Mangano, and the director and his wife, a famous Russian actress, who was greatly upset because her two scenes in *Waterloo* had landed on the cutting-room floor, were in the reception line. I was placed in between them, in case the Queen or one of the royal party spoke to them.

The Queen obviously had not been briefed that there would be an interpreter, but as she spoke to Bondarchuk, my job was to translate what she said into Russian. This seemed to surprise her; she looked at me with her beautiful, very wide cornflower-blue eyes as if to say, 'Who is this foreign woman, speaking out of turn?' I felt I had to explain. 'I am the interpreter Ma'am, the director does not speak English.' The Queen smiled and continued the conversation through me. Prince Philip, always ready for a quip, joined in and asked me if had I done the translating for all the film. I denied it, laughing. I became very conscious of the fact that the presentation was for the stars, and the conversation was about me. The producer dashed out of the line, interrupting emphatically, assuring everyone, 'No, no, she only interpreter here'.

The royal party moved on. The Russians asked me what the Prince had been talking about, and were disappointed that it was about interpreting.

The film was one of those worthy failures, with too much money spent, too many bosses, too many different opinions. But it was fun for me to be once again part of a big Hollywood promotional display. After the gala, there was supper at the Hilton, with stars, reporters, and Peter O'Toole curious to meet me, as he was Peter's drinking pal. Rod Steiger kept the Mirabelle restaurant open for hours, expanding his philosophy of life and his intense theories about acting. The Russian director, for the first time, was able to express his thoughts through me.

But with the sparse success of the film, once again I had seen a demonstration that the film industry is a precarious business. I went back to my engineering: cylinders, fertilisers, steelworks – and demonstrating incandescent furnaces for crematoria. We saw pigs' corpses being burned, their legs extended forward, stiff, the lid not fitting the coffin. We were told that anatomically a pig's structure is the nearest to a man's; a sheep's skin is covered in wool, a dog is too small, but a pig takes exactly 90 minutes to burn, like a man. This furnace produces none of the smoke that can occasionally upset relatives glancing up at the building, and the ashes are guaranteed to be the burnt body's. I classified that as another of my useless bits of information.

One party of guests visited the Edinburgh Infirmary, which was researching and developing kidney transplants. The trusting beagles recovering from their tummies being slit looked pathetic. But we met many patients whose lives had been saved, and a boy in intensive care, seen through a glass enclosure, was in an advanced stage of recovery and spoke to us through his microphone. We saw, on film close-up, the whole operation in detail. Once again my mind was too busy finding the right words to be sickened by the bloody spectacle.

I could so easily have stayed a journeywoman translator in the world of engineering; but in the 1980s, by a series of happy events, my work eventually moved into a much more artistic sphere.

Translating for the Bolshoi

Although I had been teaching some ballet classes in London after my divorce, by 1980 I was feeling a little out of the mainstream of London ballet life. Then I was invited to be an examiner in the Karsavina Syllabus at the Royal Academy of Dancing, which I did from 1981 to 1983. I also started writing monthly articles for *The Dancing Times*.

But my big 'break' came through the efforts of a friend, David Palmer, the feelance press officer, who recommended the managements at Covent Garden and Glyndebourne to use me as a translator. As a result, I was asked to become an interpreter for English ballet and opera companies travelling to Russia, and for Russian cultural groups during their tours to Great Britain. One of the most memorable of the latter was the Bolshoi Ballet's visit to London in 1986.

My first assignment with the Bolshoi was at the Henry Wood Hall in Borough High Street. The augmented Sadler's Wells Orchestra was rehearsing Sergei Prokofiev's *Ivan the Terrible*, conducted by Alexander Kopylov. The maestro could speak a few scattered words in several languages. His enthusiasm and bright personality glowed as his expansive gestures accompanied and illustrated his *moderatos, fortissimos, Panken leiser mit crescendo, vite içi, une fois more.* The orchestra, some of whom were reading the score for the first time, rose to the occasion and played splendidly. The hall shook at the sound of the bells, cymbals and timpani. The maestro was pleased and expressed his feelings over a cup of coffee.

My second call was for 8 a.m. on stage at Covent Garden. This was to be the day to set up the rest of the season and I was to help with the hanging and lighting of the scenery. I met a group of Russians: stage technician Sergei, chief electrician Boris, chief mechanic Nikolai. Nikolai's main concern was to see that three winches placed on a grid above the set were properly balanced, so that they could take the weight and provide adequate support for the three enormous revolving circles of the *Ivan the Terrible* set. These circles were huge iron structures, the frames for black nets that were constantly being manipulated to open and mask consecutive scenes of the ballet. So we went up to the catwalk above the stage, first in a lift and then continuing up a spiral staircase. The stage crew below were completely dwarfed from our lofty vantage point.

Next day was reserved for lighting the set. Although I am no stranger to the stage, I nevertheless prepared a little list, a glossary, of English–Russian expressions: footlights were floats, the iron bars from which the projectors were suspended were battens, the side lights were lanterns and Fresnels. The colours were all numbered, and Boris, in charge, knew all his instructions by rote in English; but he had no words in between. I supplied those. I learned that British stage electricians never say 'switch off' – the expression I quickly picked up was 'lose that one'.

A very agitated Russian stage manager arrived: Alexander Alexandrovich. His job was to inspect all the dressing rooms, rehearsal rooms, wardrobes and actual space allocated on stage for dancers who had to make quick changes. This is when I realised what tremendous improvements had been made backstage by the addition of the new wing at Covent Garden. The new dressing rooms were perfect. The stars' rooms, which are on the same level as the stage, each had a sofa bed, a piano for opera singers to practise, a shower, and mirrors galore. There are enough dressing rooms to house an opera company and a ballet together, and thus enough for the Bolshoi's 120 dancers. The two rehearsal rooms on the fourth floor could not be bettered, having grand pianos, barres for short and tall dancers, lights and mirrors – and also a bar for coffee and fruit juice with soft lounge chairs for resting. (In my time, when the stage was being set we had to rehearse in the Crush Bar above the foyer.) Alexander then inspected the electronic panel on the prompt side of the stage, and once he had reassured himself that from 20 July the entire Opera House would be given over completely to the sole occupation of the Bolshoi, he declared himself satisfied. (When he had arrived, the stage was being prepared for a Royal Ballet School performance.)

So, back to *Ivan the Terrible* as it resonates with me now, remembering it all so vividly. By now the winches are turning the iron circles efficiently; all seems well, until the designer Simon Virsaladze appears. Microphone clasped in his hand, he declares from the auditorium that the whole thing looks cramped. It hasn't the 'grandeur of the Bolshoi'. The false proscenium must be removed to open up the set; the borders raised; the cyclorama hung farther back; the flies moved back; the wings enlarged. His set is suffering. What about the dancers and the stage crew, with no room in the wings? No matter: the set is of prime importance. Keith, the British stage manager, says, 'We've been wanting to get this proscenium removed for years – now we're glad to see the back of it.' To the mumbled disapproval of the British stagehands, we re-hang the set, whose proportions had been so meticulously measured. We now have 'deads' – that is, limit marks for ropes and pulleys. It is lunchtime now, and this cools tempers a bit. The restaurant-cafeteria is also a colossal improvement on conditions years ago. Hot dishes, salads, sandwiches, beverages, all at unbeatable prices. It is quite amazing how the staff can serve some sixty people or so in a matter of minutes.

Although the season opens with *Ivan,* we have to hang and light *Raymonda,* as there will be so little time once performances start. Eventually *Raymonda* is all done; then Mr Virsaladze yells, 'The columns are not straight, has no one eyes to see?' We re-hang, adding weights to steady the columns.

Now I have to help in the dome. This houses the very topmost spotlights that follow the dancers on stage. Normally the lush pale-blue and gold ceiling of the theatre forms a perfect circle, but for these performances two elongated windows are opened, and four electrical engineers, behind the spotlights, have to know not only the whole continuity of the ballet but every entrance, every group, every dancer's solo – and every shade and number of light to use on them. Along with Sasha, another member of the team, I climb again: up and up we go, over the covered roof of the theatre until we descend an iron ladder backwards into a cubbyhole. Both teams, Russians and British, under the command of Guerman, are so efficient. The Russians describe every entrance and exit of the dancers, with colour-numbers for the spots. It is fully written down and in no time we all retire into a small smoking room, well stocked and with a kettle on the boil.

Guerman and Sasha get a blasting from their supervisor – apparently, I had been needed on stage. Sergei, responsible for the entire décor, has been getting urgent calls from the administrative panel in the auditorium, but had not been able to work without an interpreter. Mikhail, the Russian artistic director on stage, without whose approval nothing is passed, shouts too. He finds the British crew slow, as they have to get their orders through their chiefs. The working methods of the two countries are totally different: the one does one job at a time, the other issues three or four instructions at once. Tempers tend to rise. The British swear under their breath, the Russians shout humiliating remarks at one another. And it is Tamara here, Tamara there, Tamara, Tamara. We have six interpreters for the company, but each is delegated to a particular task: I am the one on stage.

On Monday 21 July, the Bolshoi company arrives at last; we are once again with the revolving set for *Ivan.* The rehearsal is about to start. Yuri Grigorovich, the Bolshoi's artistic director and principal ballet master, greets me warmly with three Russian kisses and hugs; my hand is kissed too, a charming habit no longer practised in England. A tall, distressed young man is looking for a trunk containing his rehearsal clothes, and is very agitated; later I discover that he is Yuri Vasyuchenko, one of the brilliant stars. I lead him offstage to the huge glass-roofed hall that was formerly the original fruit and vegetable storage bay of the market. We look for his trunk in vain; it hasn't arrived from Dublin. He is almost in tears: 'What will I do? What will I do?'

Grigorovich is calling for the rehearsal to start. I said I would explain to Grigorovich. Vasyuchenko says, 'No explanation ever works – I have to have my clothes.' But the rehearsal is hardly needed for the dancers: it is for the sets, the lights, the props, the revolving circles and the throne that has to appear and disappear in seconds and is giving trouble. The cyclorama is too heavy to be lifted all at once and requires bigger counterweights. The press patiently waits for Grigorovich to ask his dancers to pose for photographs. The first cast is saving its strength while the second cast dances; my young man is in a tracksuit, but no matter. Grigorovich dismisses his dancers. We stay and work until the stagehands get their (optional) tea break.

While alone on stage, I see and recognise a figure: Mme Galina Sergeyevna Ulanova. I approach her and ask if I can be of any help. 'Yes, please, I am so glad you are available. I should like to revisit the dressing room I occupied in 1956.' I take her to the 'opposite prompt' side of the stage where the old dressing rooms are, remembering myself that I used to have to climb many stone steps. Mme Ulanova's had been at stage level. Those old dressing rooms are barely larger than an average bathroom. Although recently repainted, they still look old and tired, with creaky floorboards and poor equipment. Galina Sergeyevna looks into first one, then another, then another, until she finally finds the one that had been hers. She can recognise it because hers had a ledge two feet by three masked by a curtain. Ulanova tells me that one morning as she was changing for rehearsal the curtain parted and a smiling young girl said to her, 'I hope, Madame, you do not mind, but I hid there last night and slept there so I would be sure to meet you this morning.' Mme Ulanova is very moved by her recollections, and even more so when a couple of former stagehands, now technicians in charge, approach her and say how well they remembered her season and the standing ovations she received. Mme Ulanova is here to supervise the dancing of the leading ballerinas.

The BBC is making a film in the rehearsal rooms; I am wanted to translate an interview. Nina Semizorova is being interviewed, and is full of praise and appreciation for Madame's help and supervision. She considers herself the luckiest dancer alive. There is another interview too, this time with Ludmila Semenyaka for the London *Evening Standard.* Semenyaka is grace personified, dressed all in pale pink with a wrap-over black shawl, which she handles expertly as she poses. There is a point when she wants to discard it, and the photographer asked her to keep it; she protests, 'But it is just my little old black rag', then uses it in a Spanish manner for him.

dancers, and each practises his or her particular solo piece, limbs working in perfect harmony. Their balance is astonishing. Mme Struchkova's class is one of precision, grace, beauty and inspiration. Madame herself does not sit still – she runs, she dances, she talks, explains, inspires. It would be impossible in her presence to dance indifferently or without expression; all dance has meaning, she says, otherwise 'it is dead'. Watching both these classes is an immense pleasure.

One day after class, Mme Struchkova, Nina Ananiashvili and I went shopping to help Nina choose a fur coat. Nina tried on a great many and found it hard to make up her mind. When we got back to the theatre, we learned that a soloist, Elena Molokova, had had her handbag snatched, with £200 in it. She was very distressed. It had happened right in the middle of the day, at the junction of Bow Street and Floral Street. I took all the particulars I could from her – 'a bearded white man in tattered jeans' – and went to Bow Street Police Station, just opposite the Opera House, to tell the story. The police were amazing. The man was caught, had up before the magistrate and sentenced, and the bag and money were returned intact. *The Times* wrote it all up the next day. (They just didn't add that she thought the British police were *wonderful!*)

As the programmes had all been mounted in turn, work for the interpreters eased off, and I was able to give myself over to the pleasure of watching the performances. After all the busy backstage turmoil, it was a complete change for me to translate for a question-and-answer session at which Galina Ulanova talked in response to points raised by members of the London Ballet Circle. This took place in the Waterloo Room of the Royal Festival Hall on the last Saturday of the visit. Ulanova had accepted honorary membership of the Circle, and the questions had been sent in beforehand but not put to her then. It was my task to interpret both ways: I had to tell Ulanova what each of the Britons had said, and then translate her replies. It was a great privilege and a great honour to have done this for her.

Irina and Gerry

Irina Baronova is my personal goddess. One of her great achievements is that she has remained unaltered throughout her life, from child dancer to star, from formative years to motherhood and grandmotherhood. She was and is uncomplicated, kind and generous. Her friendship is a thread that has run through almost my whole life, and we have shared much. I should like to finish my story by telling something of hers.

The press and public worshipped Balanchine's baby ballerinas from the moment of their 'creation' in 1932. The three outstanding ones included Tatiana Riabouchinska, an ethereal dancer, specialising in light, joyous portrayals, commanding the admiration of dreamy, romantic young men and women, and described by critics as the 'spirit of the dance'. But in daily life with us, her colleagues, she was aloof and uncommunicative, keeping within a small circle of her own. Her adolescence was unhappy. The leading dancer David Lichine loved her, but married another. The consequent lives of husband, wife and lover were dramatic, with attempted suicides, rows and tears galore.

Another of the three was Tamara Toumanova, a strong personality made even stronger by the over-protection of her mother, who guarded her and her rights with an intense jealousy, being ambitious and demanding on her behalf. If any unfortunate young man in the company so much as dreamt about Tamara, she was forbidden to speak to him and could never be found alone to allow him to pursue his romantic ideas.

Irina, however, was friendly, human and – most important – had a great sense of humour. She was not afraid of authority, either, and one could count on her speaking her mind in a lusty Russian way. On one occasion when it was not her turn to dance the Swan Queen at Covent Garden, she came into our general dressing room to say hello. I was suffering from unusually severe monthly pains; having applied my make-up and my feather crown, I had wrapped myself in my dressing-gown and curled up on the floor for a bit of comfort, trying to nurse the pain in my back and body. As I was then a member of the corps de ballet, there was no replacement for me, nor did anyone dare tell the severe disciplinarian *régisseur* Serge Grigoriev that a swan was incapacitated. Irina marched up to Grigoriev and announced to him that she was taking my place in the corps de ballet. Grigoriev's stern reply was a firm 'No!'. On her insistence, he came into our dressing room, told me off for being on the floor (and in my head-dress too) and said it was all nonsense: there was no such thing as a dancer being ill, nor would he allow a prima ballerina to replace her.

He was the management, and as such he took the decisions: he simply forbade it. One of his reasons was that the public would recognise Irina, the ballerina in the front row of the corps de ballet. But he couldn't stop her. She accused him of not understanding how much dancers suffered from pains. I personally had never been ill before; all girls danced even at death's door.

Irina put my costume on, removed the feather wings from my hair, took me into her dressing room, made me lie on her couch with a hot water bottle, and stuffed me with soothing tablets. Not to enrage Grigoriev too much, she rearranged the corps de ballet rows and took a position in the very last one – in Russian called 'near the water', a throw-back to the Imperial days when every set had a lake at the edge of which the weaker dancers were placed. The audience did not notice a thing.

Irina was also instrumental in passing down to me some of her solo roles, such as the *midinette* in *Le Beau Danube*. Without my knowledge, she had gone to the management to say that she was dancing enough, that I could spin and turn well, and that the role should be mine. From then on, it was.

Some years later, after my personal success during the first Australian tour, when I rejoined the main company only to find that all the leading roles had already been allocated and so there was no opportunity for me, she insisted that I should dance the leading role in Balanchine's *Cotillon*, saying that I had worked with Balanchine and that the role suited me better than it did her. All such things she did unsolicited and of her own accord.

In the early years of the ballet, German (Gerry) Sevastianov joined our company. Gerry came from a very distinguished Russian family. His father was a famous opera singer in the Imperial Theatres, while his mother belonged to the Alexeyev family, wealthy textile factory owners who first introduced to Russia the fashionable, embroidered golden materials that became the rage of the aristocracy. Gerry's mother was the sister of Konstantin Sergeyevich Stanislavsky of the Moscow Arts Theatre, who had changed his name so as not to create strife in the family, and who developed 'method acting'.

After an unhappy childhood due to his parents' separation and the Russian Revolution, Gerry found himself in Paris. He eventually joined the travelling company as a chauffeur-cum-*homme-à-tout-faire* to the director, Colonel de Basil. Vassili Grigorievich de Basil was myopic, and had had a series of car crashes; it was a miracle that he was still alive. Gerry filled the post of chauffeur to perfection. As well as having a flair for the theatre and an understanding of music, decor and ballet, he also had a pleasant manner, spoke five languages fluently and was an excellent and careful driver. By degrees, de Basil relied on him more and more, very soon letting him act on his behalf with contractual and managerial discussions, letting him use his smooth diplomatic approach, whether in persuading wealthy sponsors to produce additional capital or in pacifying and charming anxious creditors.

Gerry managed it all splendidly, and within a year his status changed: he became joint director of the company. Later, de Basil had to retreat from the limelight and keep low for a time because of debts, court cases and bankruptcy. For legal reasons and to avoid complications, the company took a new name and Gerry became Director.

By this time, the administration of this huge, expensive and temperamental company had no more mystery for him. He could deal with the lawyers, the unfortunate sponsors, and the impresarios and management of Europe, America and Australia. He could handle the orchestra and its conductors, along with all the complexities and expenses and concessions of travelling arrangements. He could commission new ballets, order costumes to be made, and, hardest of all, keep the dancers happy by listening to their personal problems and complaints and manoeuvre people in such a way that none would feel unwanted, neglected, underpaid, under-publicised or outshone by any other. (It was in strong contrast to the situation today, when large ballet companies are helped by government subsidy and sponsored by large commercial organisations.)

His private life was active too, paralleling his spectacular rise in the world of ballet. At the age of thirty-four when he began to spread his wings from his post as private chauffeur, he won the hearts of a few girls amongst the dancers by his personal charm, his good looks, his big, black velvet, calf-like, loving eyes, his gallant approach to women and his knowledge of classical poetry, which he often quoted in beautifully spoken Russian, and the romantic songs that he often sang at parties. He discreetly loved a few girls, gave them great joy while his love lasted, and caused them to shed tears and have tantrums when it ceased.

The gossip within the company rose to a high pitch when he fixed his attention on Irina, the junior baby ballerina then aged sixteen. She was impressed by him too, very flattered and head over heels in love. He had just abandoned an older dancer, and Irina, a mere child, had his undivided love. The gossipmongers scoffed at the possibility of it lasting. Irina was closely guarded by her mother, and her father was travelling with the company too, working in the scenic department. Gerry's intentions were honourable: he wanted to marry her and asked her parents' permission. The reply was 'No': she was underage, and no arguments were accepted.

This dramatic situation reached a climax when we were on tour in the USA. As the curtain went down on the ballet *Les Sylphides*, there was a public row, and then a tearful confrontation between Gerry's previous love and Irina. Nasty words were spoken; Irina was upset and decided to accept the sacrifice and give Gerry up. He wouldn't hear of it. Many tears were shed and obviously matters had to come to a head. When the whisper ran around like a bush fire that they would elope together, the whole of the company was agog. That evening everyone danced on tenterhooks, with feelings of expectation, fear and excitement. Everyone knew of the secret. Except Mama and Papa...

The plot was that after the performance, while Mama was at the hotel and Papa still busy supervising the scenery, Irina would dress in a hurry, leave the theatre in a waiting taxi, be driven to the local airport, board a plane and from Columbus, Ohio, fly to Cincinnati, the next city on the Ballet's itinerary. This she did, leaving a letter for her parents telling them of her whereabouts and her intentions. The parents were quite convinced that she could not marry because of her youth. However, when the Cincinnati taxi driver discovered that they were heading for their wedding ceremony, he asked Irina how old she was. She replied innocently, 'Sixteen'. He said, 'You mean eighteen...'. The young lovers then knew that by lying about her age they would have no difficulty in securing a licence. And so they were married. Two days later the ballet company arrived in Cincinnati, and Irina's parents had to accept the reality.

Gerry and Irina were happy in the years that immediately followed. She with her talent, personality and artistry became the most appreciated and beloved ballerina, who inspired choreographers Léonide Massine and Michel Fokine to create ballets for her in which she was irreplaceable.

As the company's co-director (a title he had had to share when de Basil was re-established), Gerry ran it efficiently, with a man-of-the-world polish that gave it more 'class'. With his friendly manner and offering the company's prestige, he could gather around him titled people who impressed the Americans: Counts, Grand Dukes and Georgian Princes, along with writers, artists, composers and the cream of the Russian émigrés in the arts and amongst the aristocracy.

But the war interfered with everyone's lives and wrecked the Ballet at its height. De Basil's company was badly affected by the war, and their bookings became less attractive. Irina then danced for four years as a ballerina with Ballet Theatre in America, and Gerry managed to become director of that company, too. When she left, it was because of pressures imposed by him that exploited her talent and position. There were also deep-seated personal reasons and her desire to widen her range and become an actress.

Gerry joined the United States Army. Very soon he was promoted to the rank of Captain, and as a multi-lingual interpreter was assigned to the headquarters of the Army of Occupation in Europe. His knowledge of Europe and its culture was very useful to the army during the invasion and penetration of Europe.

He had an adventurous and enjoyable time after the liberation, working with administrators when hostilities ceased and the celebrations started. But back home in the States, his private life was not going too well. In uniform he looked devastating; his overwhelming charm drove ladies to distraction and he basked in their admiration. But that no longer impressed Irina, who had to deal with her problems alone.

Work in her chosen new career was hard to find. Because she needed to support her parents and because she wanted to prove to herself that she could survive on her own, she took an engagement in Radio City Music Hall, where she had to dance five times a day, starting at eleven a.m., to fit in between showings of a film. Then, at last, she performed as an actress in summer stock in the play *Dark Eyes* and went into musical comedy with *Follow the Girls*. Because it was hard to break into a new profession, she had to return for a time to ballet and joined Massine in a concert group. It was nothing but hard work to keep the wolf from the door.

She came to England with Massine to appear in *A Bullet in the Ballet*, but the play never reached London. There was no immediate work on offer in

London, and she was completely broke. A friend, the playwright Noel Langley, wanted to help by offering accommodation, but his house at Kingston-upon-Thames was already full. She gratefully accepted an alternative, though – a tent pitched in his garden. Langley was writing and finishing a play called *The Farm of Three Echoes*, and offered Irina the part of a South African tart, which she accepted gratefully. While waiting for the production to start, she slept in the tent and worked as a barmaid in the local pub. A mutual friend asked her to call on Cecil Tennant; she did so, and they became instant friends.

The play folded and there was nothing to do but return home to the States. As soon as she arrived, her London agent Bill Linnit cabled her to return to London, as there was a strong possibility that she would be given the part of a temperamental pianist in a Michael Balcon film, *Train of Events*. After her return journey and a quick test, she was cast in the part. Waiting for her in her hotel room was an enormous bunch of flowers with a note informing her, not asking her, that she was having dinner that night with Cecil Tennant.

At that very time, Peter and I had just arrived in England full of hope and expectations about Peter's career. The film director Harry Watt was instrumental in introducing Peter to Michael Balcon, head of Ealing Studios. Through Harry's recommendation, Peter was given a role in the same episodic film.

Cecil Tennant was Peter's agent and connected with Laurence Olivier Productions. One evening after coming back from the Studios, Peter told me that Cecil had asked me to go and visit an ex-dancer from the de Basil Monte Carlo ballet. He believed I might have met her; she was alone in London and ill in a hotel room. She was also a Russian. Impatiently I rushed to the Pastoria Hotel in Leicester Square – to find that it was Irina. We had not seen one another for ten years. To preserve her voice, she had been forbidden to speak aloud; she had a very bad throat infection and had been alone and miserable. We whispered the evening away.

Cecil was happy that I could be there to provide a little company for her. She managed to finish her episode in the film, then left London mysteriously. I had her confidence and kept her secret: having fallen in love while looking after her, Cecil had persuaded her to marry him and had sent her to Wyoming to get a quick divorce. Irina was in love with him too. She stayed the required four weeks to establish residence in Wyoming, and Cecil arrived there the day before the court hearing. They came back to London shortly afterwards as a married couple.

From then on, retired from the profession, she became the perfect wife and later the perfect mother to three children: two girls and a boy. Still very young, she could have continued her dancing and acting career now that she was married to one of London's leading theatrical agents, whose clients included the Oliviers, Michael Redgrave, Edith Evans and many other great actors. She could have had a fabulous social life, travelling the capitals of the world, attending world premieres of films and plays and entertaining the stars; but her family was so important to her that she hardly left her comfortable home, busy with children's parties, shopping, dogs, cats and all the paraphernalia of a busy young housewife.

Gerry, in the meantime, was miserable. The abundant fringe benefits of his war ceased. Without Irina, his power in the re-formed ballet companies was nil. Each American ballet group had its established director or wealthy sponsor. After vegetating for a time in the States, he came back to Europe, as his Russian soul yearned to be near Paris with his old Russian friends, or London with its culture and Irina, or Monte Carlo with its memories of glories past.

Gerry was jobless. He tried his hand unsuccessfully at various ventures, and when in London always telephoned me. How was Irina, was she happy, how could she be happy married to an Englishman, how could she (being so Russian, and an artist) just be nothing but a housewife? Did she ever speak of him, regretting the old days? Yes, Irina was happy, no, she didn't regret the old days. No, she didn't want to dance again. Would I go out with him to a show, to dinner? Yes, I would. Could we talk about Irina? We always did; that was inevitable.

When Gerry was in London and completely broke, he occupied a pied-à-terre belonging to a friend. When he had no money, which happened often, I would cook dinner for him at my place, or we would go to his and he would prepare for us a casserole of buckwheat *kasha* (porridge) cooked in butter, or macaroni cheese, followed by lemon tea – all reminiscent of our lean days in Paris when the stomach had to be filled cheaply. We talked about Irina, of course.

On one of our Russian evenings, while listening to records of Alexander Vertinsky, a Russian *chansonnier* with the ability to conjure up the emptiness of existence, the futility of yearning and the disillusionment of life, Gerry proposed marriage to me. I replied, 'But Gerry – you love Irina.' 'Yes,' he said, 'but it is hopeless. You are her friend. You are Russian too. Let's go to Bali or Surabaya, forget the world and start a business there with pearl divers.' He had a connection somewhere in that part of the world, and had been assured that easy fortunes could be made. I laughed, and said I wouldn't consider it for a minute; and besides, it would spoil our friendship. He said the trouble was that my heart was still full of Peter, and his heart full of Irina; we laughed and cried together a little, and that evening we were very close in spirit.

Later, as I described in a previous chapter, I became an interpreter. My first job was at a very large British Trade Fair in Moscow in 1961. On returning to dinner at the hotel one evening, I was astonished to find Gerry at an adjoining table. He was there with a French textile-machinery firm, also, like me, as an interpreter – French into Russian. A French exhibition was to follow the British one. We had dinner and Sovietsky champagne ... and talked about Irina.

He, full of confidence, asked me to stay and work at the French exhibition. I told him my visa was running out and my daughter expected me back. He assured me he could arrange everything, get my visa extended, arrange for phone calls back to England... but I went home.

A couple of months later Gerry was in London again and phoned me – from the Savoy, no less: could I be called for at seven o'clock tonight? We would go to a ballet at Covent Garden, then to supper at the Savoy. He was entertaining a French textile tycoon and his wife and they would be happy of my company. The evening was a delight, the French couple being overjoyed at not having to struggle with the English language. My fluent friend helped.

I was recruited for the next few days, for visits to Westminster Abbey, the Tower, the Tate Gallery and shows and dinners, all made comfortable by the fact that a large black car was at our disposal. I was asked to go to Mulhouse in eastern France to be a representative for their knitting machines.

Over the next few years Gerry visited London at least four or five times a year, staying at the Savoy. He had meetings there with French, British and Swedish businessmen, and with Soviet officials negotiating enormous deals. I was often present, a reliable companion; and besides, he always wanted to know how Irina was faring.

To me this was fun. Gerry introduced me to dozens of colourful people, and now he could once again entertain on a scale familiar to him. His old Hollywood friends were often in London too.

Gregory Ratoff, a larger-than-life character who took a particular interest in me, wrote me no less than three hundred letters full of poems and romantic ideas, and followed me to the south of France where I was holidaying with my daughter. He was a compulsive gambler who could not keep away from casino tables but lost more money than he won. In desperation he would pick up the phone and dial secret numbers to place bets on horses; he knew every doorman and every bookie, had accounts and debts in every capital of Europe, and was afraid to return to the United States because of the alimony he owed his ex-wife.

The movie actor Akim Tamiroff, another great friend of Gerry's, was in London too. So were Boris Chaliapin – an artist with *Time* magazine, and the son of the great Feodor – and George St. George, a Hollywood writer then negotiating to make a film in the Soviet Union with Anthony Asquith, featuring the Bolshoi Ballet. Gerry brought many of these people to my home and much colour into my life.

There were Soviet delegations too – visits to shoe manufacturers, chemistry plants... 'But Gerry,' I said, 'I don't know anything about chemistry!' 'You don't have to,' he answered, 'they know what they're looking at.'

Every time, there were the inevitable questions about Irina. 'Is she happy? 'Yes, Gerry, she is.' Gerry gave me a special little book with various telephone numbers through which he could be found at any time of the day or night in whichever city he was, and an itinerary of his business travels, all in case Irina should want to get in touch. I was to give her the information immediately.

By now, and in just a few years, Gerry had become an enormously wealthy man. He had opened an office in the Hotel Metropole in Moscow and been able to make deals with various Soviet Ministries, with whom he arranged the installation of complete plants and the equipment to fill them: machinery from Britain, steel from Sweden, textile know-how from France. His reward was a percentage of the contract monies, to be deposited for him at banks in Switzerland and Luxembourg. He was a middleman for deals the Soviet Union made through their trade delegations. Gerry knew trade well; and what he didn't know, he had the confidence to find out.

On a couple of my trips to Moscow as an interpreter with British firms, I visited Gerry's office at the Metropole. It was comfortable, almost luxurious, with a lovely young secretary who was obviously very devoted to him. His office walls were covered by framed enlargements of photographs of Irina in her many dancing roles. Was she still happy, how could she possibly be? Yes, she was.

After another few years, Gerry moved out of the Soviet Union because business had become slack; the Russians were now working through their own trade ministries both in Paris and in London, and were dispensing with middlemen.

Gerry now had houses in Malta and an office in Luxembourg, as well as property in Switzerland. On his visits to London, money was no problem at all. He had a great deal of it. His generosity in entertaining was limitless; but he was bored, neurotic. He would get the best tickets for an opera or ballet and walk out in the interval; order caviar, lobsters and chateaubriands and hardly touch them; chain-smoke and yearn for Russian music and Russian people, and ask me to play my Russian records to him; and always the inevitable questions about Irina.

Late one night in July 1967 my phone rang. It was Gerry from Switzerland. He had just been told by his cousin, another of his informants, that Irina's husband Cecil had crashed his Jaguar into a tree that evening. The front of the car had been split by the impact, and Cecil was believed killed. Two children, his daughter Irina and son Bobby, had been severely hurt in the accident. Gerry wanted to know if there was anything he could do for Irina. He would wait for my phone call. But I could not contact Irina then, as she was at the hospital.

Later I found out more details. Cecil had attended Vivien Leigh's funeral that day, came back home and offered to drive home a friend of his son's who had been visiting them. The children jumped into the new E-type Jaguar for the ride and the friend was deposited at his own place. On the way back the Jaguar failed to negotiate a bend in the road and crashed into a tree. The car had gone completely out of control, but at the inquest neither the garage mechanic nor the coroner could say why it had happened.

Irina's story of events was hair-raising. The guest's home was only a couple of miles away, so the car and her family should have returned within twenty minutes. As time went by, Irina was seized with inward panic. Purely driven by instinct, she ran out of the house and down the road. She came upon police signs indicating that an accident had happened. Her heart pounding, she tried to proceed further but was stopped by the police and forbidden to do so. To her horror she saw two ambulances, and bodies in a field covered with bloody sheets. She knew before she was allowed near that they were her husband and two children. The police kept her at a distance. She begged, pleaded, cried and fought. She was only able to go near them when her daughter Irina was moved by the ambulance men and cried out to her. The police then allowed her to enter one of the ambulances and be driven to hospital with her family.

Her husband had died on impact. Her son Bobby was unconscious, and her daughter had suffered multiple injuries. How Irina withstood such ordeals, God only knows. The vigil over her son went on for many months. The injuries to his head were extensive, and at first it was impossible to say whether he would survive. It took a year to get him better. Her daughter needed a few stitches but mended more quickly.

In the meantime, asking every day for bulletins that I was unable to supply, Gerry phoned, phoned and phoned again. He was in London or Switzerland or Luxembourg, but always at the end of a line to me. How was she? She would not answer his letters or his calls; her mother did not answer the phone, but kept Irina away.

When I saw her during this period, there was nothing one could do to help. She was completely shattered. She aged considerably, her cheeks stayed pale and drawn, her silhouette in profile was pencil-slim, her eyes were permanently red and swollen. She was a spectre of the woman she had been. The severity of her black clothes added a tragic note to her figure. But her strong maternal love and instinct prevailed; she survived because she had to for her children.

Two years went by until Gerry wore me down. Keeping it secret from her mother, I told Irina that Gerry was begging me to get them together, to arrange a meeting – where else but at my place. I had to agree to this; they were adults and could work out their own salvation. I was simply giving them the opportunity to do so.

Under the pretence that she was coming to my home for tea, she travelled to London from Chertsey. Gerry arrived first, his arms laden with presents for me, including a beautiful and enormous Caucasian cashmere shawl with hand-knitted lacework. The story about these shawls is that in the Caucasus they are given as dowries to young brides, and the test both of the fine work and of the couple's future happiness is that the whole shawl can be threaded and pass through the circle of a wedding ring. Mine did. It was clear that psychologically the present was really meant for Irina, but he could not summon the courage to offer it to her.

When Irina arrived and kissed my daughter and me at the front door, she was shaking like the proverbial leaf in an autumn breeze. They greeted one another clasping both hands, voices trembling, finding practically nothing to say. They had not seen one another for some twenty-two years, having before that been married to one another for fourteen.

After making polite chit-chat to break the awkward silence, serving coffee and opening a bottle of Armenian brandy that Gerry had brought, my daughter and I disappeared. I did not even want to know what the results of my engineering were.

Gerry was very eager just to walk back into her life; he considered that she was his, and had always been his. She was hesitant. Her children meant so much to her; she was not alone as she had been in her younger days, and the initial shock to the children had to be considered as they readjusted to life without their father. They needed her constantly, and she had to be at hand when they wanted her. It was a difficult time for everyone, and Gerry, depressed, visited me again, asking me why she was not thinking more of herself and of the pleasant life she could have with him; now that money for him was no problem, he could offer her anything she wanted.

As time went by, her two daughters were married and Bobby went to college. Irina collapsed and underwent a serious operation. Gerry was out of his mind with worry, and, using all his persuasive charm, proposed a round-the-world cruise to Irina as convalescence. It turned into a very happy time for them both. Gerry, with love and pride, had informed all their mutual friends of their voyage. They stayed in Lebanon, in Singapore, in Bangkok, and were feted everywhere. Australia, too, treated them royally. Her admiring public there remembered her well. Invitations poured in: everyone was happy for them.

The cruise ended in Istanbul, where they spent a further few days. For three years before the voyage, Gerry had not been well and had been diagnosed as having a virus that affected his lungs. He suffered a setback in Istanbul and they decided to fly back to London, where I saw them again. She was radiant, looking young and beautiful, her blue eyes like cornflowers, her hair blonde and girlish, a ready smile on her lips, the occasional colourful word adding spice to her conversation. Gerry had made the mistake of dyeing his lovely, thick silver hair black, which did not suit him and made his face look sallow. He did not talk much, but was constantly looking at Irina with admiration.

They returned to their base in Switzerland, but the virus never left his body, and he needed serious medical attention. Irina took him to see specialists, then to a private clinic and then to hospital in Montreux. The virus attacked his liver, kidneys and bladder; he was losing weight and needed blood transfusions. Finally his lungs became infected too.

For six months in 1974, Irina nursed him every day. She was always present, and shared a room with him at the hospital. His last few months were very painful. He had tubes inserted for feeding, tubes for passing water, tubes for blood transfusion, a machine to pump his lungs. He would not let the nurses feed him, but would accept food only from Irina. She often snatched an hour's sleep sitting in an armchair, aware of the slightest sound from him. Her night's sleep was interrupted by the need to give him constant care. For six months she hardly slept. His communication to her was through a few words scribbled on a writing pad.

When the end was near, and he was hardly capable of moving, he joined his thumb, forefinger and middle finger together, trying to make the sign of the cross. She rushed to the writing pad and put a pencil in his hand; he scribbled something incomprehensible. Gerry died with his hand in hers, looking into her eyes and worshipping her.

I was one of the first of their friends to receive a telegram from her. She has the note he was trying to write, but neither she nor I nor any other of the few people who have seen it can make out what he wanted to say.

Magic and heartbreak

From the early twenty-first century, I can look back at the ballet of the previous century, and indeed at my own life, with a perspective that was impossible while I was so actively living through a crucial part of it.

Like a sudden violent storm, Nureyev had burst into the West in 1961, sweeping away complacency in ballet in his wake. His impact on the dancing world was a source of inspiration mixed with fury. People had heard about Nijinsky, but they could see Nureyev. Male dancers aspired to his perfection, and ballerinas' standards rose to his demands. Audiences once again screamed deliriously. Television gave him worldwide coverage, and films were made of his performances, rehearsals and classes. Every step became familiar to the public, every interpretation critically assessed. Little girls dreamt of being magic swans, boys of showing their virility. Other brilliant personalities also defected from the Soviet Union. Never has Western Europe been so involved in dance.

Several decades ago in the USA, Balanchine's talent and dedication created a voracious appetite for dancing. Styles and schools sprang up nationwide and audiences grew, enlightened by ballets developed by other superb choreographers. Techniques improved, perfection sparkled. Yet it all started from the same beginning: traditional training, discipline, barre work, endless centre exercises, never-ending pirouettes, experienced teachers transmitting that glorious Russian system.

In the late 1930s in Australia, when the de Basil Company performed and its success inflamed the continent like a bush fire, a Melbourne eye specialist, Dr Joseph Ringland Anderson, proved his enthusiasm by filming whole scenes of the ballets. Eventually the reels of film were handed to the Australian Ballet archives, and in 1974 were compiled into a documentary for Australian Broadcasting Commission called *Another Beginning*.

I was asked to identify some of the dancers and the ballets now forgotten. When the film was shown at the London Ballet Circle and at the Victoria and Albert Museum, I was further asked to introduce the film with a lecture about the de Basil Ballet. Then I sat back to watch. There we all were, young, strong, bright-eyed, indefatigable, exercising continuously, loving it all so much that even as guests of Dr Anderson we danced on his lawn, leaping high, supported by partners, and dived into his pool in balletic postures.

We could see fleeting moments of Baronova, Toumanova, Riabouchinska, Massine, Dolin and various other soloists, including me; *Scheherazade, Carnaval, Danube, Femmes de bonne humeur, Thamar* – a lively, enthusiastic company, appreciated for our skill, artistry and tradition. I knew then that we had been the link – the vital link – after Diaghilev's death. Had it not been for the thousands of refugees from Russia in Paris, ballet would not have developed so much in the West. Had it not been for the much later but also brilliant refugees from the Soviet Union, ballet would not have achieved its present perfection.

At the Royal Academy of Dancing, when I was examining candidates taking the Karsavina syllabus for their teacher-training course, I talked to them, and in my little way tried to transmit that feeling for the dance, that precious legacy.

My own pleasure is still in watching marvellous dancers. When I saw the perfection of Makarova, it was obvious that technique has advanced so much with time. But I also remember the chic of Danilova, the lightness of Riabouchinska, the soul and artistry of Baronova. One of my proudest moments in recent years was in 1997 when, onstage and in front of thousands of people, Yuri Grigorovich presented me with the Diaghilev Medal in Moscow, where I had been serving as a juror for the World Ballet Competition. I felt so honoured to be joining the ranks of such distinguished recipients as Baronova and Lifar.

Of my other life and career, to any young person contemplating learning a foreign language, I can recommend the job of interpreter. In this age of computers and push-button technology, it is still a profession where a person cannot be adequately replaced. There is an anecdote of two computers being programmed, one to translate and the other to retranslate back into the original, the sentence 'The spirit is willing, but the flesh is weak'. The result came out as 'The vodka is strong, but the meat has gone off'. Perhaps one of the computers was Russian.

Epilogue

Magic and heartbreak are part of my background. Intermittently for ten years, Mama had asked the Home Office's permission for her sister Lydia to immigrate. Finally it was granted, and in 1962 an old, small, round-shouldered, white-haired lady, carrying a bundle, arrived but was not recognised, and Mama could not find her at the airport. Hours later, in a bus journeying towards London, the conductor had trouble collecting a fare and trying to understand a miserable-looking lady, who was repeating 'No money', 'Romania'. Mama, still unaware, from a few seats away, said, 'I pay for her'. Seconds later, the two sisters were in one another's arms, crying. From an excited Mama, the other passengers heard the story of her frustrated day searching amongst thousands of faces.

Once Lydia was with us, long sessions of family reminiscences followed. In 1940 Bessarabia had been overrun by the Russians. All the inhabitants were considered White Russians, and most sent to Siberia. Grandfather was guarding his cellar during the advance. Soldiers forced their way in, got drunk, then destroyed the barrels and bayoneted him. He died in Grandmother's arms. He was 88. She followed Evgraf and his family to Siberia, and died on the way there.

Lydia's husband Kolia died of hunger in exile, as did Evgraf, though he lasted a little longer and his wife and sons survived. Lydia made her way into Romania. After the war, she brought up a busy doctor's children. They had grown up, and she was destitute when the permit to enter England arrived. Lydia's personality had been crushed. She spoke in whispers, was afraid of crossing the road, was embarrassed at Mama's generosity. She died three years later.

And so to tie up the loose ends in my own story. For three years after my divorce, I strongly needed to feel that another person cared for me – I had quite a few proposals, but was not attracted to these men. Nevertheless, I realised that sexual love was necessary to me, and eventually I met a very interesting man, an artist. He fell in love with me too, and painted me many times. I posed fully dressed, but next day would find his sketches repainted featuring me au naturel. We meant a lot to one another: sex, affection and companionship, particularly when spending days in his manor house. He loved Anita too and made a fuss over her, her love of animals and her childish demands, even giving her a much-loved though disobedient beagle dog.

But he was extremely jealous of me and particularly of the visits Peter made during his second marriage. My lover would prowl outside my house at night, watching for Peter's frequent visits, then phone me, crying hysterically and making threats. Our affair lasted some four years but then I ended it, feeling, as I often have in Britain, that I was simply too foreign for him and his aristocratic upbringing. He never asked me to marry him; we just drifted apart. Later I read in the papers that he had married a titled lady, a very wealthy widow.

But by then I had met another man who totally satisfied some of my artistic needs. We went to exhibitions and lectures together and travelled to China, an unknown world then. He showed me Prague, which I had never visited during my world-wanderings. Although he was single, we did not have a sexual relationship; he never proposed to me and died unmarried. Perhaps he was not the marrying kind. Perhaps again I was too foreign for him: uneducated, unexpectedly melancholic and not 'in line' with British ways.

There was however, one man I knew who could have fulfilled my various demands. We were attracted to one another – though we never made love – and in our togetherness we shared a vast interest in the variety of life, books, discoveries, events, people and travels. He was happily married, though by his gifts, his plans, his letters, his eyes, I knew he cared. But it was not to be.

In my later years, I have had a loyal companion, an honest and good man – but I am the difficult one. Although I realise one must work at a perfect relationship, I still feel I am at fault. We see one another as much as we can. He was a neighbour of mine in London and used to help me to crank my Morris Minor in the 1960s. He still lives in England, while I now live in Spain.

In my mind, even Peter's peccadilloes are redeemed. In 1977 he wrote to Anita inviting her to visit him in Hollywood. She received the letter a day after his death. Perhaps he felt he wanted to get closer. What a pity that he was not persuaded to have heart surgery. There was still so much good acting in him, and as a man, who knows? He could have found greater depth in his relationship with his children.

My daughter has always been a source of happiness to me, and looking after her filled my life for many years. She grew up beautiful and intelligent, was a good scholar, went to Bristol University, became an actress, and married a lovely American, Val Harrison, whom she met when they were both working in Marbella on the Costa del Sol. Having several separate careers may be something that runs in the blood, for while they lived in California she became a psychotherapist and set up a private practice in Beverley Hills.

For me, the wrench of letting go of beloved people has been the hardest: first releasing Peter, then losing Mama, then letting go of Anita when she married. These I have found most painful.

But what a wonderful compensation close friends are! – those with whom I can cry and laugh together, those who listen to every day's trivialities, those with whom one can discuss opinions or exchange a warm hug when in need. And now Anita and Val have moved from Los Angeles to Europe to help look after me (I became quite lame after a fall in 1998), and we have settled happily in the warmth of Marbella, overlooking San Pedro and the Mediterranean. Anita continues to practice analysis and psychotherapy here.

I now watch the sky, the trees, the changing seasons, the expanse of the sea's horizon, and I am grateful to be still alive and to have had a full and interesting life with wonderful, magical memories. The love of those close to me obliterates past heartbreaks and sets them into perspective for me. It is a life I am glad and thankful to have lived.

November 2006

I am now 87. On a sunny day here in Spain last week, my half brother Alexander and I met for the first time. He is 77 and came from Moscow with his daughter Ludmila, to meet the sister he had for 60 years been searching for. All of us felt apprehensive. It is strange to meet someone you are so closely related to, someone whose existence you did not know about two years ago.

We invited them for lunch at our house and Val cooked a Mexican chilli con carne, which gave us something to talk about to break the ice. Eventually our fears melted away and we asked each other direct questions about Father, questions to which both he and I had sought answers for years. We discussed and compared our very different lives. We talked of many things – music, art, books. This stranger, Alexander, had the qualities I love in a man – intelligent, articulate, interested in everything. Ludmilla was a good looking woman, smart, fluent in English and very easy to relate to. I found out about the troubled years they had lived through in Russia. It emerged that when I was working as an interpreter in Moscow, I had unknowingly many times walked down their street, in fact when I was a judge at the International Ballet Competition in 1997 we were working in the theatre right in front of their apartment. The week of their visit passed quickly. I was so happy that they were able to make the trip. I certainly wouldn´t have been able to go to Moscow again. It is good to know that we are of the same blood and akin in spirit. Alexander told me things about our father I had not known, that he spoke many languages, that he was very intellectual and respected. We were both so young when we last saw our father, that many questions remain. Why was he shot by Stalin? Did our mothers know that he was a spy? Was he really a spy? Was he a counter-spy? Alexander has just published a book in Russia, all about our father, which he believes clears his name and restores his reputation as a brave man who just wanted peace and freedom. Perhaps neither of us will ever know the full truth, but at least we have been able to fill in some gaps for each other. How strange that both of us were in some way writing about our father at the same time on other sides of the world. How wonderful that we were able to meet towards the end of our lives. One has to wonder about Fate.

Afterword

My thanks for my interesting life go to:

My beloved Mama, for her courage, initiative, support, upbringing and love.

My father, misguided sentimentalist, whose blood I feel in my veins, who brought a world of magic into my early life, and who advised me to read, write and dream.

Irina Baronova, for being such a loyal and helpful friend, showing and giving me some of her roles. From childhood to old age, we have been and remain great friends.

Arnold Haskell, for writing words of praise at the right time in my career.

Edouard Borovansky, for appreciating my efforts at taking up ballet once more by giving me leading roles when I was still somewhat out of practice.

Dayna Goldfine and Dan Geller, for producing the wonderful documentary *Ballets Russes* that has been such a success all over the world, reminding ballet lovers of the glorious days of the 1930s and 1940s when our ballet company fascinated Europe and America by reviving the Diaghilev classics and adding original productions, particularly the unforgettable symphonies of Massine.

David Palmer, for advising the managements of Covent Garden and Glyndebourne to use me as their interpreter for Russian ballet and opera companies visiting Britain, and for English companies travelling to Russia. David saved me from being stuck as an interpreter specialising in automobile technology, machine tools and assembly lines.

Anthony Dowell and Maina Gielgud, for being such wonderful artistic directors while touring Russia with the Royal and Australian Ballets under severe technical difficulties, eased (I hope) by my explanations of the differences of habit, behaviour and technology to both sides.

Hilary Condron, for introducing me to Russian ballet teachers, and for making our trips to St Petersburg such a pleasure.

Dr Michelle Potter of *Brolga* magazine, for welcoming me to Australia in words and deeds.

Olive Harding, Peter Finch's agent, who made Peter sign over our London house to me after our divorce, and arranged for the mortgage when I had not demanded anything.

Kathrine Sorley Walker, writer and historian, for telling George Dorris about my autobiography and encouraging me to write more.

George Dorris and Jack Anderson, for choosing snippets of my draft book so well and publishing them in *Dance Chronicle* in 2004.

Mary Clarke, for correcting the grammar and spelling mistakes in my articles, and publishing them.

Elena Prokina, Russian soprano, for making me realise that I was not the only one with Russian 'sentimental moods'.

David Leonard, for publishing my book. He is a patient and tolerant man, and I trust him with organising the glorious chaos of my life.

A special thank you to my editor, Dr Rod Cuff, who made sense of my bits and pieces, put an English spin on my Russian/French turn of phrase and was hugely encouraging. He made everything come together.

Finally, I want to express my unlimited gratitude to Anita and her husband Val Harrison for having taken complete charge of me, abandoning California and transporting me to sunny Spain. Anita sees to my smallest need, and Val is patient and has a wonderful sense of humour, essential with a Russian mother-in-law.

Tamara Tchinarova Finch

Index